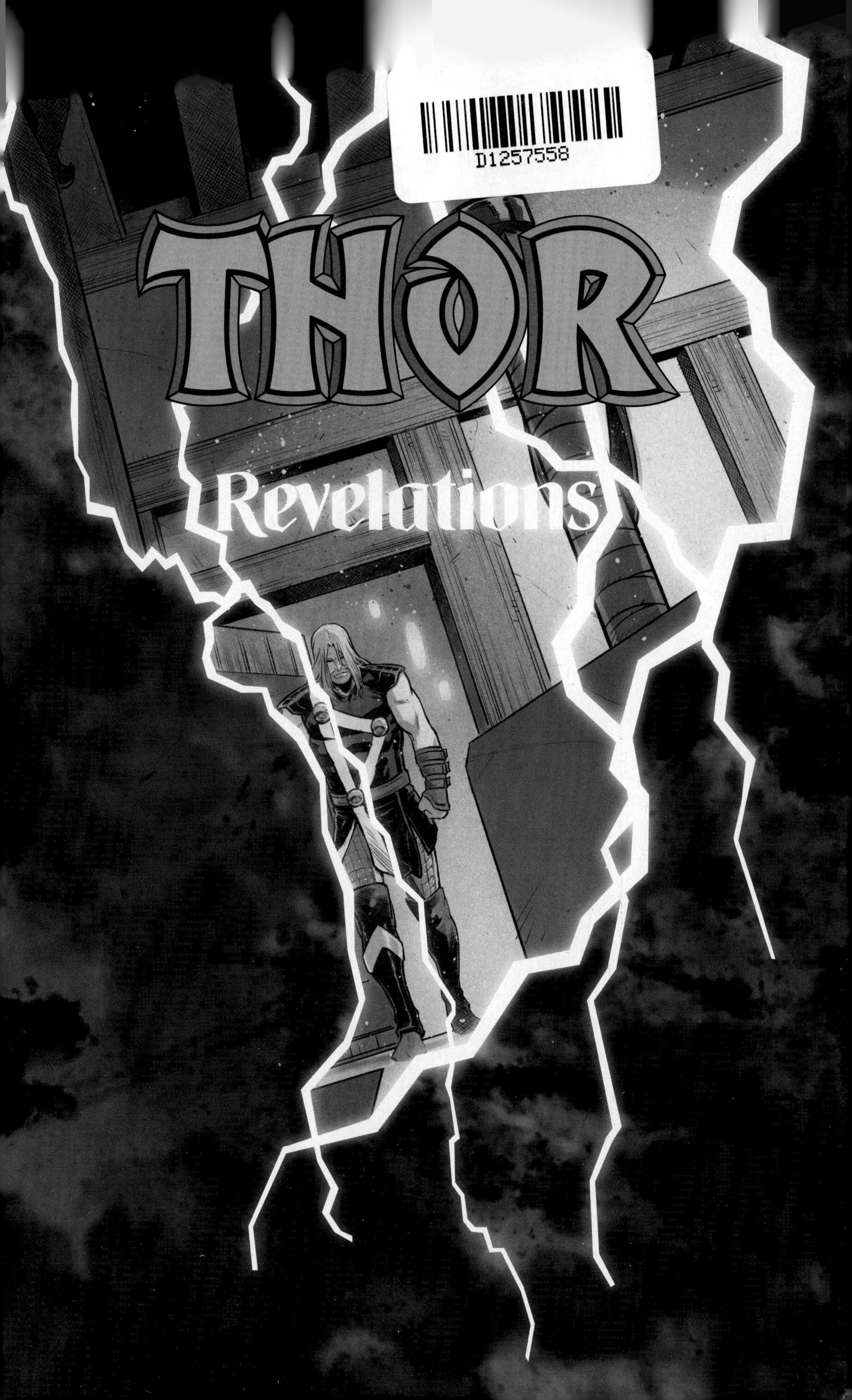
THOR
Revelations

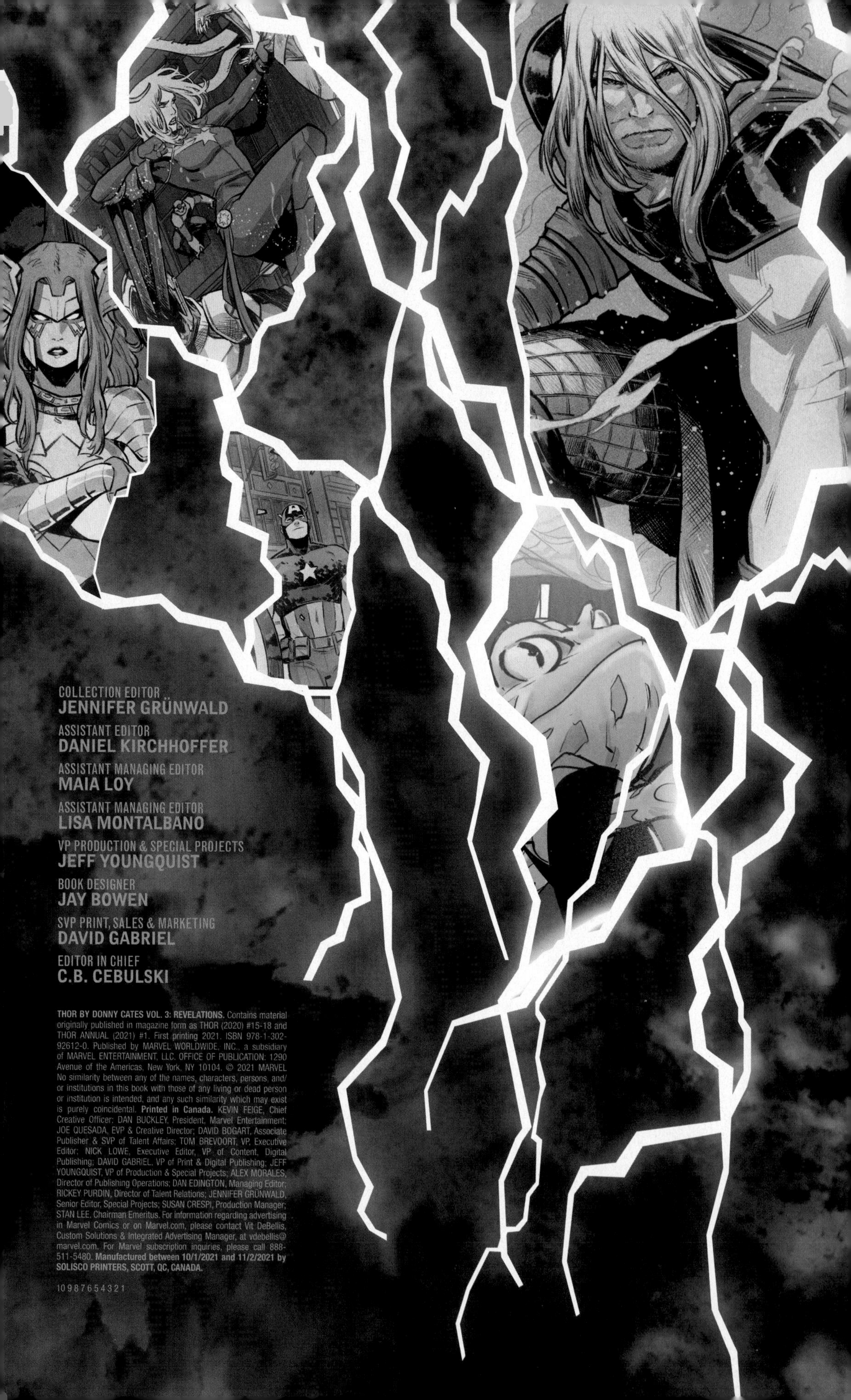

COLLECTION EDITOR
JENNIFER GRÜNWALD

ASSISTANT EDITOR
DANIEL KIRCHHOFFER

ASSISTANT MANAGING EDITOR
MAIA LOY

ASSISTANT MANAGING EDITOR
LISA MONTALBANO

VP PRODUCTION & SPECIAL PROJECTS
JEFF YOUNGQUIST

BOOK DESIGNER
JAY BOWEN

SVP PRINT, SALES & MARKETING
DAVID GABRIEL

EDITOR IN CHIEF
C.B. CEBULSKI

THOR BY DONNY CATES VOL. 3: REVELATIONS. Contains material originally published in magazine form as THOR (2020) #15-18 and THOR ANNUAL (2021) #1. First printing 2021. ISBN 978-1-302-92612-0. Published by MARVEL WORLDWIDE, INC., a subsidiary of MARVEL ENTERTAINMENT, LLC. OFFICE OF PUBLICATION: 1290 Avenue of the Americas, New York, NY 10104.

Printed in Canada. KEVIN FEIGE, Chief Creative Officer; DAN BUCKLEY, President, Marvel Entertainment; JOE QUESADA, EVP & Creative Director; DAVID BOGART, Associate Publisher & SVP of Talent Affairs; TOM BREVOORT, VP, Executive Editor; NICK LOWE, Executive Editor, VP of Content, Digital Publishing; DAVID GABRIEL, VP of Print & Digital Publishing; JEFF YOUNGQUIST, VP of Production & Special Projects; ALEX MORALES, Director of Publishing Operations; DAN EDINGTON, Managing Editor; RICKEY PURDIN, Director of Talent Relations; JENNIFER GRÜNWALD, Senior Editor, Special Projects; SUSAN CRESPI, Production Manager; STAN LEE, Chairman Emeritus. For information regarding advertising in Marvel Comics or on Marvel.com, please contact Vit DeBellis, Custom Solutions & Integrated Advertising Manager, at vdebellis@marvel.com. For Marvel subscription inquiries, please call 888-511-5480. **Manufactured between 10/1/2021 and 11/2/2021 by SOLISCO PRINTERS, SCOTT, QC, CANADA.**

10 9 8 7 6 5 4 3 2 1

THOR IS THE GOD OF THUNDER AND ALL-FATHER OF ASGARD.

OF LATE, HE HAS HAD TROUBLE WITH HIS HAMMER, MJOLNIR SOMETIMES IT IS TOO
HEAVY FOR HIM TO LIFT, AND OTHER TIMES PEOPLE LIKE HIS BROTHER LOKI ARE
ABLE TO LIFT IT DESPITE THE FACT THAT NO ONE BUT THOR SHOULD BE ABLE TO.

AND AFTER A DEADLY ENCOUNTER WITH HIS FORMER ALTER EGO, DONALD BLAKE —
WHO HAD GONE INSANE AND SOUGHT REVENGE ON ODIN AND ANYONE TOUCHED BY
HIS POWER — THOR FEELS MORE UNSURE OF HIMSELF THAN HE EVER HAS BEFORE.

SOMETHING MUST CHANGE. TRUTH MUST COME TO LIGHT...

THOR

Revelations

WRITER **Donny Cates**

THOR #15-17

PENCILER **Michele Bandini**
INKERS **Michele Bandini** (#15-17) &
Elisabetta D'Amico (#15-16)
COLOR ARTIST **Matthew Wilson**
LETTERER **VC's Joe Sabino**
COVER ART **Olivier Coipel & Matthew Wilson**

THOR #18

ARTISTS **Pasqual Ferry & Bob Quinn**
COLOR ARTIST **Matthew Wilson**
LETTERER **VC's Joe Sabino**
COVER ART **Olivier Coipel & Matthew Wilson**

THOR ANNUAL #1

WRITER/PENCILER AARON KUDER
INKERS CAM SMITH & AARON KUDER
COLOR ARTIST CHRIS O'HALLORAN
LETTERER VC's JOE SABINO
COVER ART AARON KUDER & MATTHEW WILSON

ASSOCIATE EDITOR **Sarah Brunstad**
EDITOR **Wil Moss**

THOR CREATED BY Stan Lee, Larry Lieber & Jack Kirby

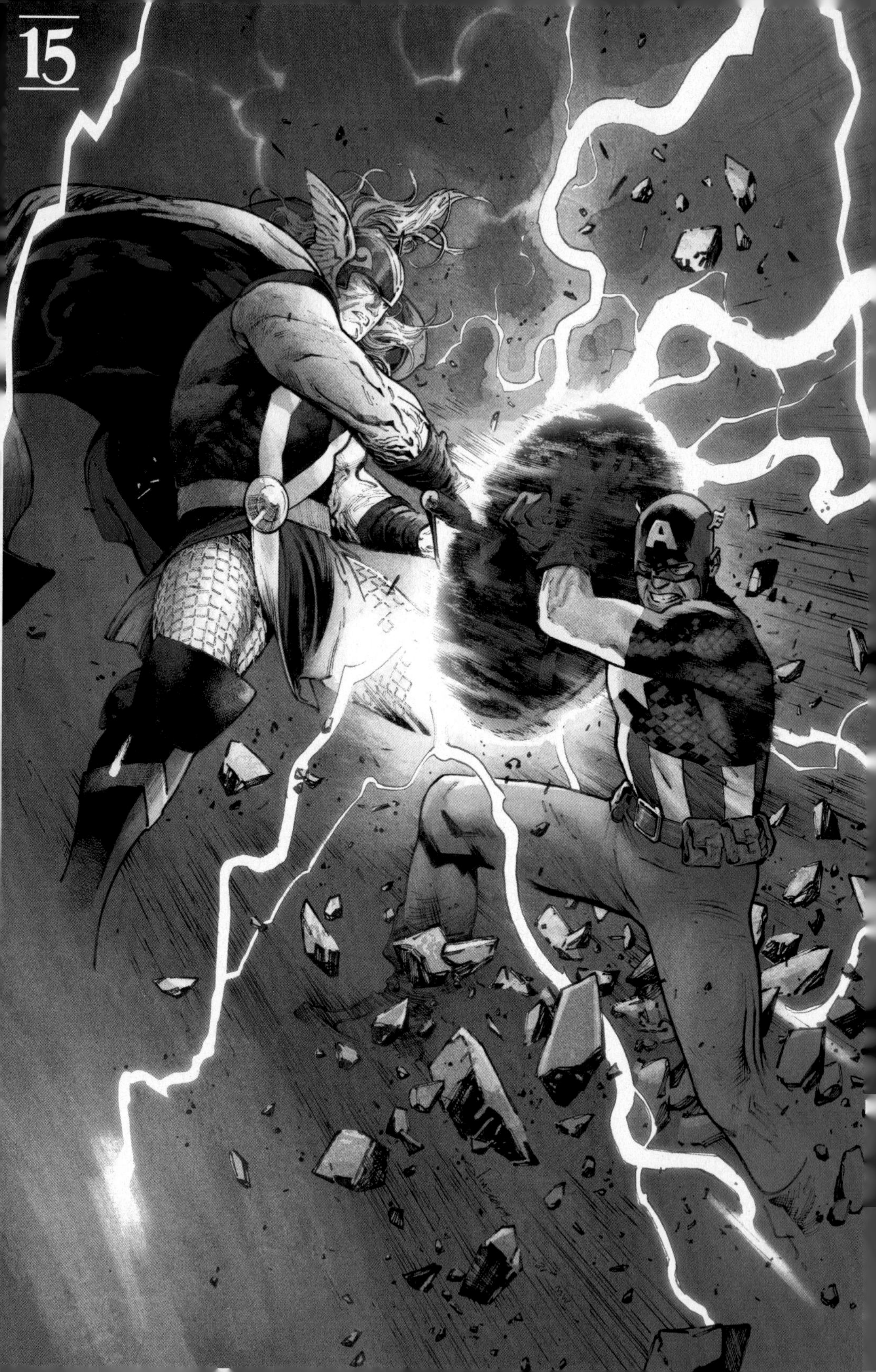
15

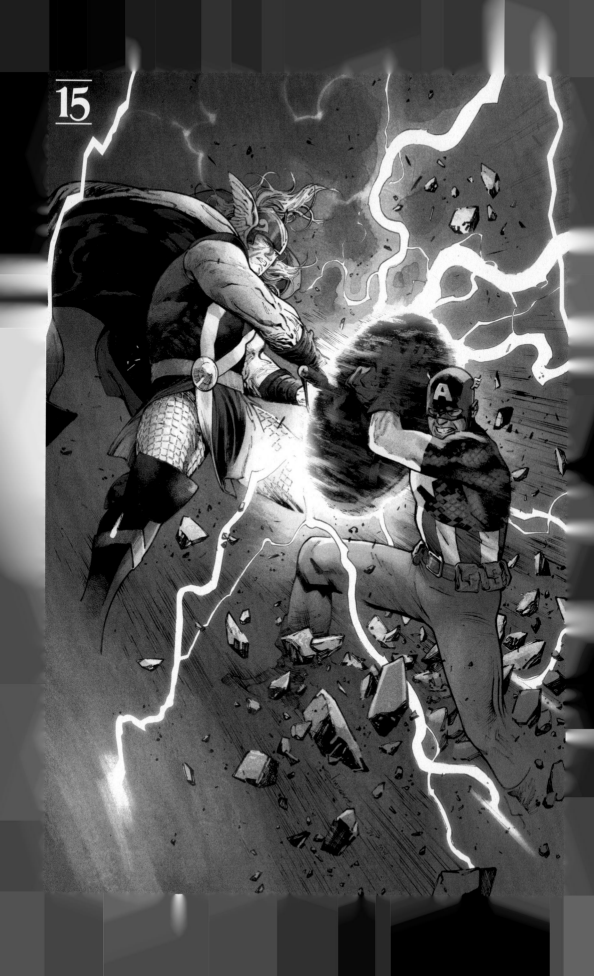

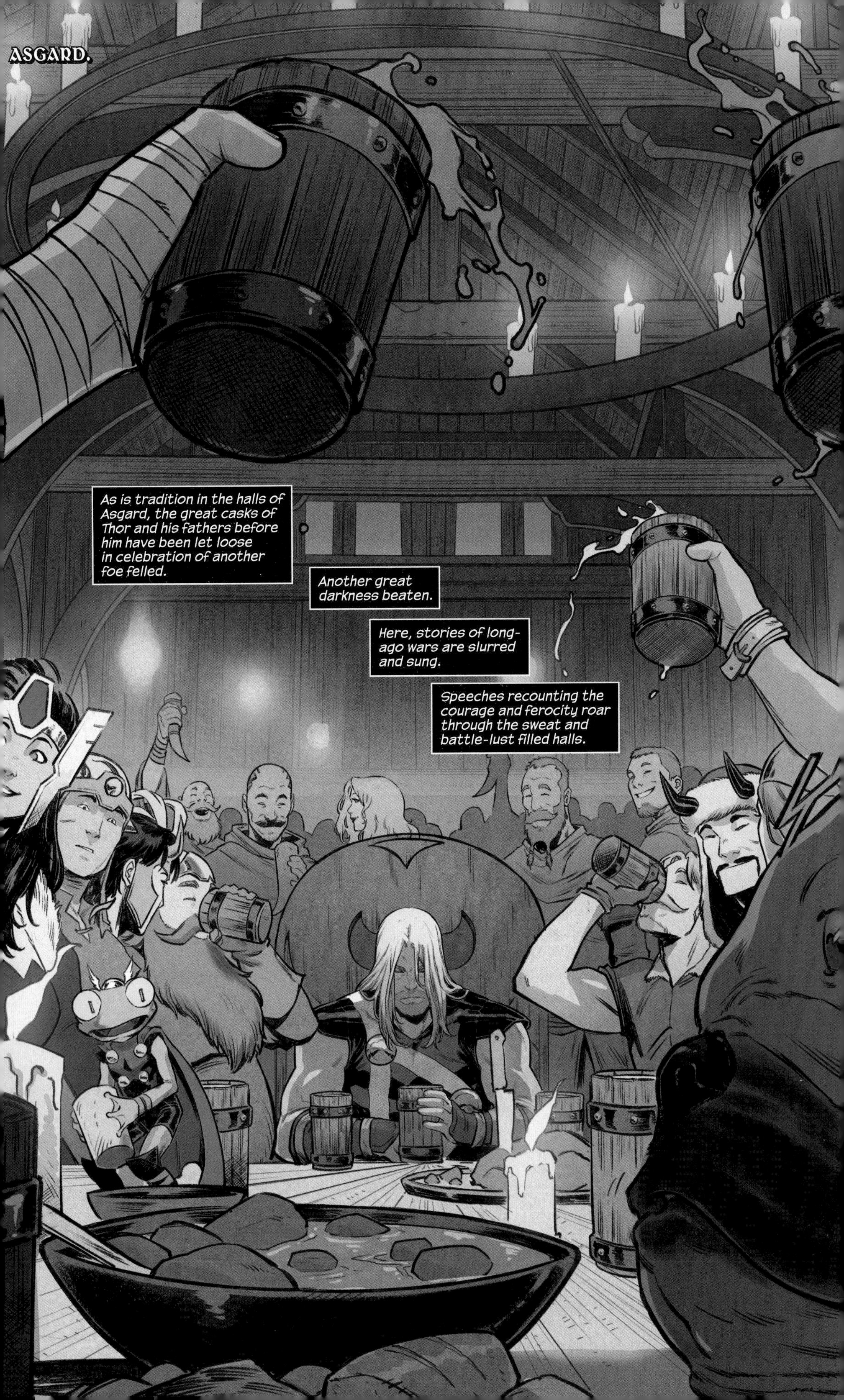
ASGARD.
As is tradition in the halls of Asgard, the great casks of Thor and his fathers before him have been let loose in celebration of another foe felled.
Another great darkness beaten.
Here, stories of long-ago wars are slurred and sung.
Speeches recounting the courage and ferocity roar through the sweat and battle-lust filled halls.

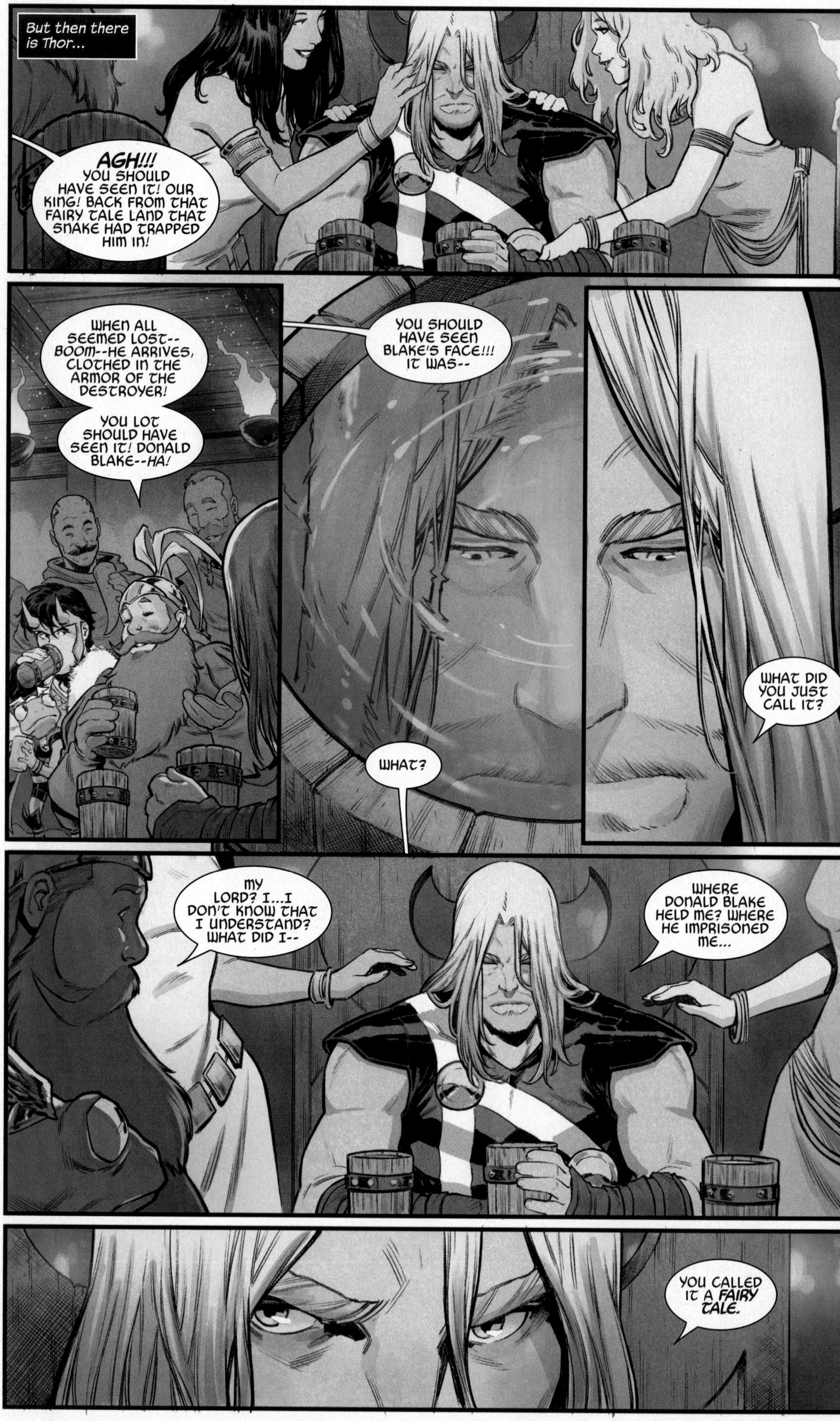
But then there is Thor...
AGH!!! YOU SHOULD HAVE SEEN IT! OUR KING! BACK FROM THAT FAIRY TALE LAND THAT SNAKE HAD TRAPPED HIM IN!
WHEN ALL SEEMED LOST--BOOM--HE ARRIVES, CLOTHED IN THE ARMOR OF THE DESTROYER!
YOU LOT SHOULD HAVE SEEN IT! DONALD BLAKE--HA!
YOU SHOULD HAVE SEEN BLAKE'S FACE!!! IT WAS--
WHAT DID YOU JUST CALL IT?
WHAT?
MY LORD? I...I DON'T KNOW THAT I UNDERSTAND? WHAT DID I--
WHERE DONALD BLAKE HELD ME? WHERE HE IMPRISONED ME...
YOU CALLED IT A FAIRY TALE.

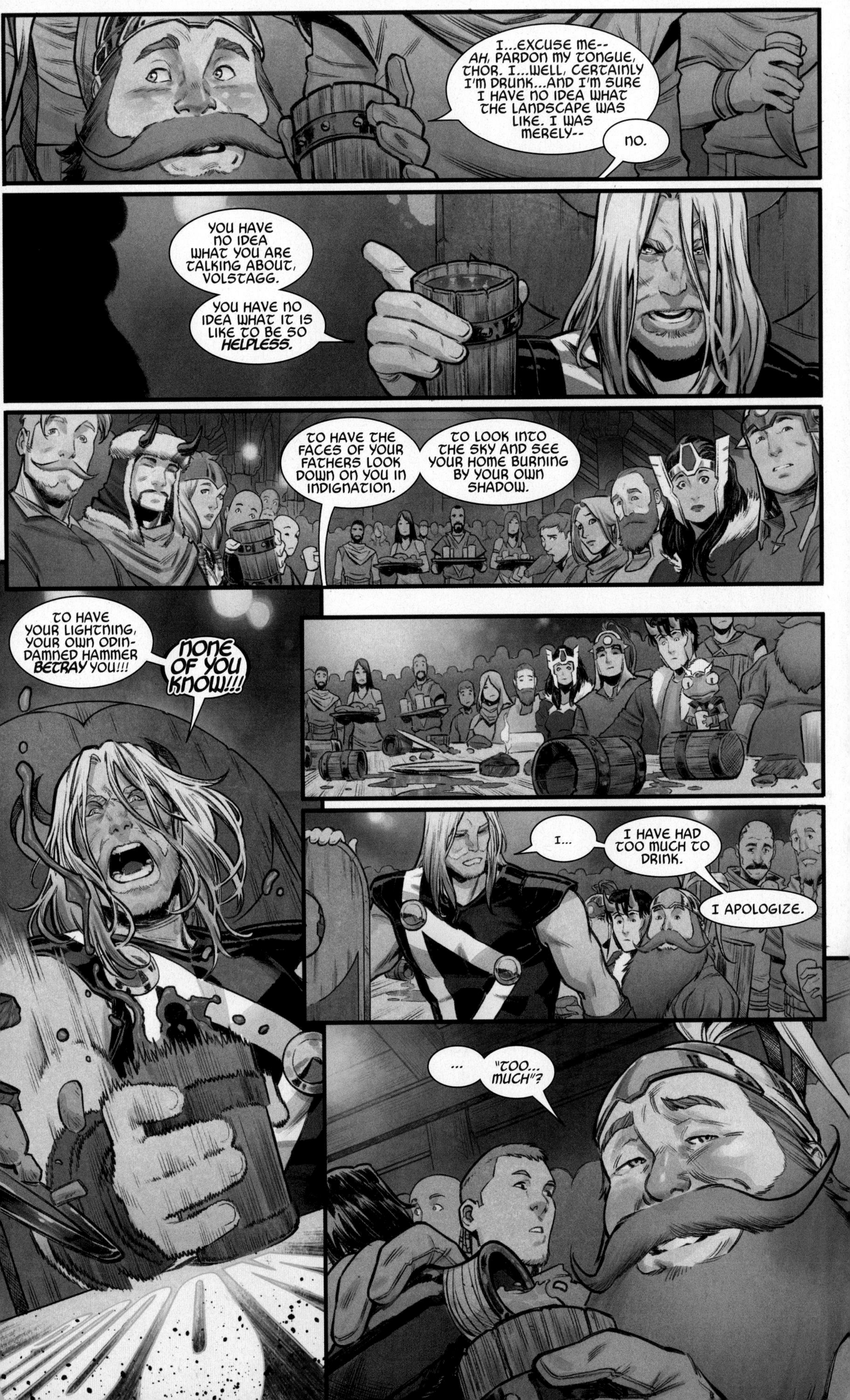

I...EXCUSE ME-- AH, PARDON MY TONGUE, THOR. I...WELL, CERTAINLY I'M DRUNK...AND I'M SURE I HAVE NO IDEA WHAT THE LANDSCAPE WAS LIKE. I WAS MERELY--
NO.
YOU HAVE NO IDEA WHAT YOU ARE TALKING ABOUT, VOLSTAGG.
YOU HAVE NO IDEA WHAT IT IS LIKE TO BE SO HELPLESS.
TO HAVE THE FACES OF YOUR FATHERS LOOK DOWN ON YOU IN INDIGNATION.
TO LOOK INTO THE SKY AND SEE YOUR HOME BURNING BY YOUR OWN SHADOW.
TO HAVE YOUR LIGHTNING, YOUR OWN ODIN-DAMNED HAMMER BETRAY YOU!!!
NONE OF YOU KNOW!!!
I...
I HAVE HAD TOO MUCH TO DRINK.
I APOLOGIZE.
...
"TOO... MUCH"?

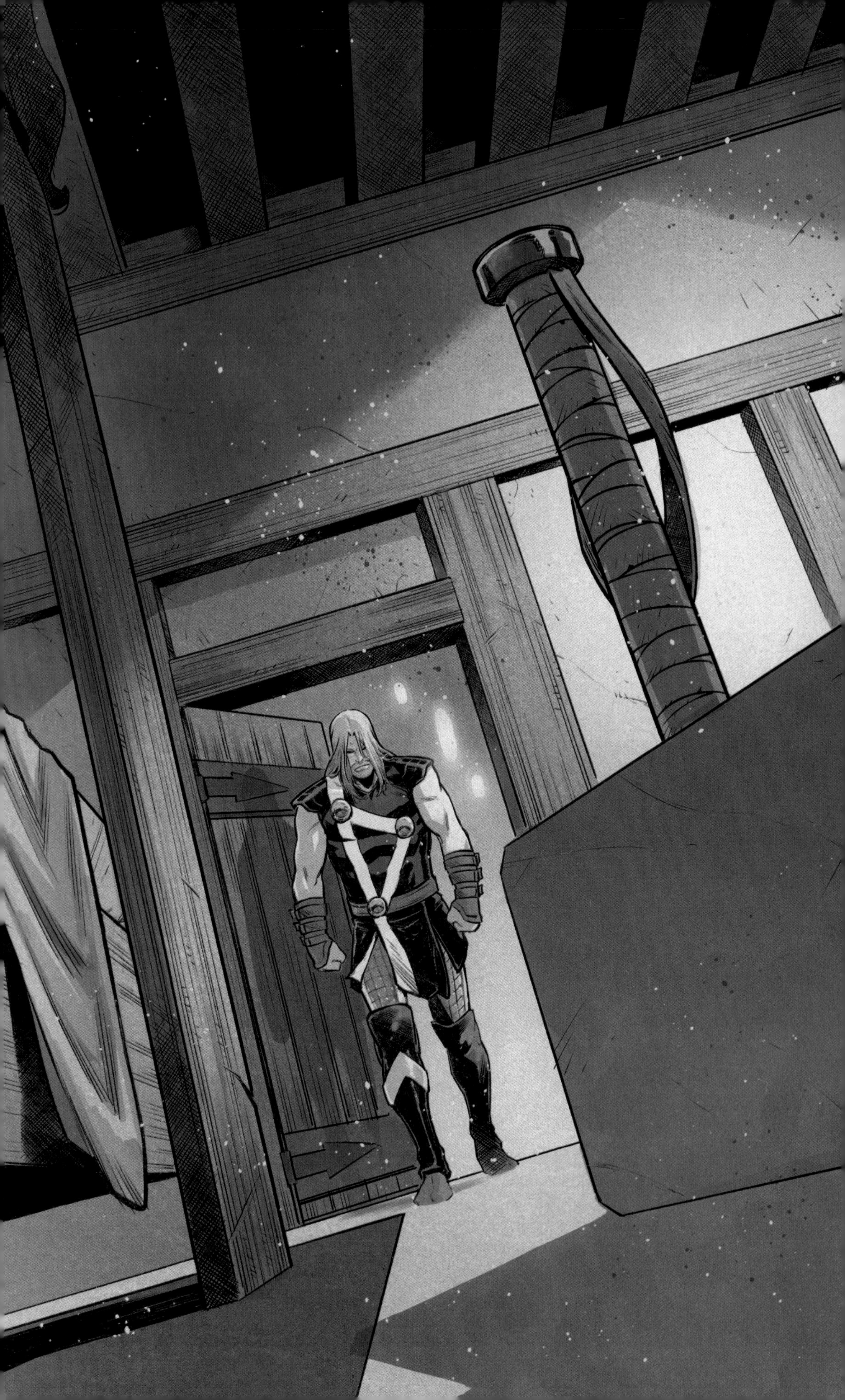

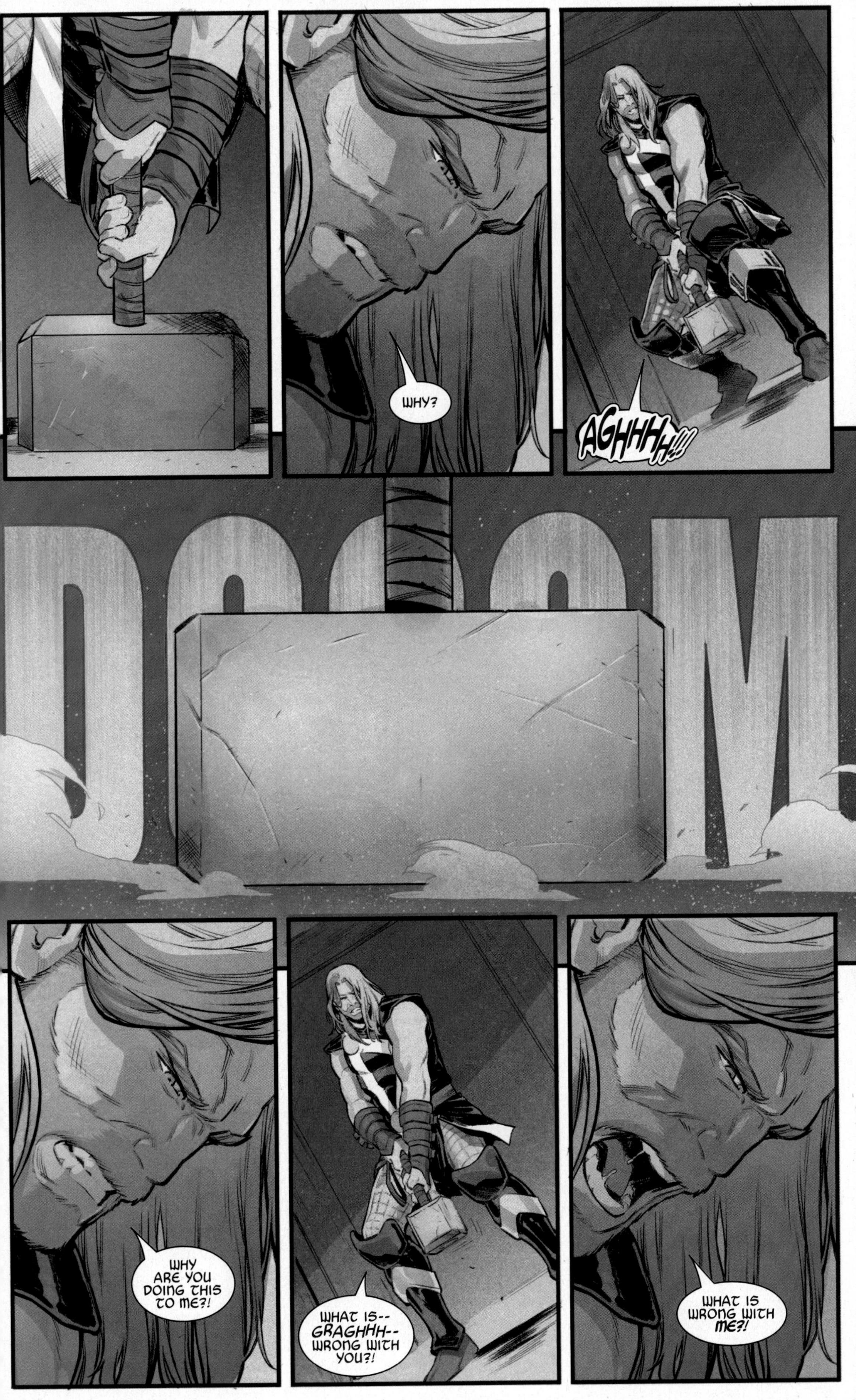
WHY?
AGHHHH!!!
DOOOM
WHY ARE YOU DOING THIS TO ME?!
WHAT IS-- GRAGHHH-- WRONG WITH YOU?!
WHAT IS WRONG WITH ME?!

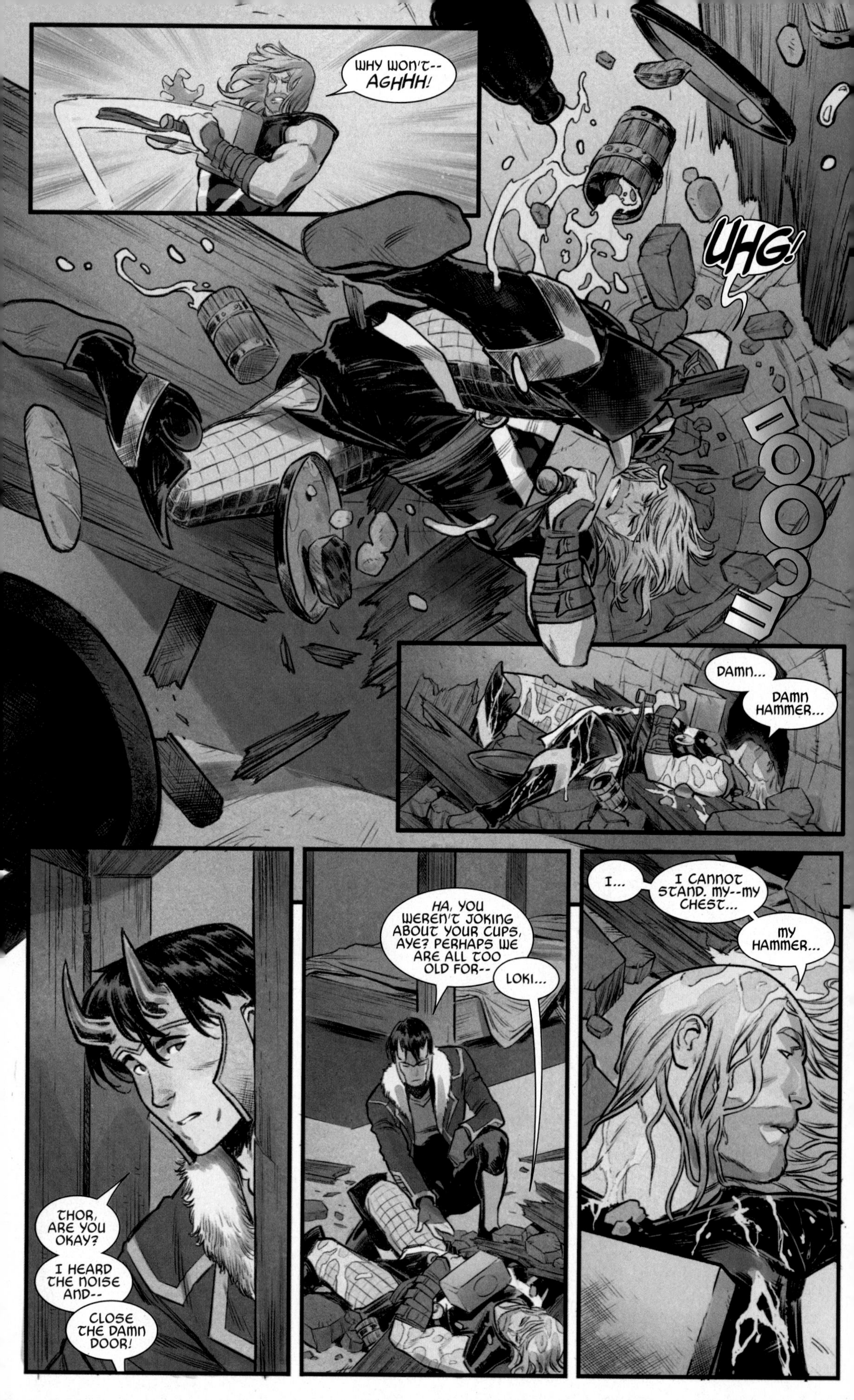
WHY WON'T--
AGHHH!
UHG!
DOOOOM!!
DAMN...
DAMN HAMMER...
THOR, ARE YOU OKAY?
I HEARD THE NOISE AND--
CLOSE THE DAMN DOOR!
HA, YOU WEREN'T JOKING ABOUT YOUR CUPS, AYE? PERHAPS WE ARE ALL TOO OLD FOR--
LOKI...
I...
I CANNOT STAND. MY--MY CHEST...
MY HAMMER...

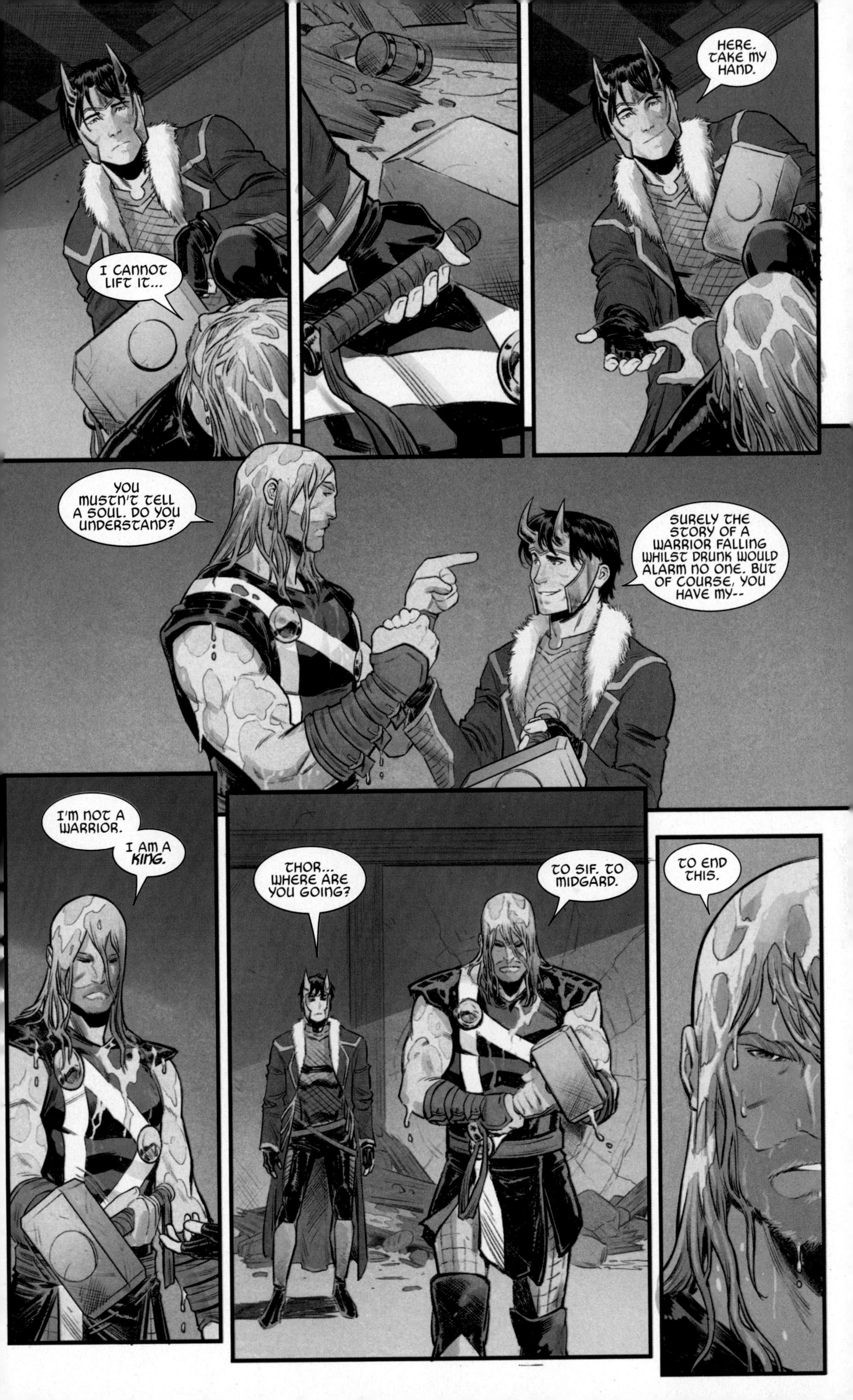
I CANNOT LIFT IT...
HERE. TAKE MY HAND.
YOU MUSTN'T TELL A SOUL. DO YOU UNDERSTAND?
SURELY THE STORY OF A WARRIOR FALLING WHILST DRUNK WOULD ALARM NO ONE. BUT OF COURSE, YOU HAVE MY--
I'M NOT A WARRIOR.
I AM A *KING.*
THOR... WHERE ARE YOU GOING?
TO SIF. TO MIDGARD.
TO END THIS.

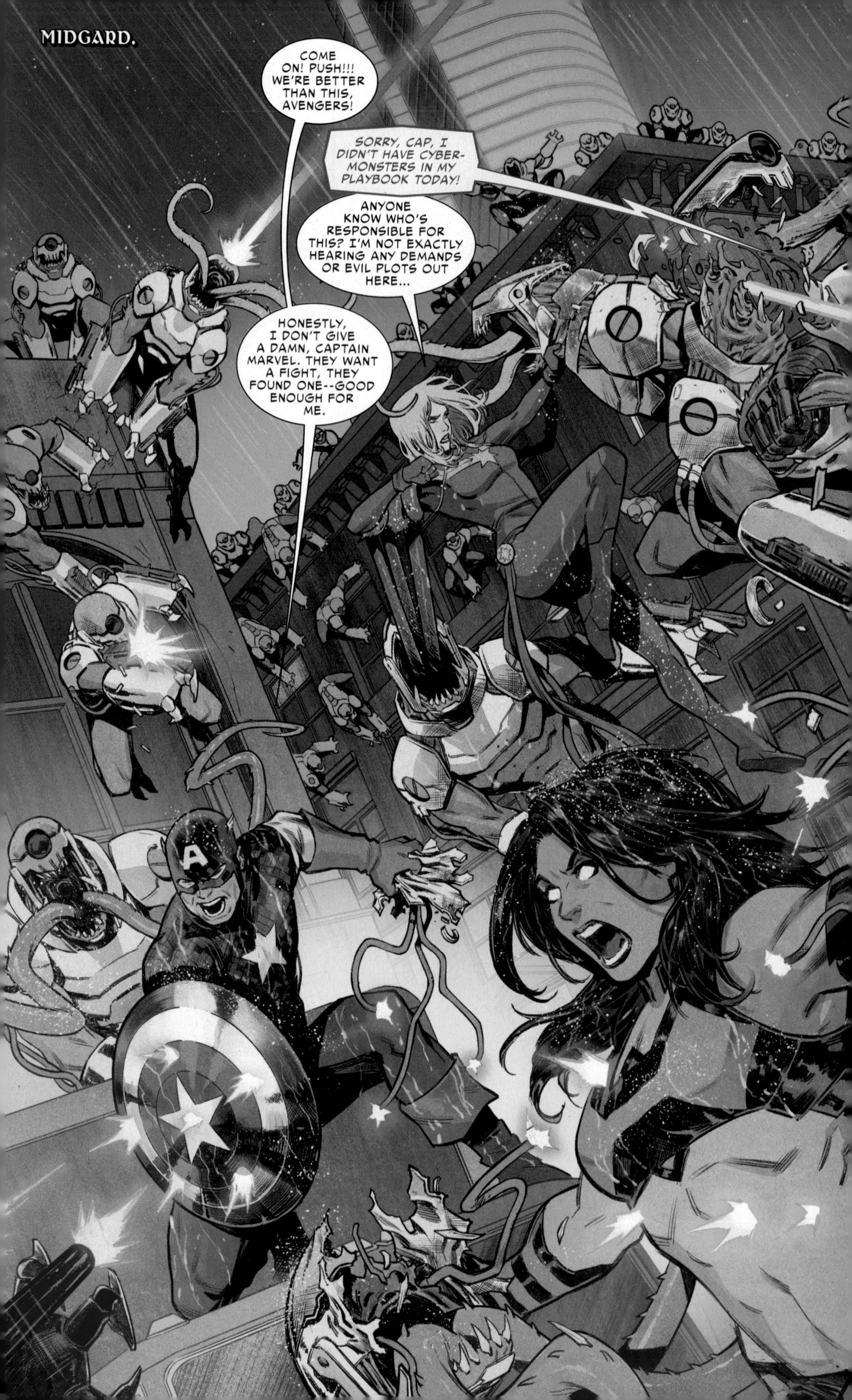
MIDGARD.
COME ON! PUSH!!! WE'RE BETTER THAN THIS, AVENGERS!
SORRY, CAP, I DIDN'T HAVE CYBER-MONSTERS IN MY PLAYBOOK TODAY!
ANYONE KNOW WHO'S RESPONSIBLE FOR THIS? I'M NOT EXACTLY HEARING ANY DEMANDS OR EVIL PLOTS OUT HERE...
HONESTLY, I DON'T GIVE A DAMN, CAPTAIN MARVEL. THEY WANT A FIGHT, THEY FOUND ONE--GOOD ENOUGH FOR ME.

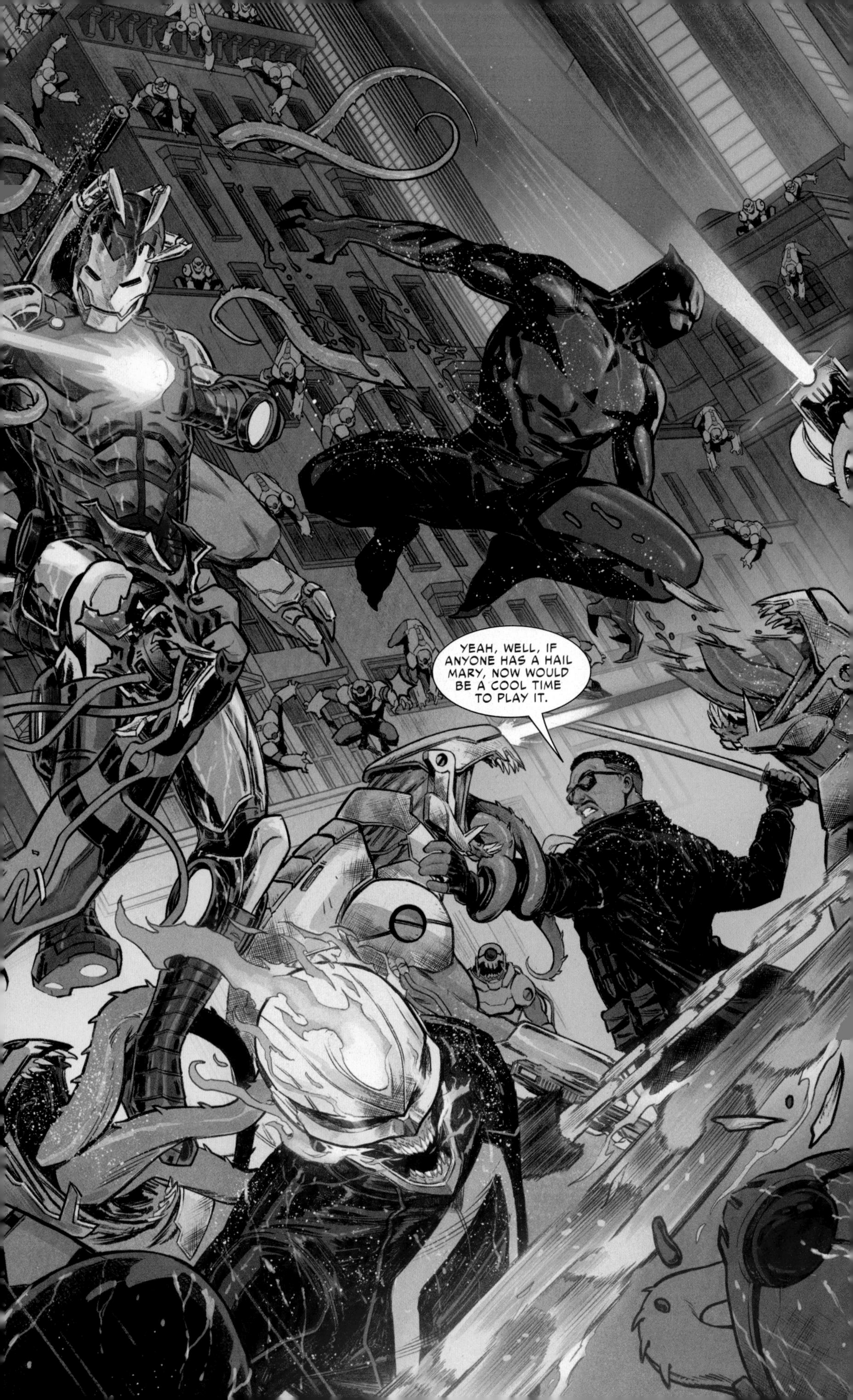
YEAH, WELL, IF ANYONE HAS A HAIL MARY, NOW WOULD BE A COOL TIME TO PLAY IT.

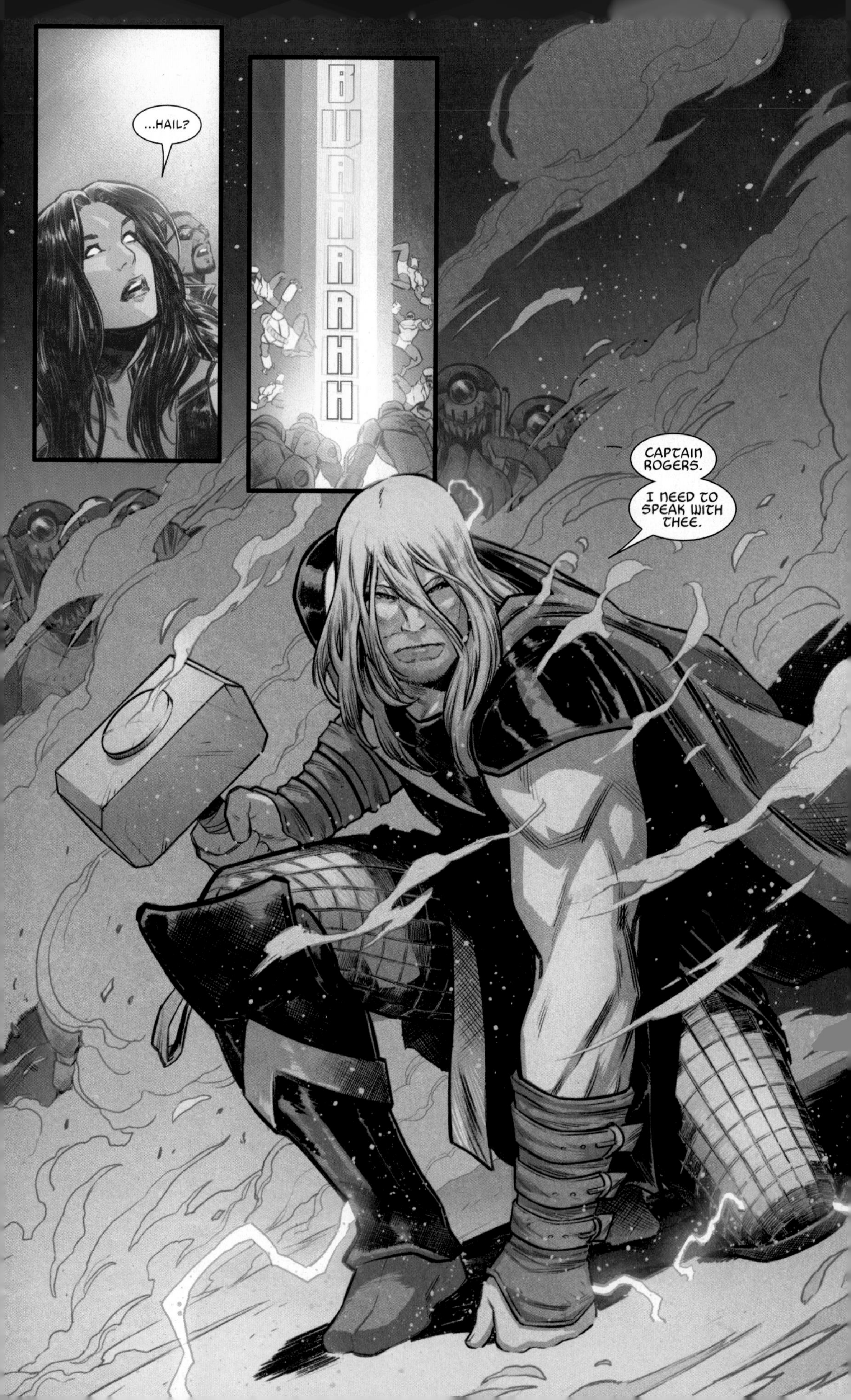
...HAIL?
BWAAAAHH
CAPTAIN ROGERS.
I NEED TO SPEAK WITH THEE.

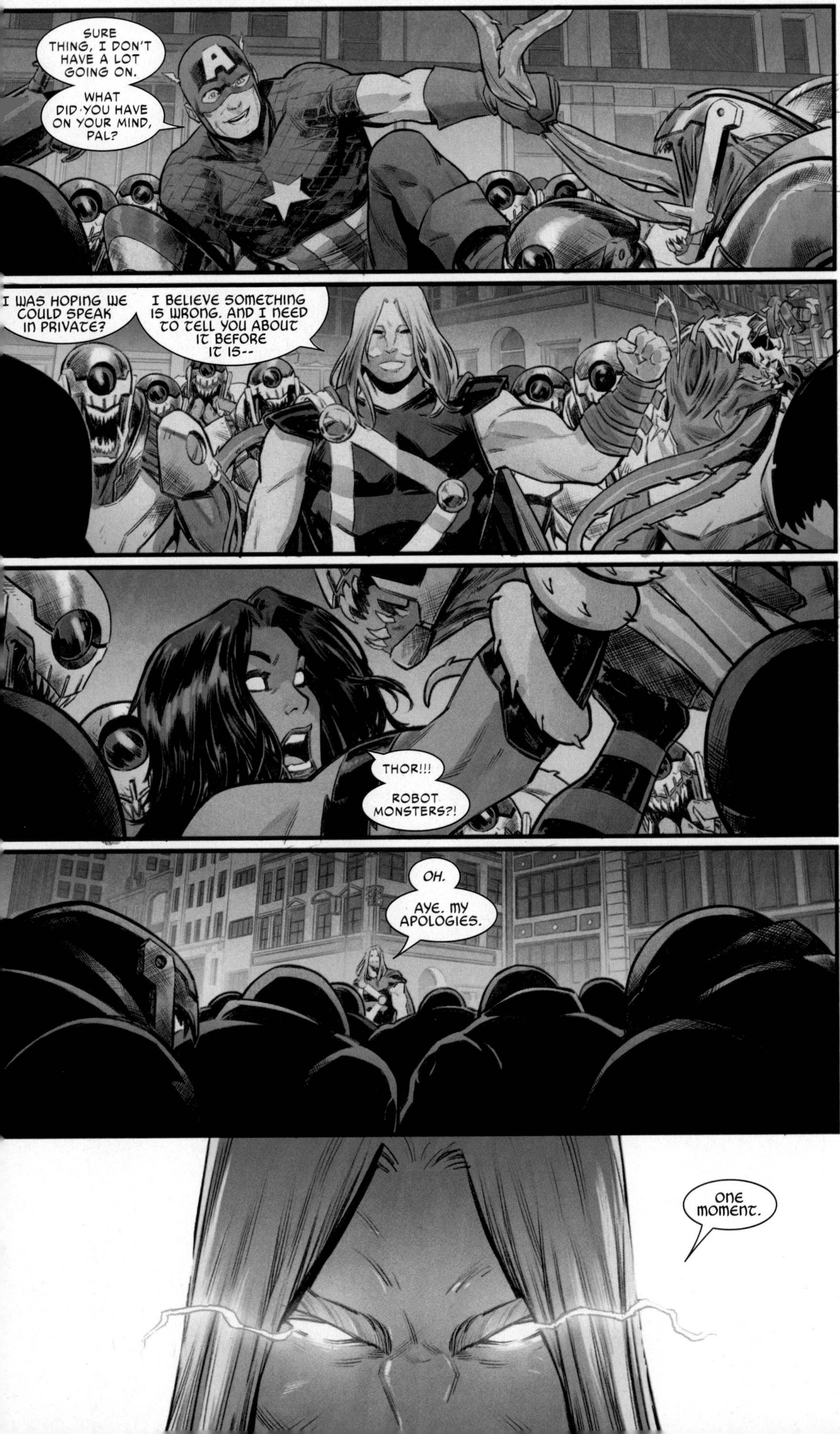
SURE THING, I DON'T HAVE A LOT GOING ON.
WHAT DID YOU HAVE ON YOUR MIND, PAL?
I WAS HOPING WE COULD SPEAK IN PRIVATE?
I BELIEVE SOMETHING IS WRONG. AND I NEED TO TELL YOU ABOUT IT BEFORE IT IS--
THOR!!!
ROBOT MONSTERS?!
OH.
AYE. MY APOLOGIES.
ONE MOMENT.

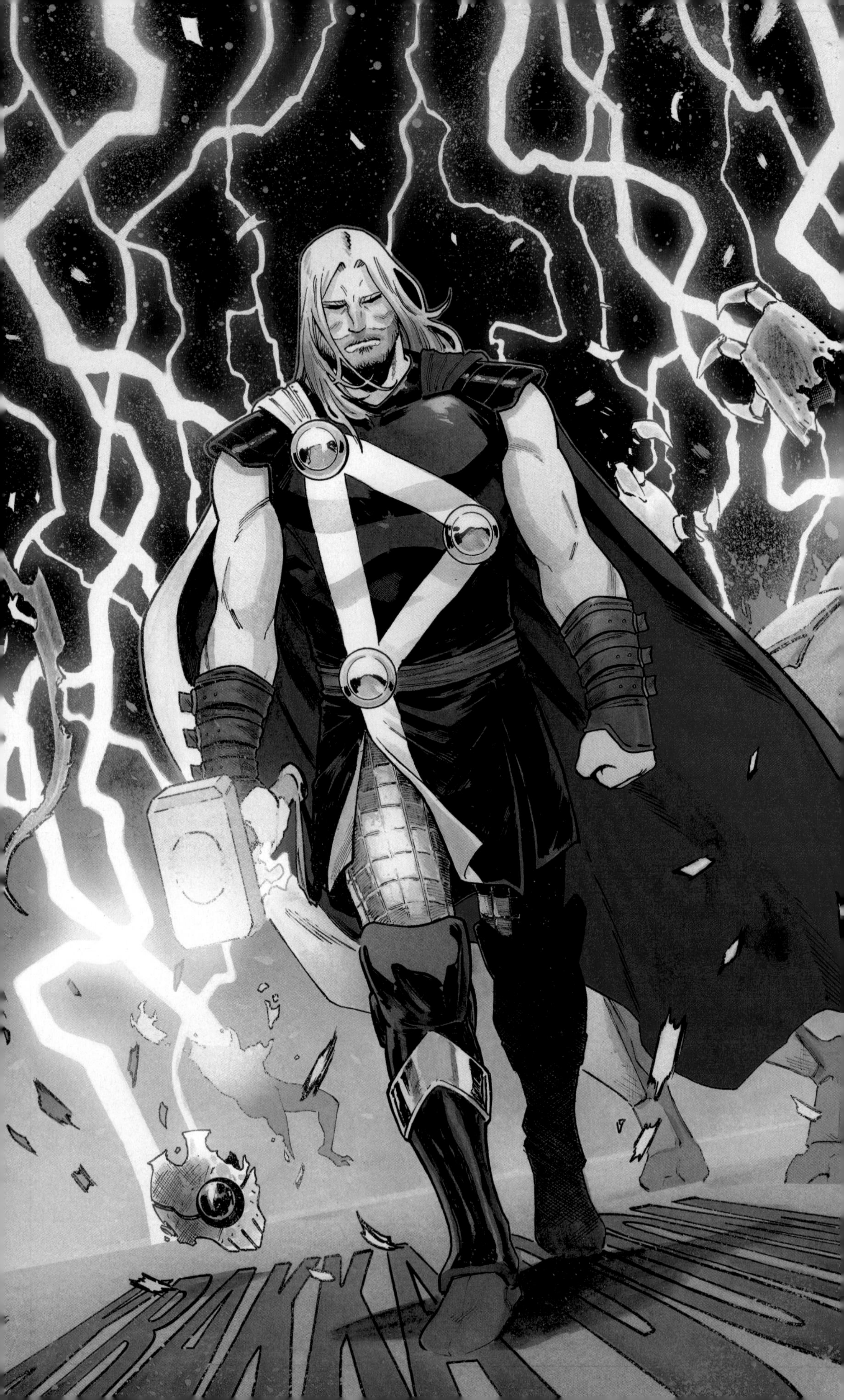

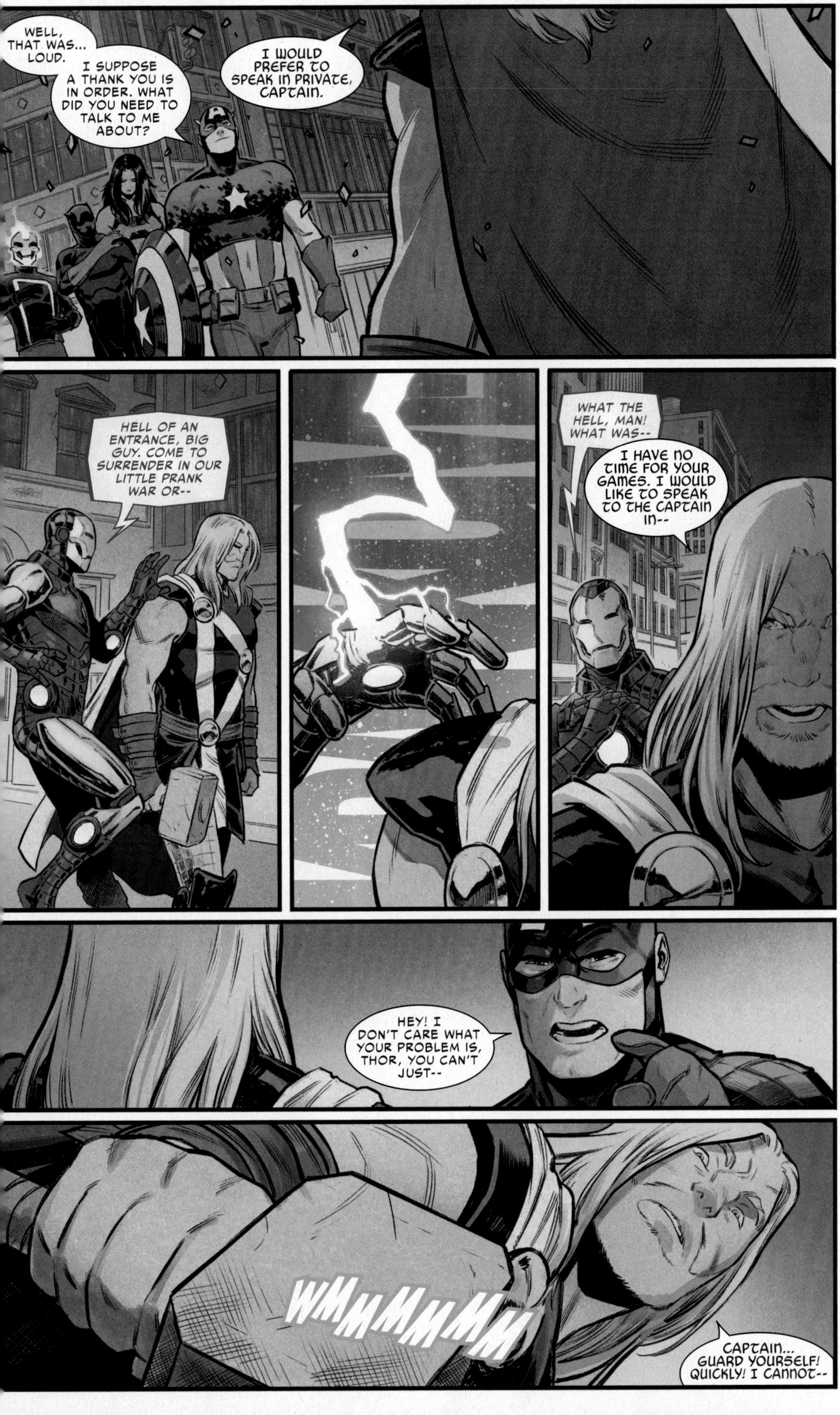
WELL, THAT WAS... LOUD.
I SUPPOSE A THANK YOU IS IN ORDER. WHAT DID YOU NEED TO TALK TO ME ABOUT?
I WOULD PREFER TO SPEAK IN PRIVATE, CAPTAIN.
HELL OF AN ENTRANCE, BIG GUY. COME TO SURRENDER IN OUR LITTLE PRANK WAR OR--
WHAT THE HELL, MAN! WHAT WAS--
I HAVE NO TIME FOR YOUR GAMES. I WOULD LIKE TO SPEAK TO THE CAPTAIN IN--
HEY! I DON'T CARE WHAT YOUR PROBLEM IS, THOR, YOU CAN'T JUST--
WMMMMMMM
CAPTAIN... GUARD YOURSELF! QUICKLY! I CANNOT--

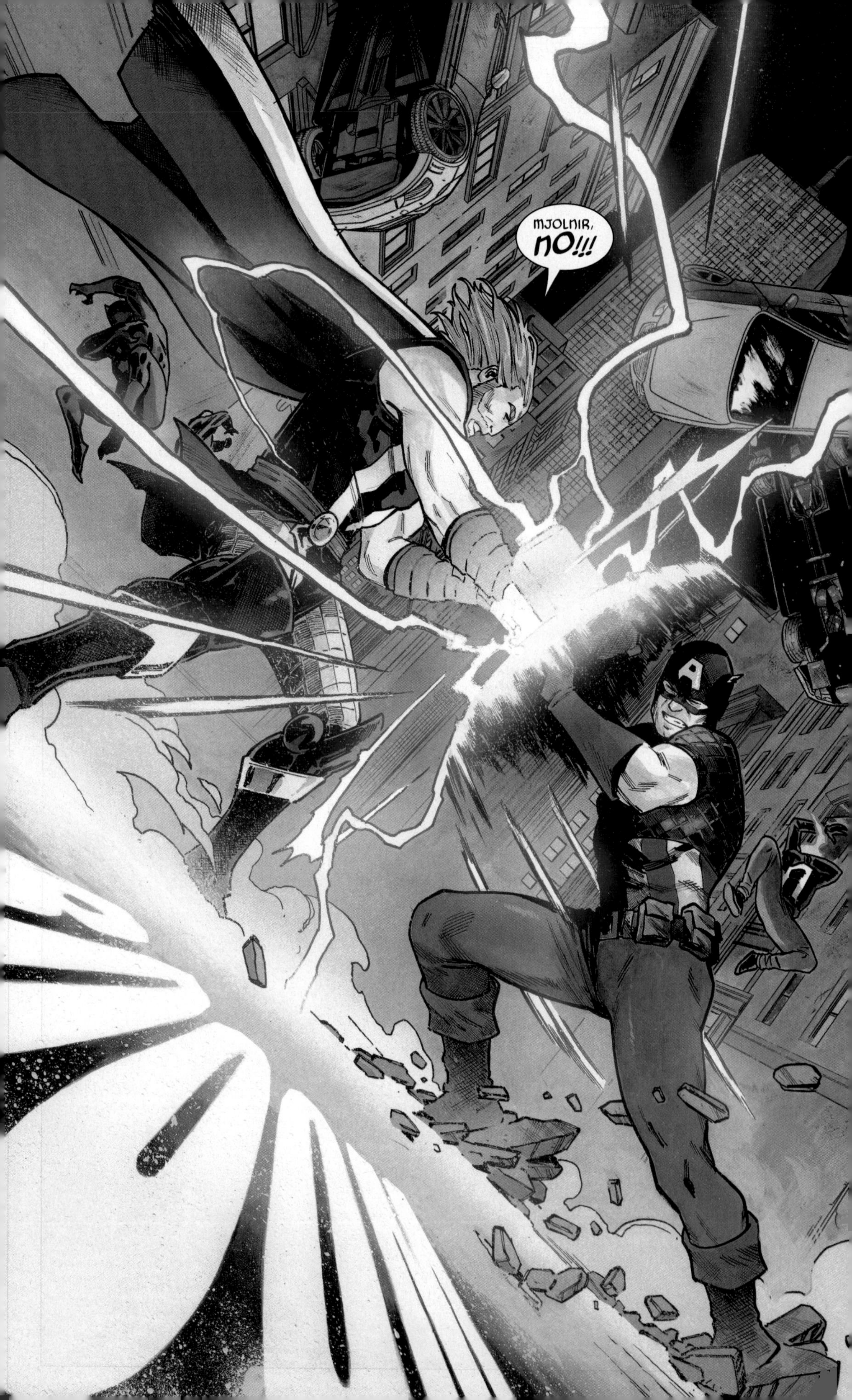
MJOLNIR, NO!!!

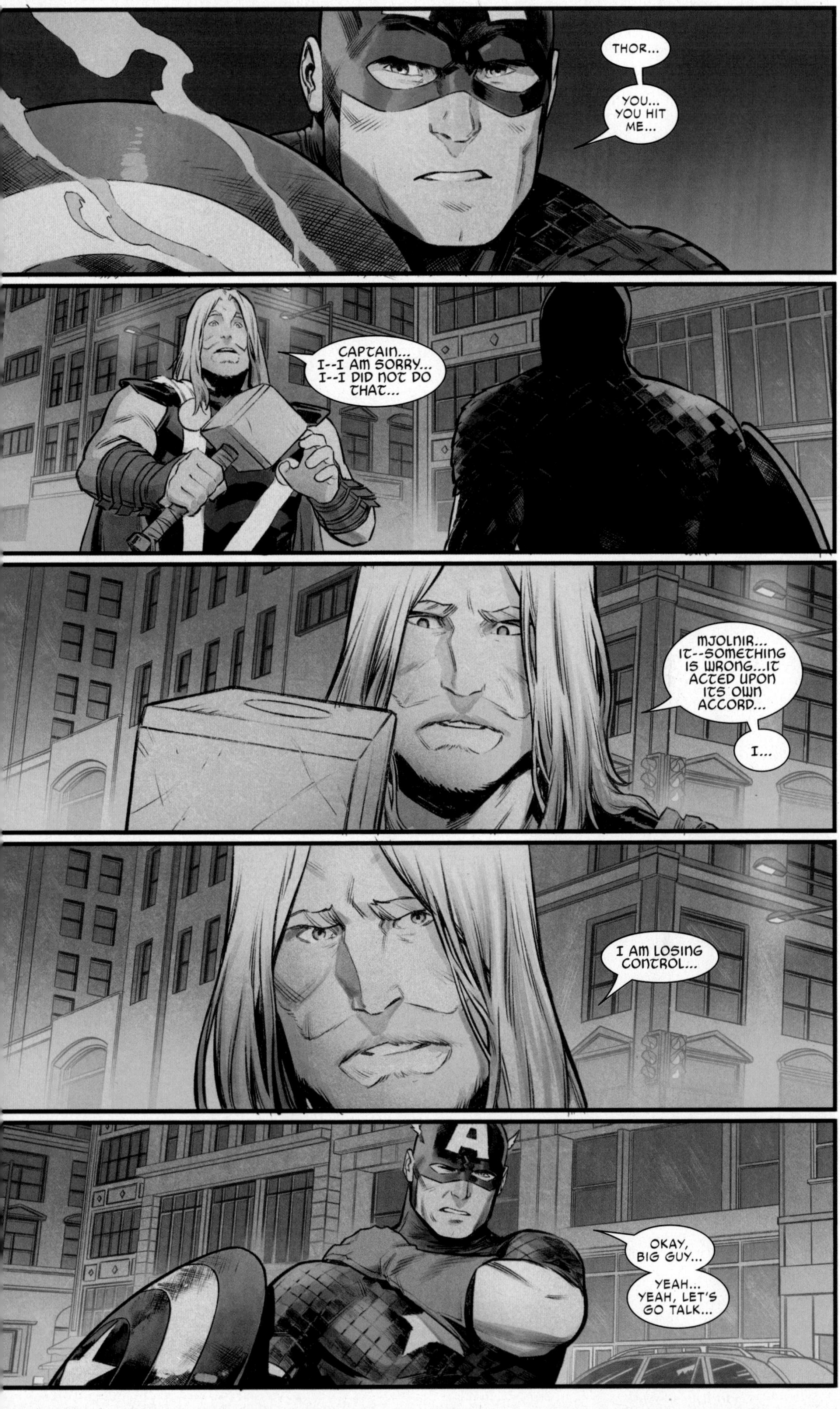
THOR...
YOU... YOU HIT ME...
CAPTAIN... I--I AM SORRY... I--I DID NOT DO THAT...
MJOLNIR... IT--SOMETHING IS WRONG...IT ACTED UPON ITS OWN ACCORD...
I...
I AM LOSING CONTROL...
OKAY, BIG GUY...
YEAH... YEAH, LET'S GO TALK...

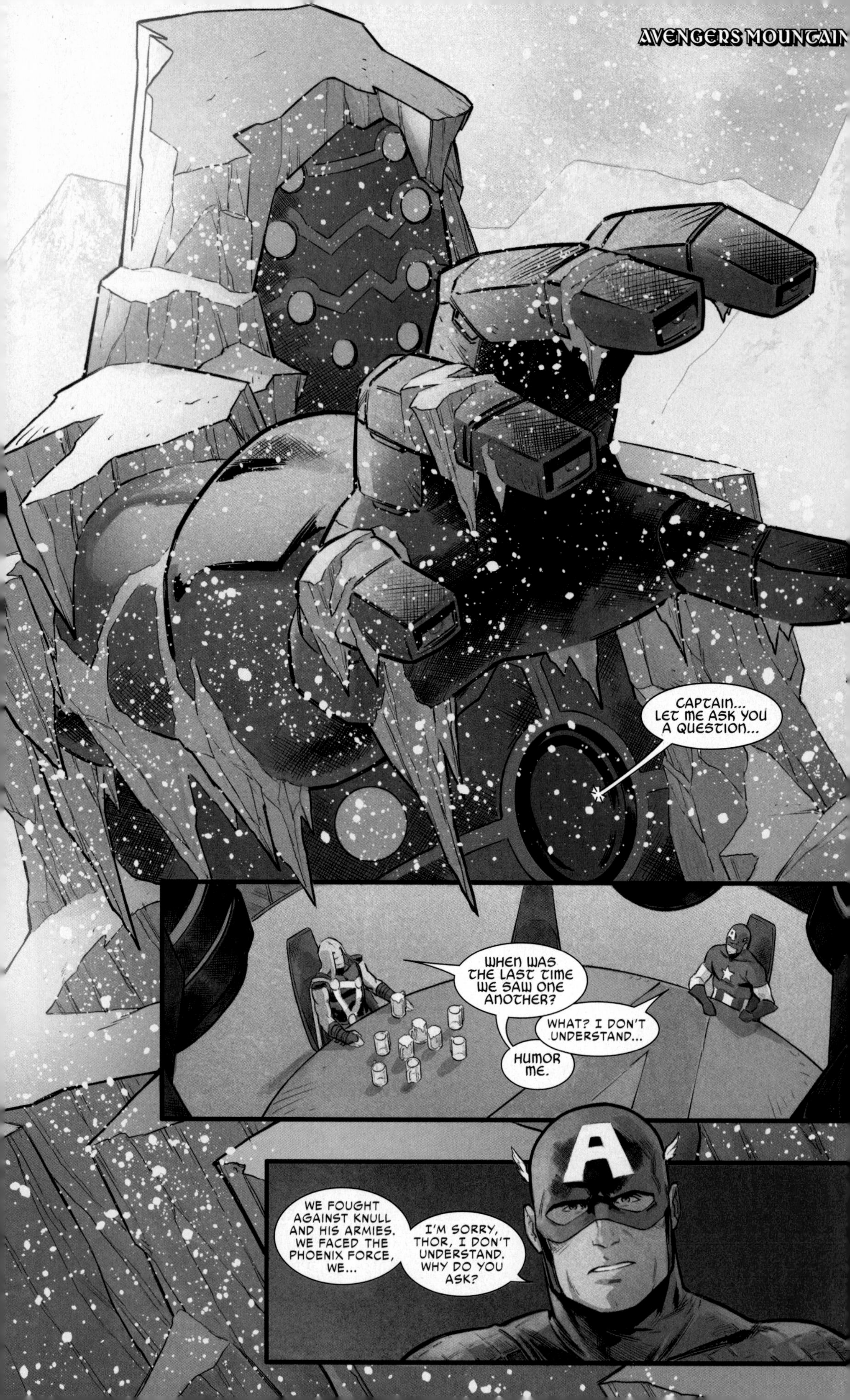
AVENGERS MOUNTAIN
CAPTAIN... LET ME ASK YOU A QUESTION...
WHEN WAS THE LAST TIME WE SAW ONE ANOTHER?
WHAT? I DON'T UNDERSTAND...
HUMOR ME.
WE FOUGHT AGAINST KNULL AND HIS ARMIES. WE FACED THE PHOENIX FORCE, WE...
I'M SORRY, THOR, I DON'T UNDERSTAND. WHY DO YOU ASK?

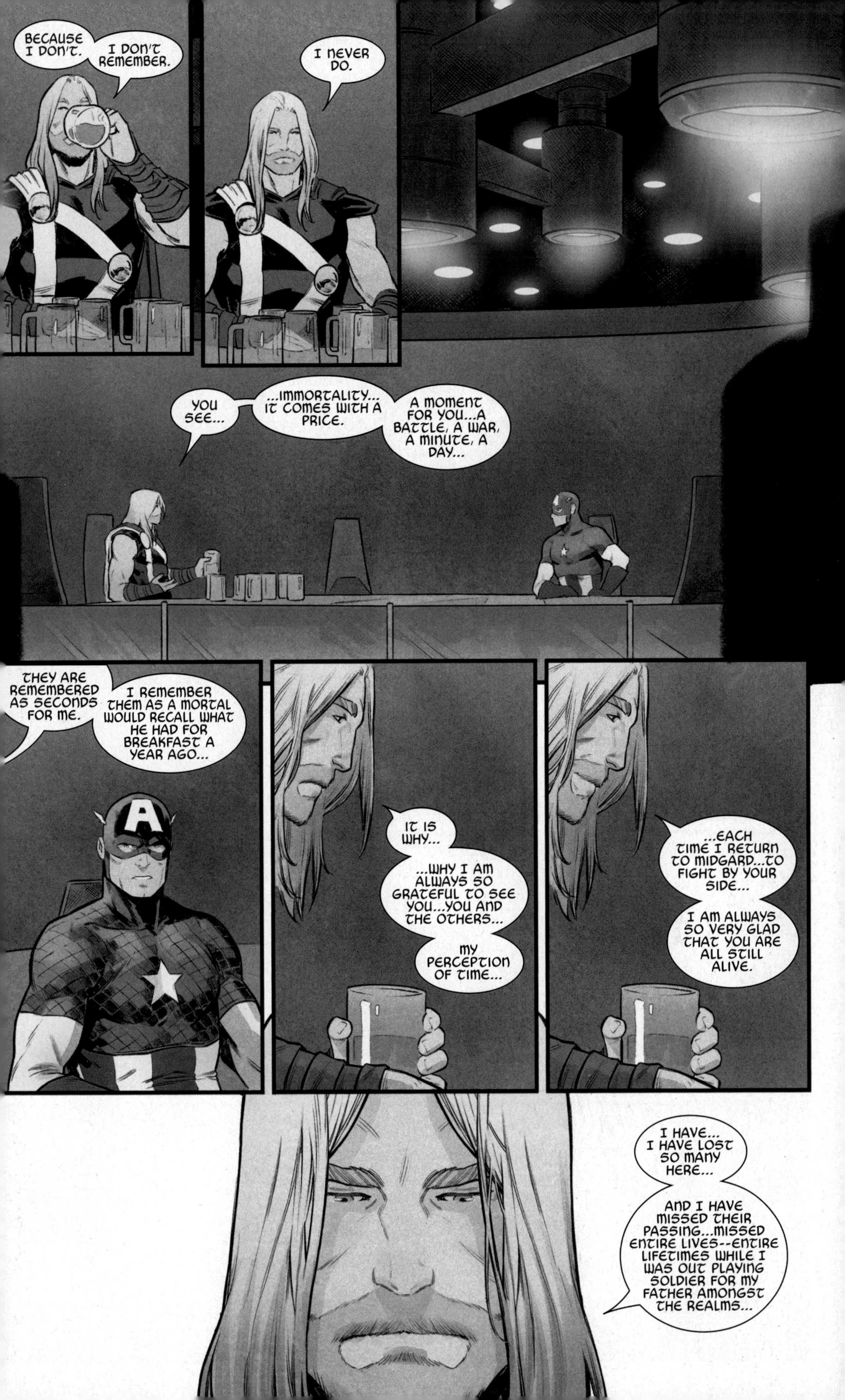
BECAUSE I DON'T.
I DON'T REMEMBER.
I NEVER DO.
YOU SEE...
...IMMORTALITY... IT COMES WITH A PRICE.
A MOMENT FOR YOU...A BATTLE, A WAR, A MINUTE, A DAY...
THEY ARE REMEMBERED AS SECONDS FOR ME.
I REMEMBER THEM AS A MORTAL WOULD RECALL WHAT HE HAD FOR BREAKFAST A YEAR AGO...
IT IS WHY...
...WHY I AM ALWAYS SO GRATEFUL TO SEE YOU...YOU AND THE OTHERS...
MY PERCEPTION OF TIME...
...EACH TIME I RETURN TO MIDGARD...TO FIGHT BY YOUR SIDE...
I AM ALWAYS SO VERY GLAD THAT YOU ARE ALL STILL ALIVE.
I HAVE... I HAVE LOST SO MANY HERE...
AND I HAVE MISSED THEIR PASSING...MISSED ENTIRE LIVES--ENTIRE LIFETIMES WHILE I WAS OUT PLAYING SOLDIER FOR MY FATHER AMONGST THE REALMS...

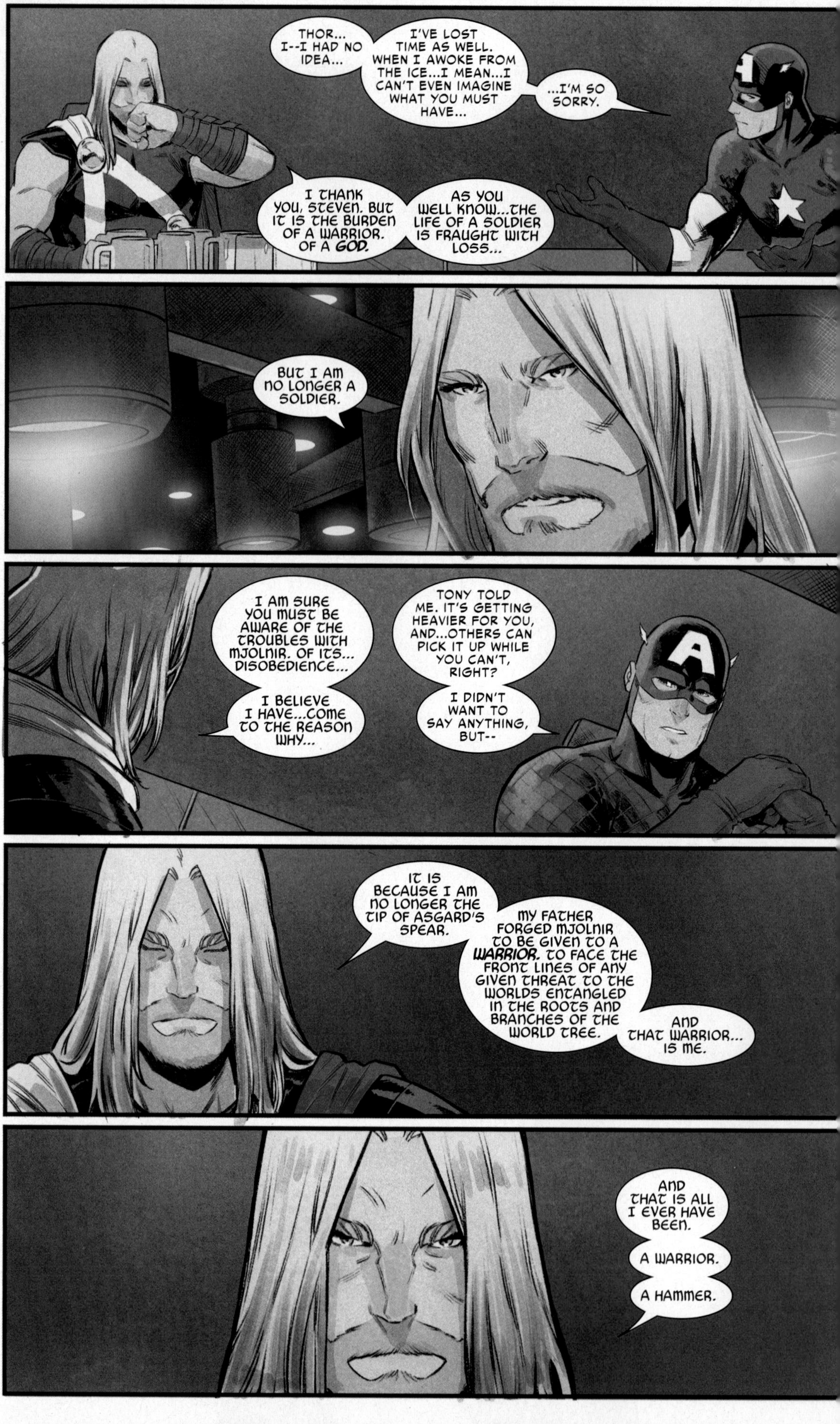

THOR... I--I HAD NO IDEA...
I'VE LOST TIME AS WELL. WHEN I AWOKE FROM THE ICE...I MEAN...I CAN'T EVEN IMAGINE WHAT YOU MUST HAVE...
...I'M SO SORRY.
I THANK YOU, STEVEN. BUT IT IS THE BURDEN OF A WARRIOR. OF A GOD.
AS YOU WELL KNOW...THE LIFE OF A SOLDIER IS FRAUGHT WITH LOSS...
BUT I AM NO LONGER A SOLDIER.
I AM SURE YOU MUST BE AWARE OF THE TROUBLES WITH MJOLNIR. OF ITS... DISOBEDIENCE...
I BELIEVE I HAVE...COME TO THE REASON WHY...
TONY TOLD ME. IT'S GETTING HEAVIER FOR YOU, AND...OTHERS CAN PICK IT UP WHILE YOU CAN'T, RIGHT?
I DIDN'T WANT TO SAY ANYTHING, BUT--
IT IS BECAUSE I AM NO LONGER THE TIP OF ASGARD'S SPEAR.
MY FATHER FORGED MJOLNIR TO BE GIVEN TO A WARRIOR. TO FACE THE FRONT LINES OF ANY GIVEN THREAT TO THE WORLDS ENTANGLED IN THE ROOTS AND BRANCHES OF THE WORLD TREE.
AND THAT WARRIOR... IS ME.
AND THAT IS ALL I EVER HAVE BEEN.
A WARRIOR.
A HAMMER.

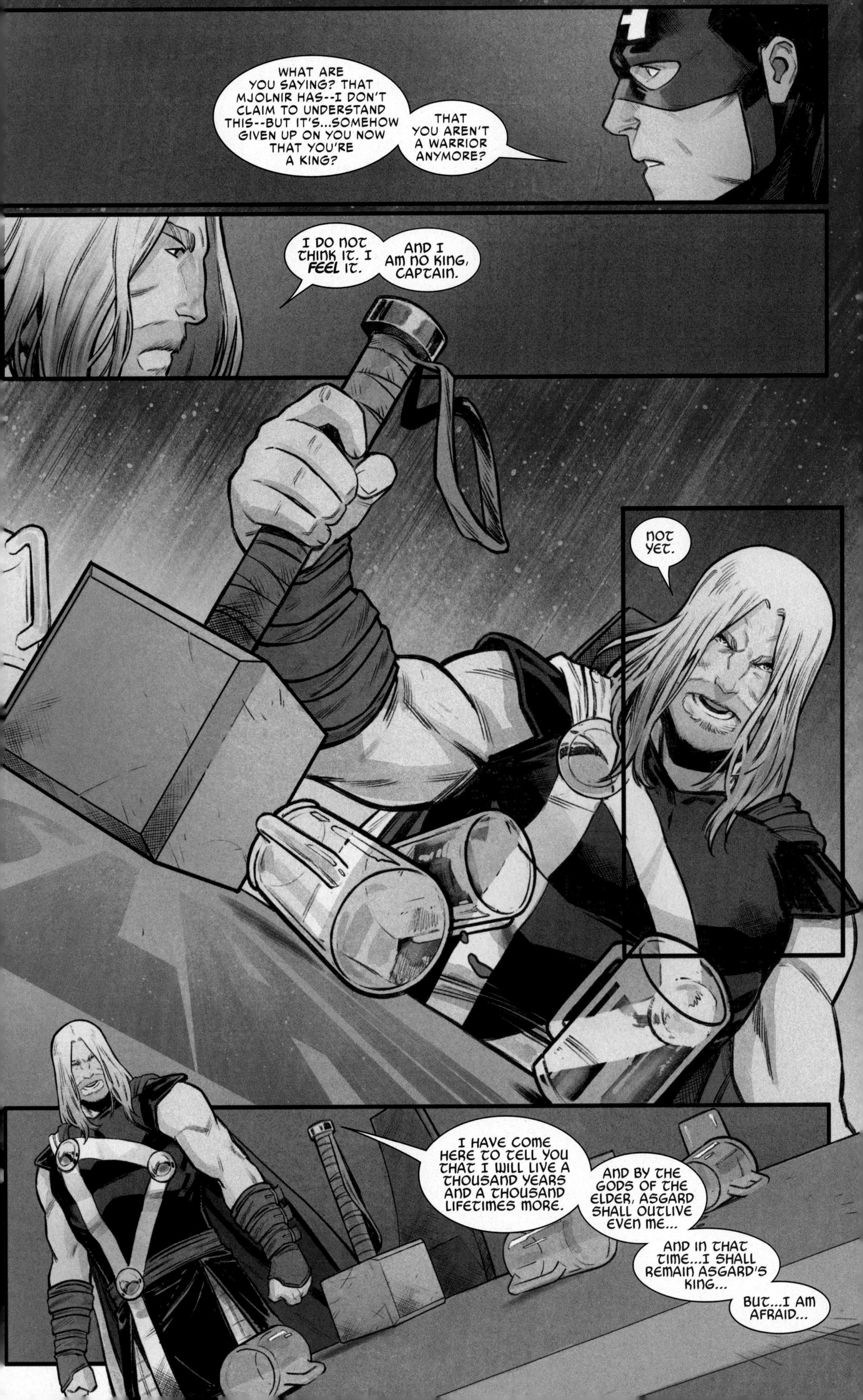
WHAT ARE YOU SAYING? THAT MJOLNIR HAS--I DON'T CLAIM TO UNDERSTAND THIS--BUT IT'S...SOMEHOW GIVEN UP ON YOU NOW THAT YOU'RE A KING?
THAT YOU AREN'T A WARRIOR ANYMORE?
I DO NOT THINK IT. I FEEL IT.
AND I AM NO KING, CAPTAIN.
NOT YET.
I HAVE COME HERE TO TELL YOU THAT I WILL LIVE A THOUSAND YEARS AND A THOUSAND LIFETIMES MORE.
AND BY THE GODS OF THE ELDER, ASGARD SHALL OUTLIVE EVEN ME...
AND IN THAT TIME...I SHALL REMAIN ASGARD'S KING...
BUT...I AM AFRAID...

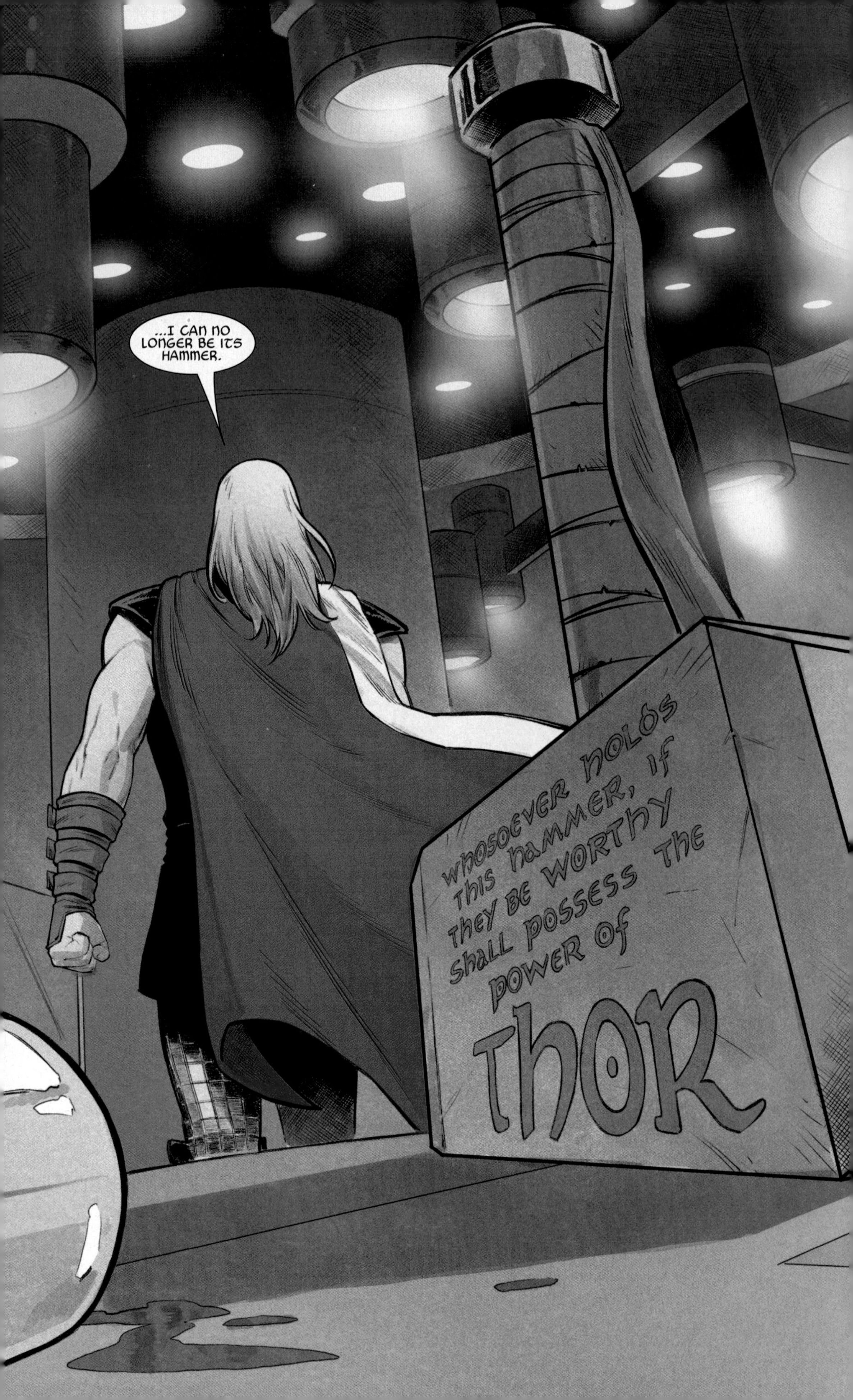
...I CAN NO LONGER BE ITS HAMMER.
WHOSOEVER HOLDS THIS HAMMER, IF THEY BE WORTHY SHALL POSSESS THE POWER OF
THOR

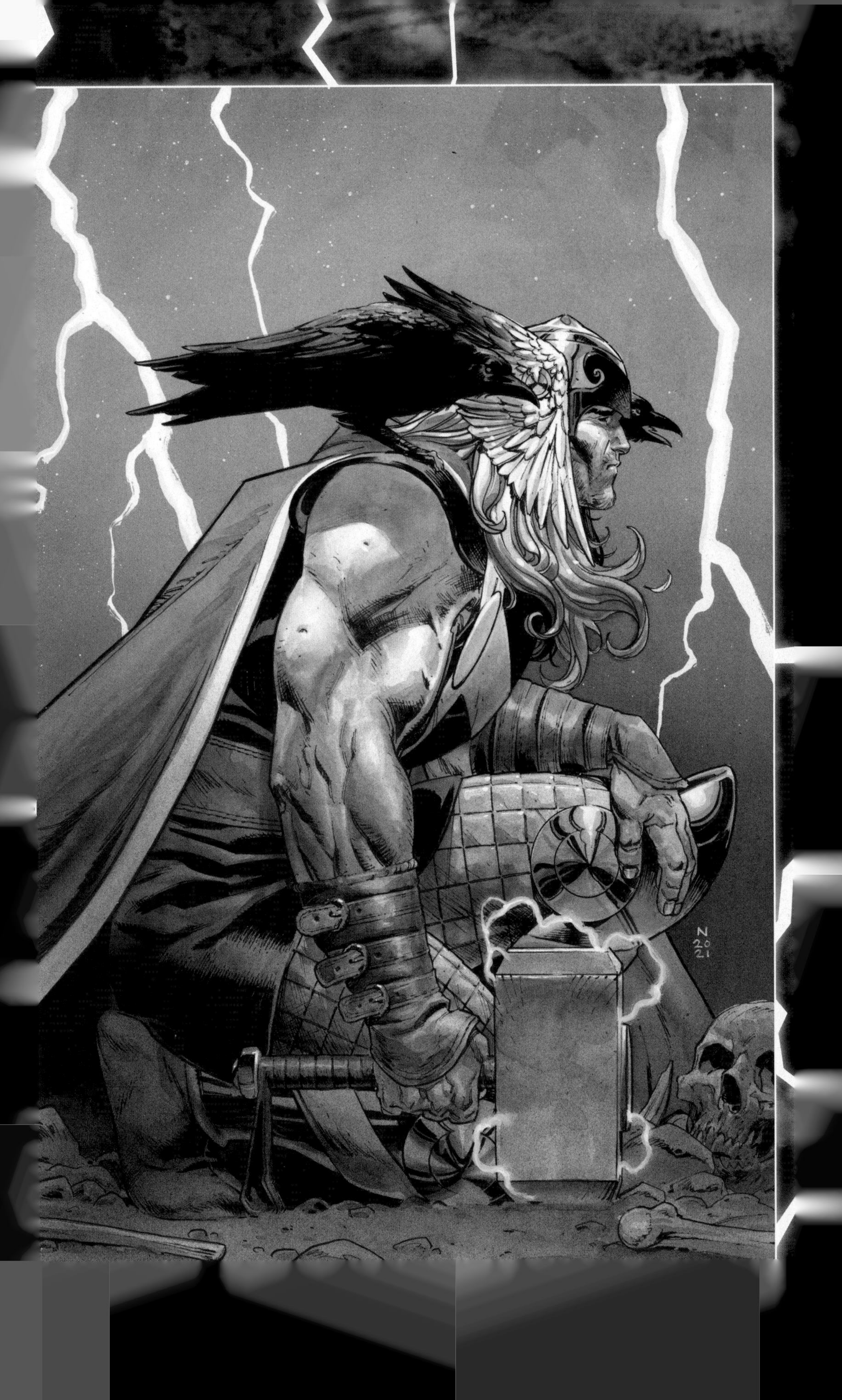

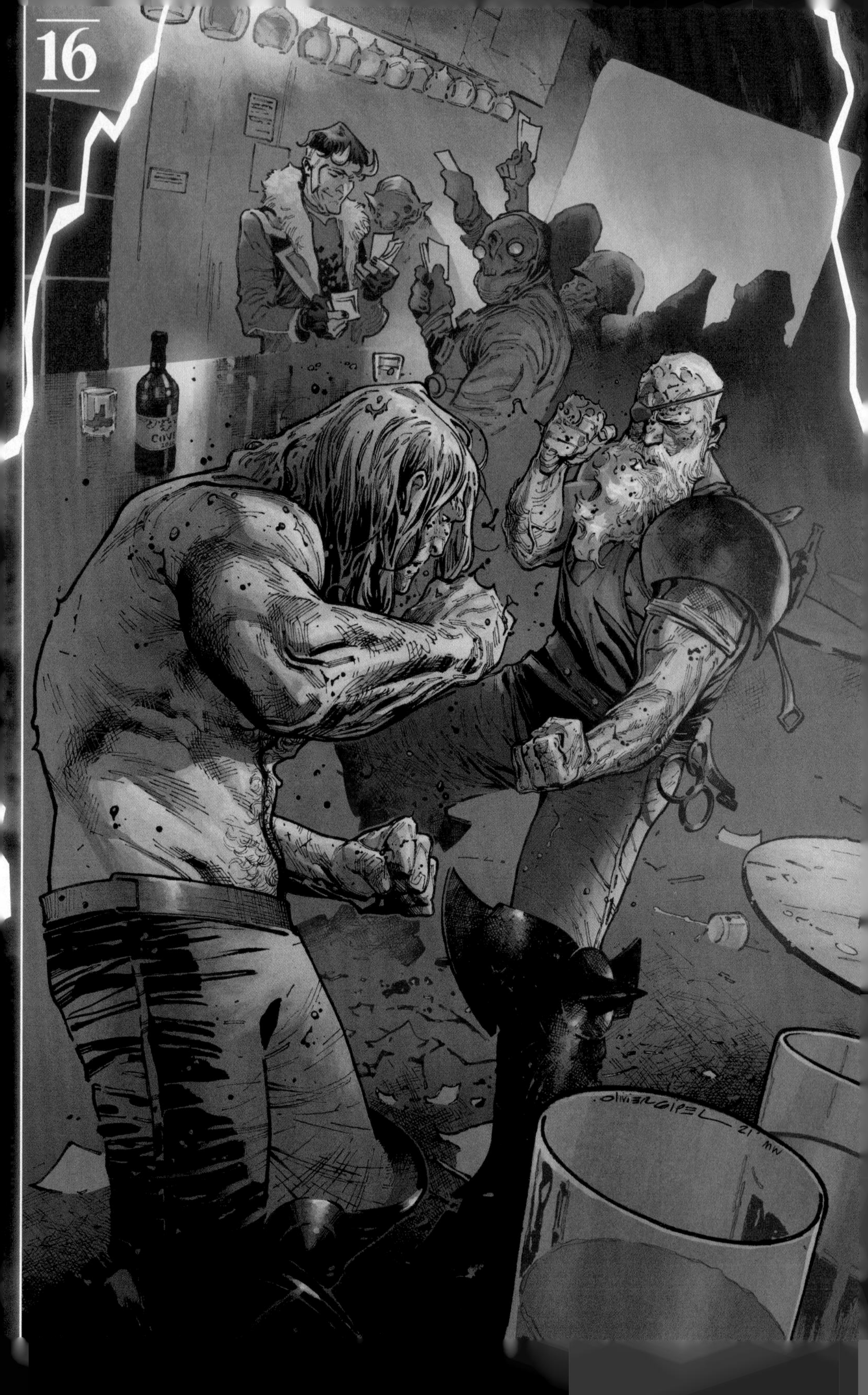
16

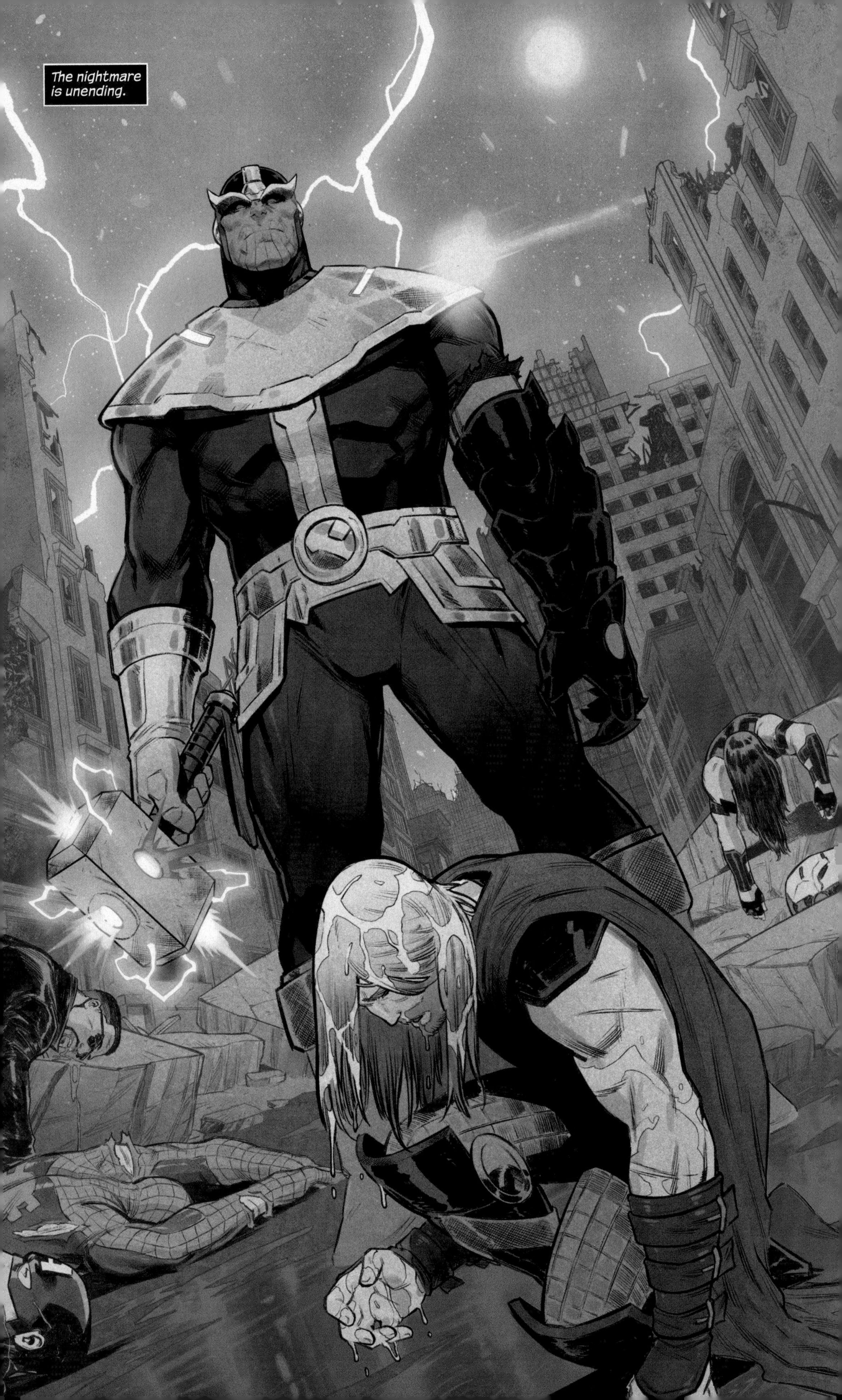
The nightmare
is unending.

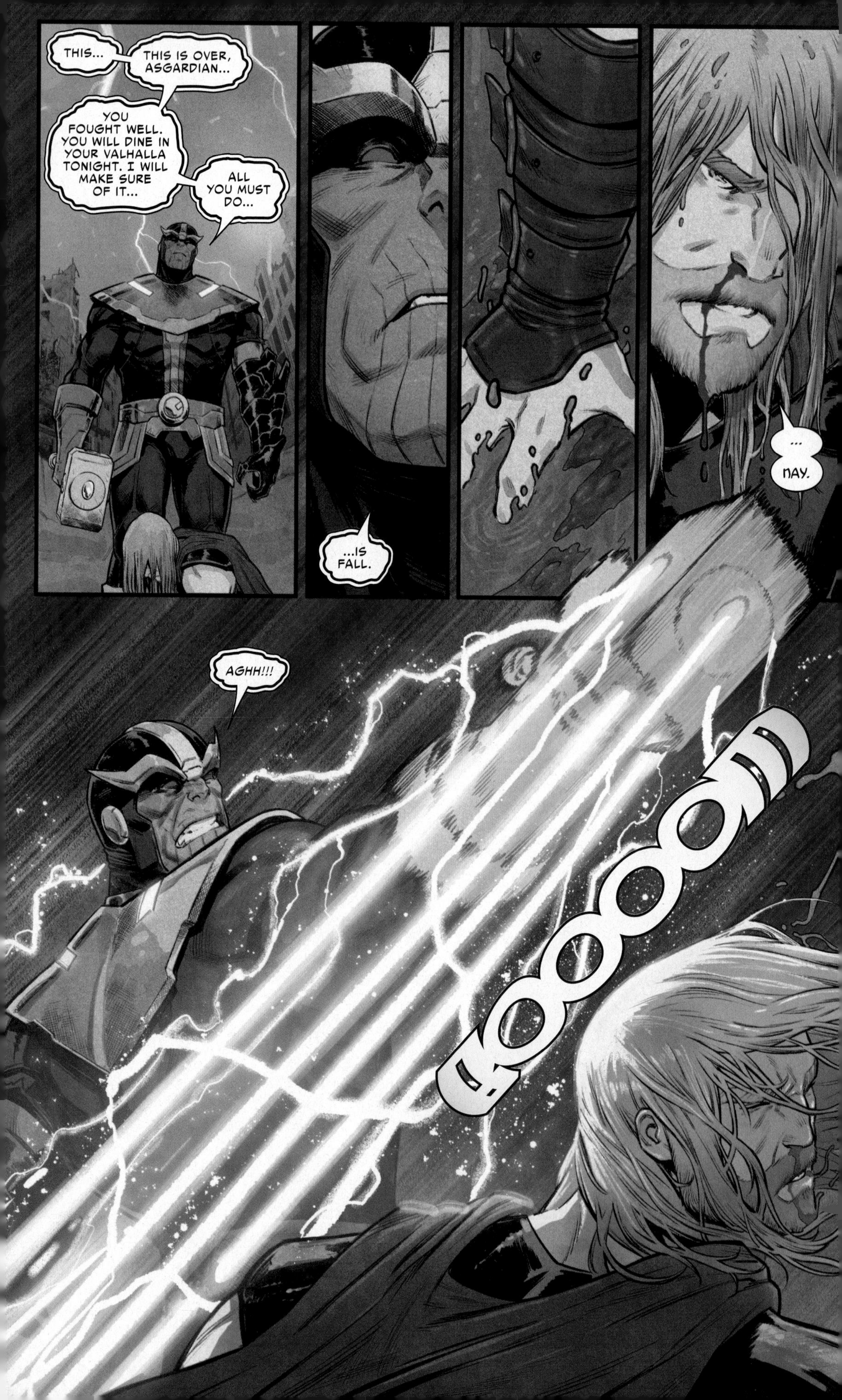
THIS...
THIS IS OVER, ASGARDIAN...
YOU FOUGHT WELL. YOU WILL DINE IN YOUR VALHALLA TONIGHT. I WILL MAKE SURE OF IT...
ALL YOU MUST DO...
...IS FALL.
...
NAY.
AGHH!!!
GOOOOOM

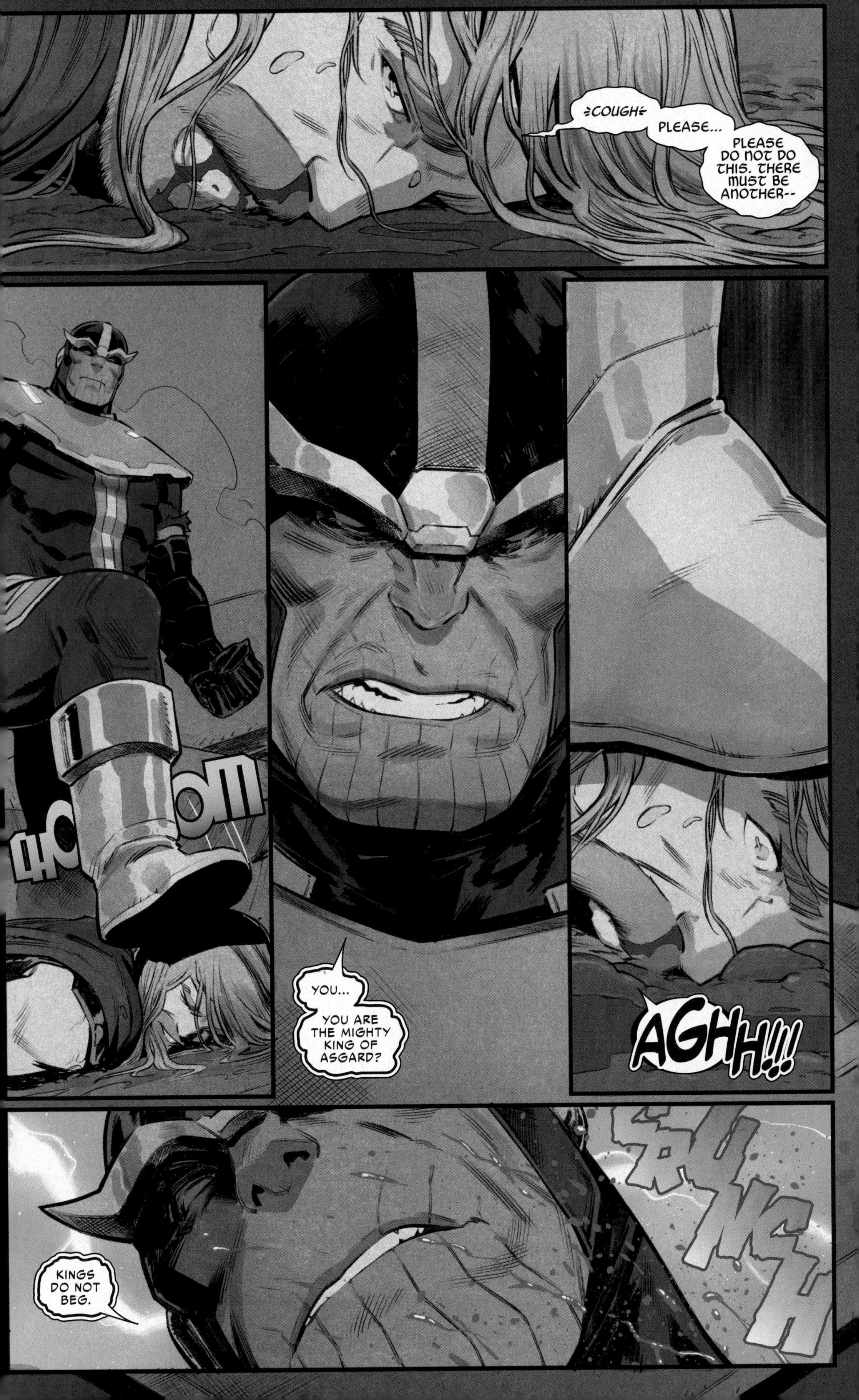

COUGH
PLEASE...
PLEASE DO NOT DO THIS. THERE MUST BE ANOTHER--
YOU...
YOU ARE THE MIGHTY KING OF ASGARD?
AGHH!!!
KINGS DO NOT BEG.

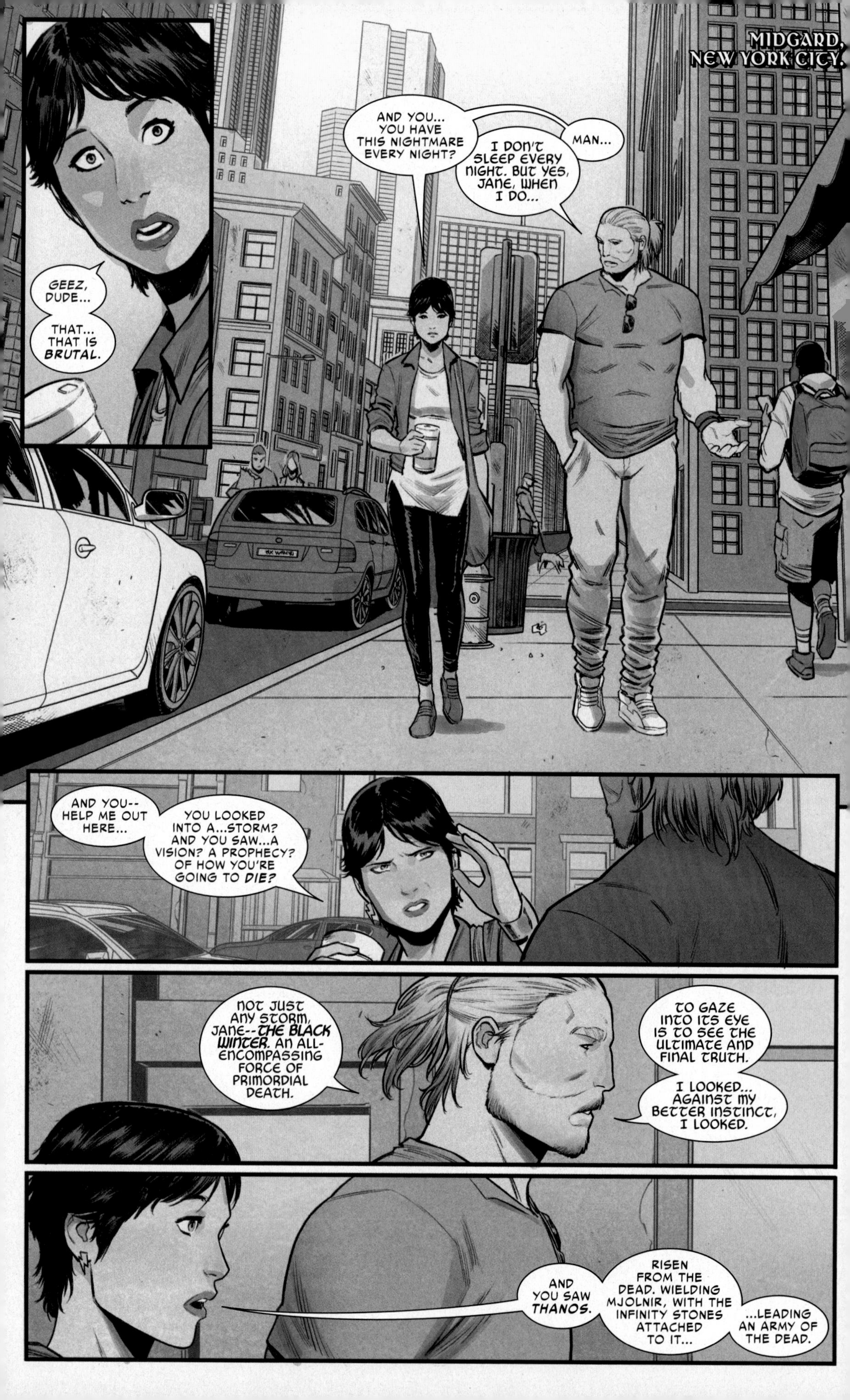
MIDGARD, NEW YORK CITY.
AND YOU... YOU HAVE THIS NIGHTMARE EVERY NIGHT?
MAN...
I DON'T SLEEP EVERY NIGHT. BUT YES, JANE, WHEN I DO...
GEEZ, DUDE...
THAT... THAT IS BRUTAL.
AND YOU-- HELP ME OUT HERE...
YOU LOOKED INTO A...STORM? AND YOU SAW...A VISION? A PROPHECY? OF HOW YOU'RE GOING TO DIE?
NOT JUST ANY STORM, JANE--THE BLACK WINTER. AN ALL-ENCOMPASSING FORCE OF PRIMORDIAL DEATH.
TO GAZE INTO ITS EYE IS TO SEE THE ULTIMATE AND FINAL TRUTH.
I LOOKED... AGAINST MY BETTER INSTINCT, I LOOKED.
AND YOU SAW THANOS.
RISEN FROM THE DEAD. WIELDING MJOLNIR, WITH THE INFINITY STONES ATTACHED TO IT...
...LEADING AN ARMY OF THE DEAD.

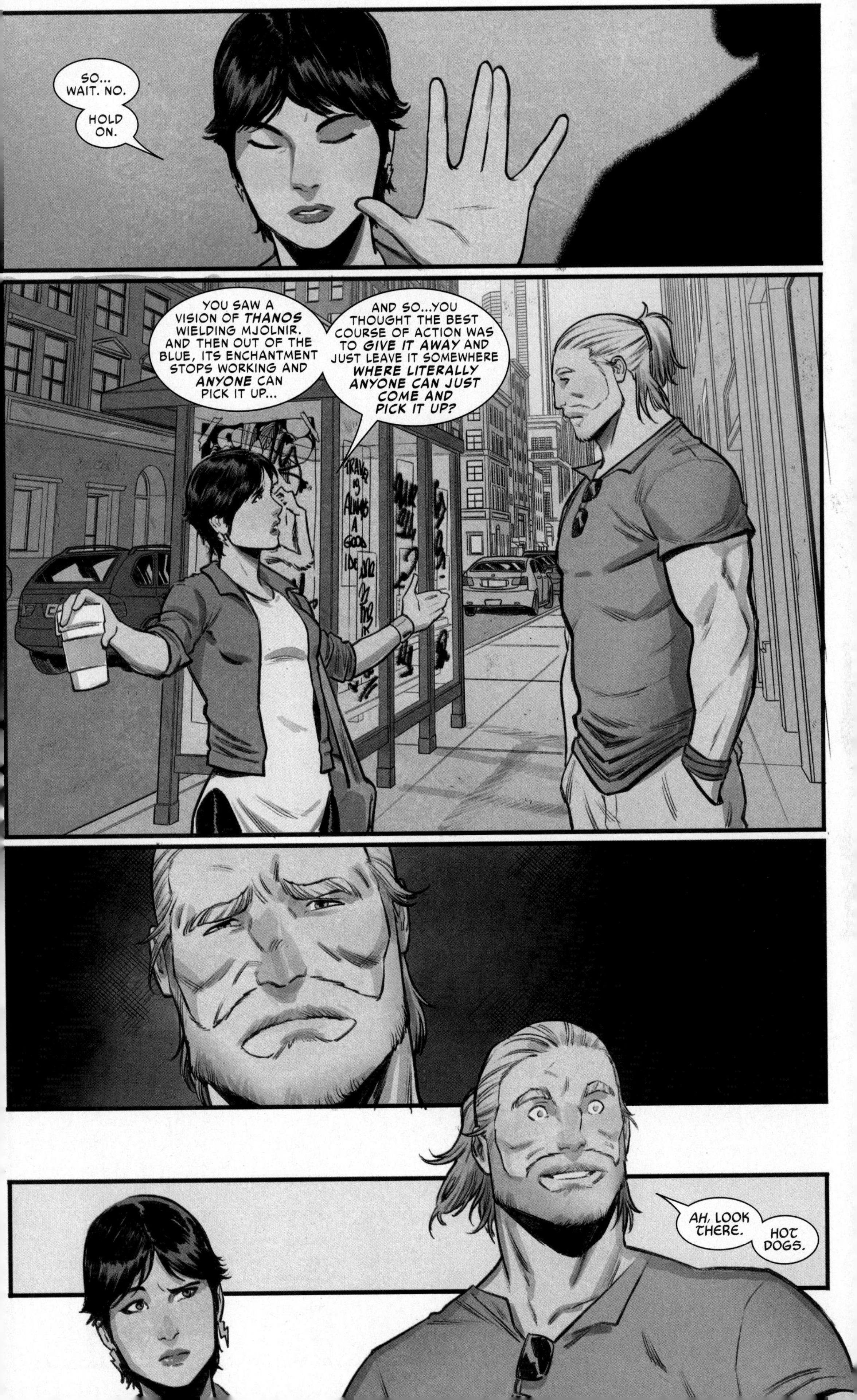
SO... WAIT. NO.
HOLD ON.
YOU SAW A VISION OF THANOS WIELDING MJOLNIR. AND THEN OUT OF THE BLUE, ITS ENCHANTMENT STOPS WORKING AND ANYONE CAN PICK IT UP...
AND SO...YOU THOUGHT THE BEST COURSE OF ACTION WAS TO GIVE IT AWAY AND JUST LEAVE IT SOMEWHERE WHERE LITERALLY ANYONE CAN JUST COME AND PICK IT UP?
AH, LOOK THERE.
HOT DOGS.

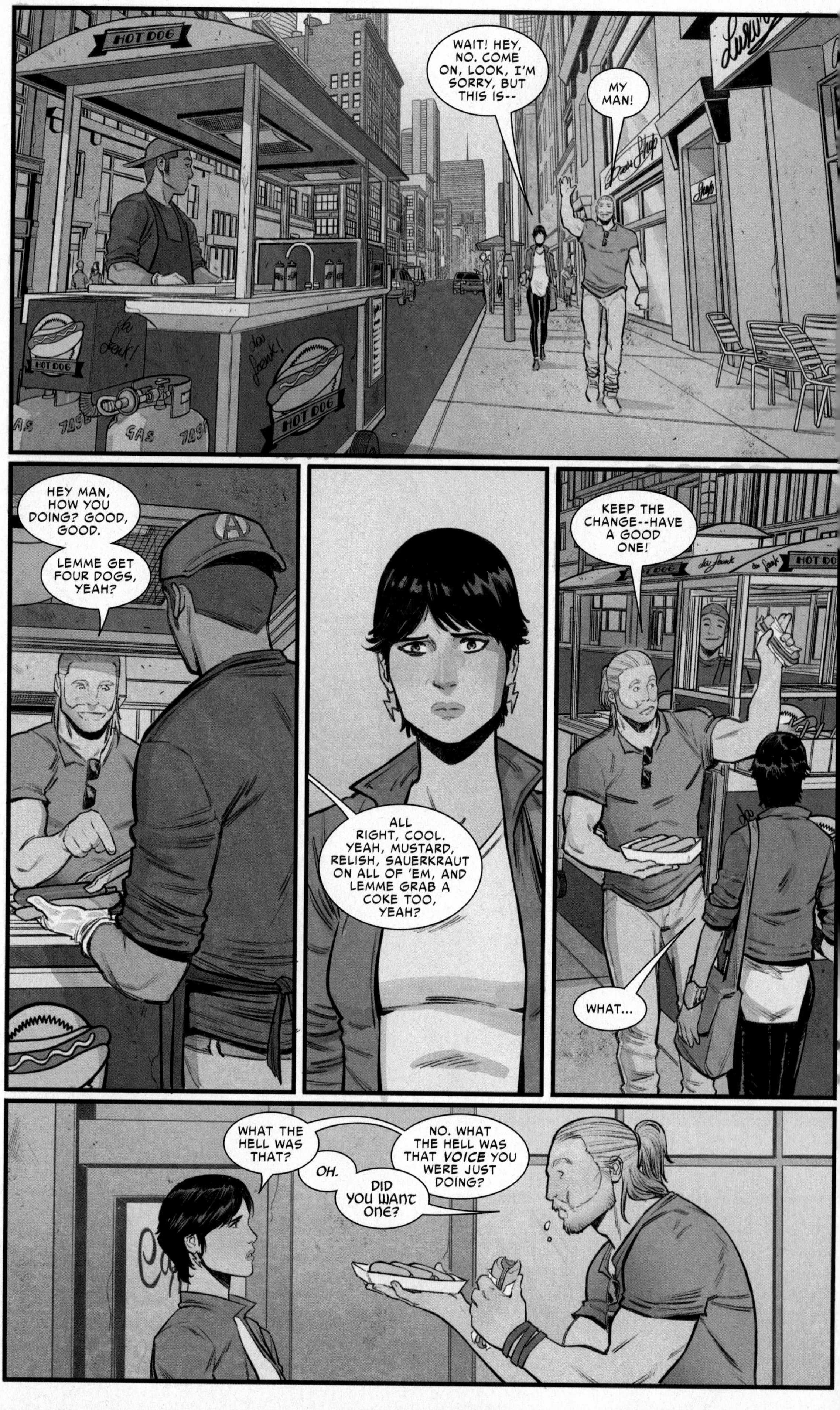
HOT DOG
WAIT! HEY, NO. COME ON, LOOK, I'M SORRY, BUT THIS IS--
MY MAN!
HOT DOG
HOT DOG
HEY MAN, HOW YOU DOING? GOOD, GOOD.
LEMME GET FOUR DOGS, YEAH?
ALL RIGHT, COOL. YEAH, MUSTARD, RELISH, SAUERKRAUT ON ALL OF 'EM, AND LEMME GRAB A COKE TOO, YEAH?
KEEP THE CHANGE--HAVE A GOOD ONE!
WHAT...
WHAT THE HELL WAS THAT?
NO. WHAT THE HELL WAS THAT *VOICE* YOU WERE JUST DOING?
OH.
DID YOU WANT ONE?

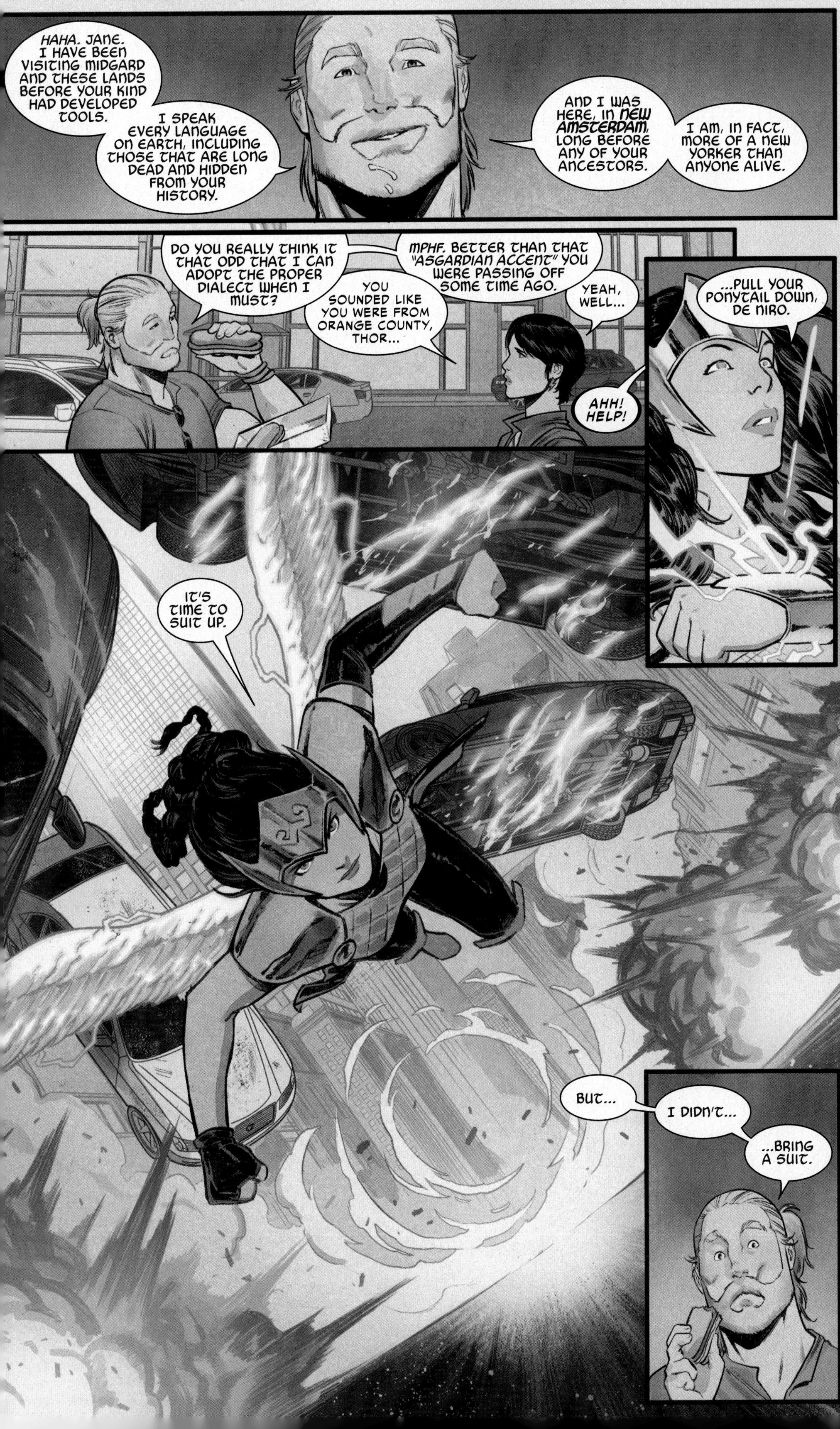

HAHA. JANE. I HAVE BEEN VISITING MIDGARD AND THESE LANDS BEFORE YOUR KIND HAD DEVELOPED TOOLS.
I SPEAK EVERY LANGUAGE ON EARTH, INCLUDING THOSE THAT ARE LONG DEAD AND HIDDEN FROM YOUR HISTORY.
AND I WAS HERE, IN NEW AMSTERDAM, LONG BEFORE ANY OF YOUR ANCESTORS.
I AM, IN FACT, MORE OF A NEW YORKER THAN ANYONE ALIVE.
DO YOU REALLY THINK IT THAT ODD THAT I CAN ADOPT THE PROPER DIALECT WHEN I MUST?
YOU SOUNDED LIKE YOU WERE FROM ORANGE COUNTY, THOR...
MPHF. BETTER THAN THAT "ASGARDIAN ACCENT" YOU WERE PASSING OFF SOME TIME AGO.
YEAH, WELL...
...PULL YOUR PONYTAIL DOWN, DE NIRO.
AHH! HELP!
IT'S TIME TO SUIT UP.
BUT...
I DIDN'T...
...BRING A SUIT.

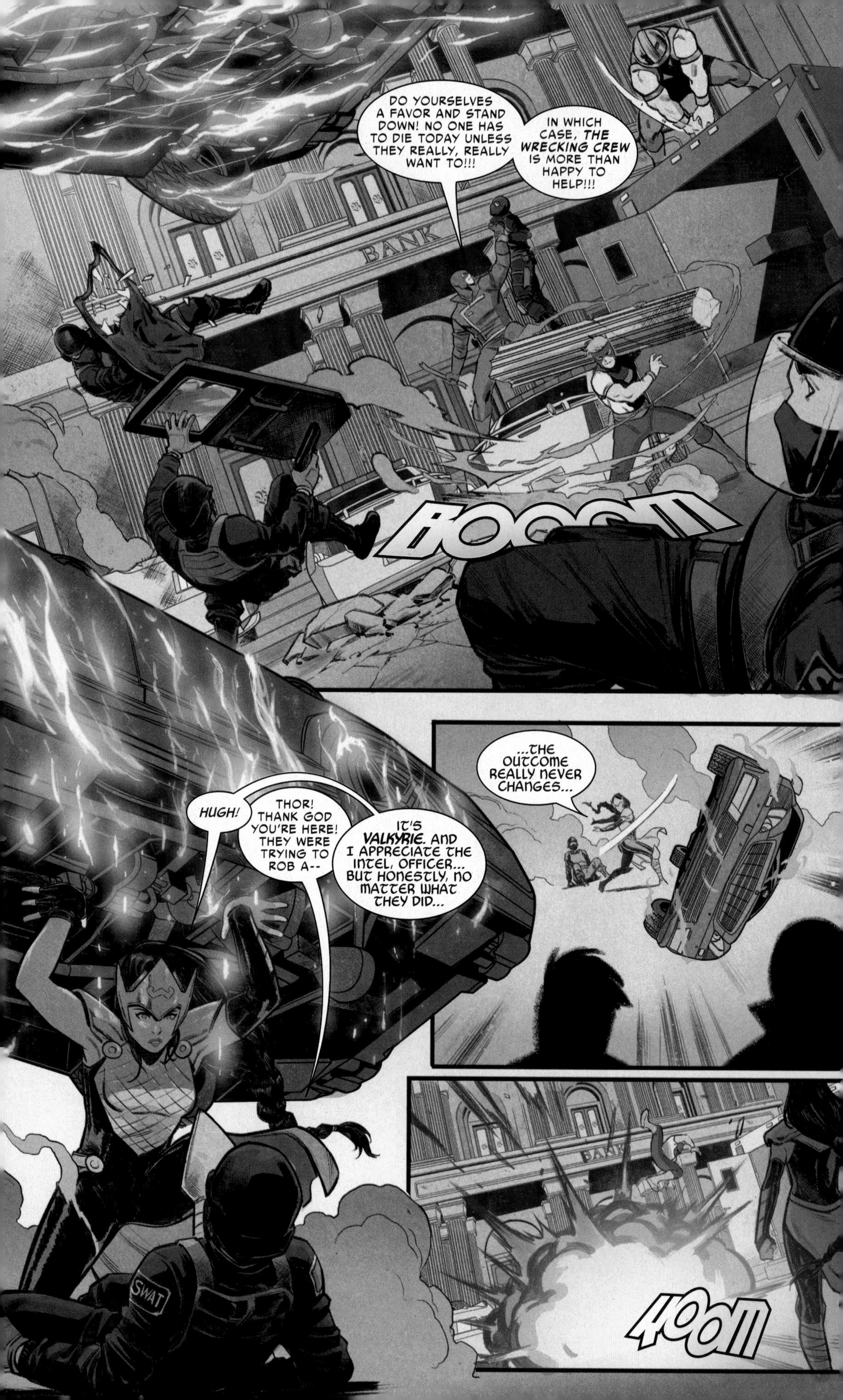
DO YOURSELVES A FAVOR AND STAND DOWN! NO ONE HAS TO DIE TODAY UNLESS THEY REALLY, REALLY WANT TO!!!
IN WHICH CASE, THE WRECKING CREW IS MORE THAN HAPPY TO HELP!!!
BANK
BOOOM
HUGH!
THOR! THANK GOD YOU'RE HERE! THEY WERE TRYING TO ROB A--
IT'S VALKYRIE. AND I APPRECIATE THE INTEL, OFFICER... BUT HONESTLY, NO MATTER WHAT THEY DID...
...THE OUTCOME REALLY NEVER CHANGES...
SWAT
BANK
WOOM

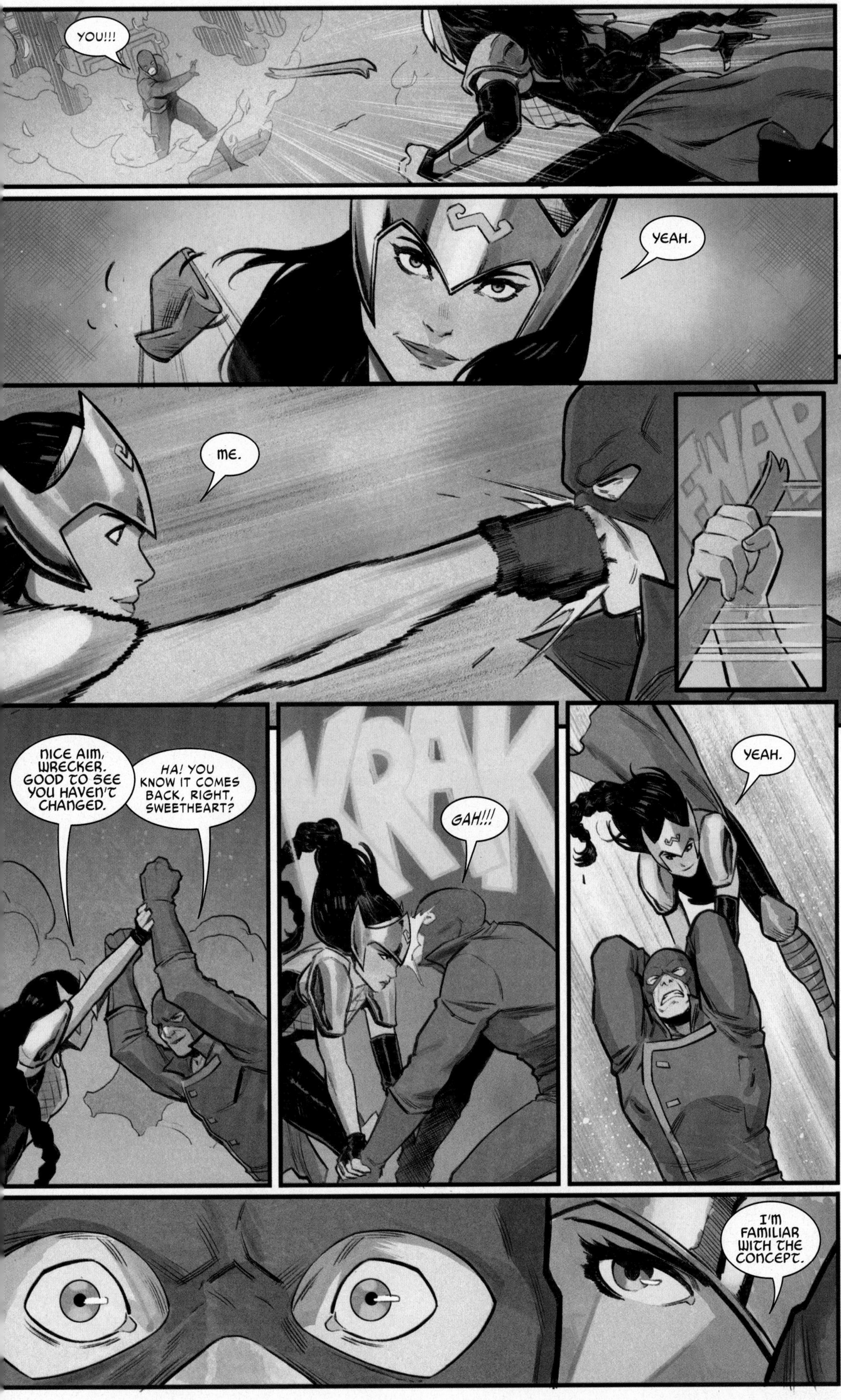
YOU!!!
YEAH.
ME.
SNAP
NICE AIM, WRECKER. GOOD TO SEE YOU HAVEN'T CHANGED.
HA! YOU KNOW IT COMES BACK, RIGHT, SWEETHEART?
KRAK
GAH!!!
YEAH.
I'M FAMILIAR WITH THE CONCEPT.

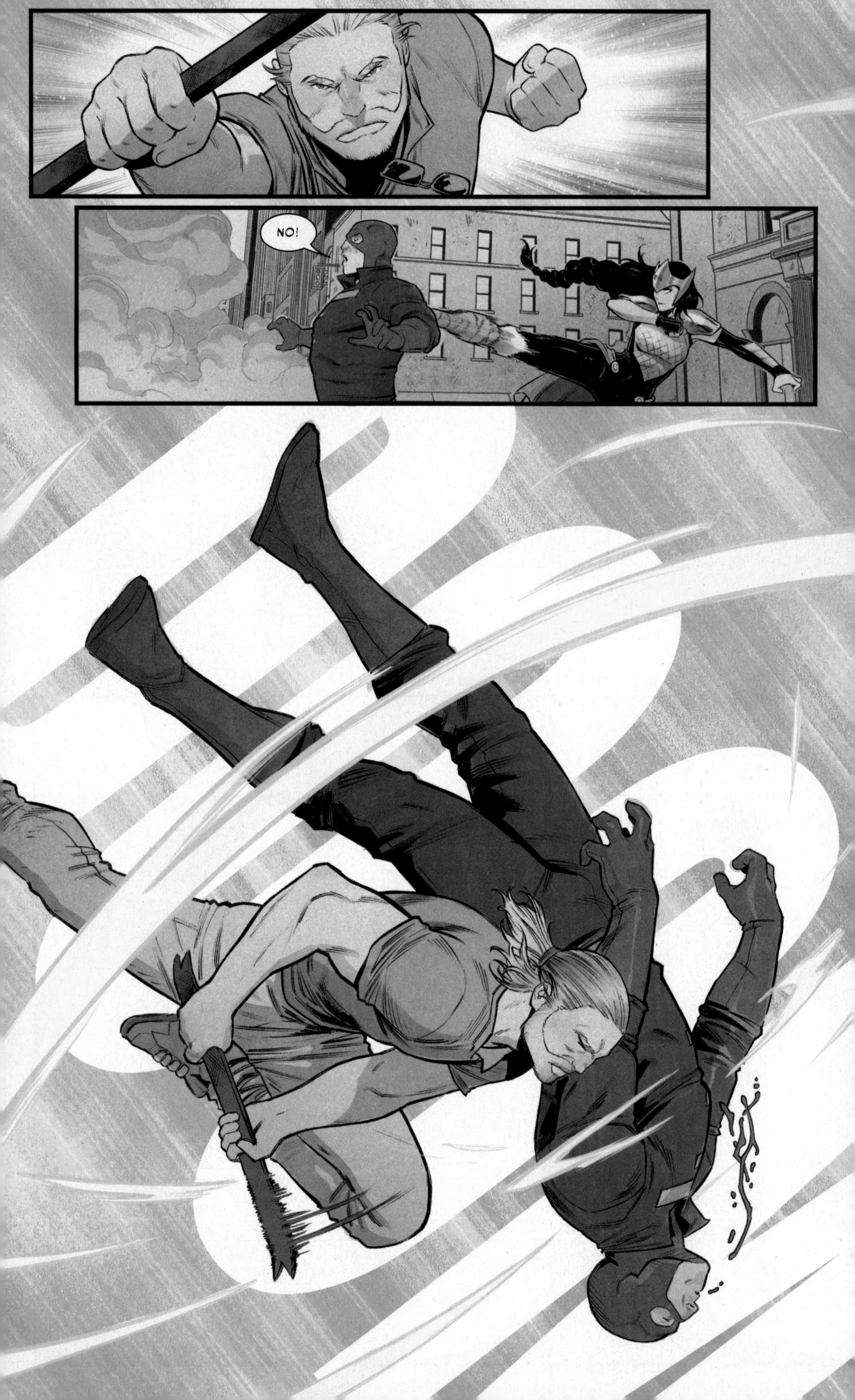
NO!

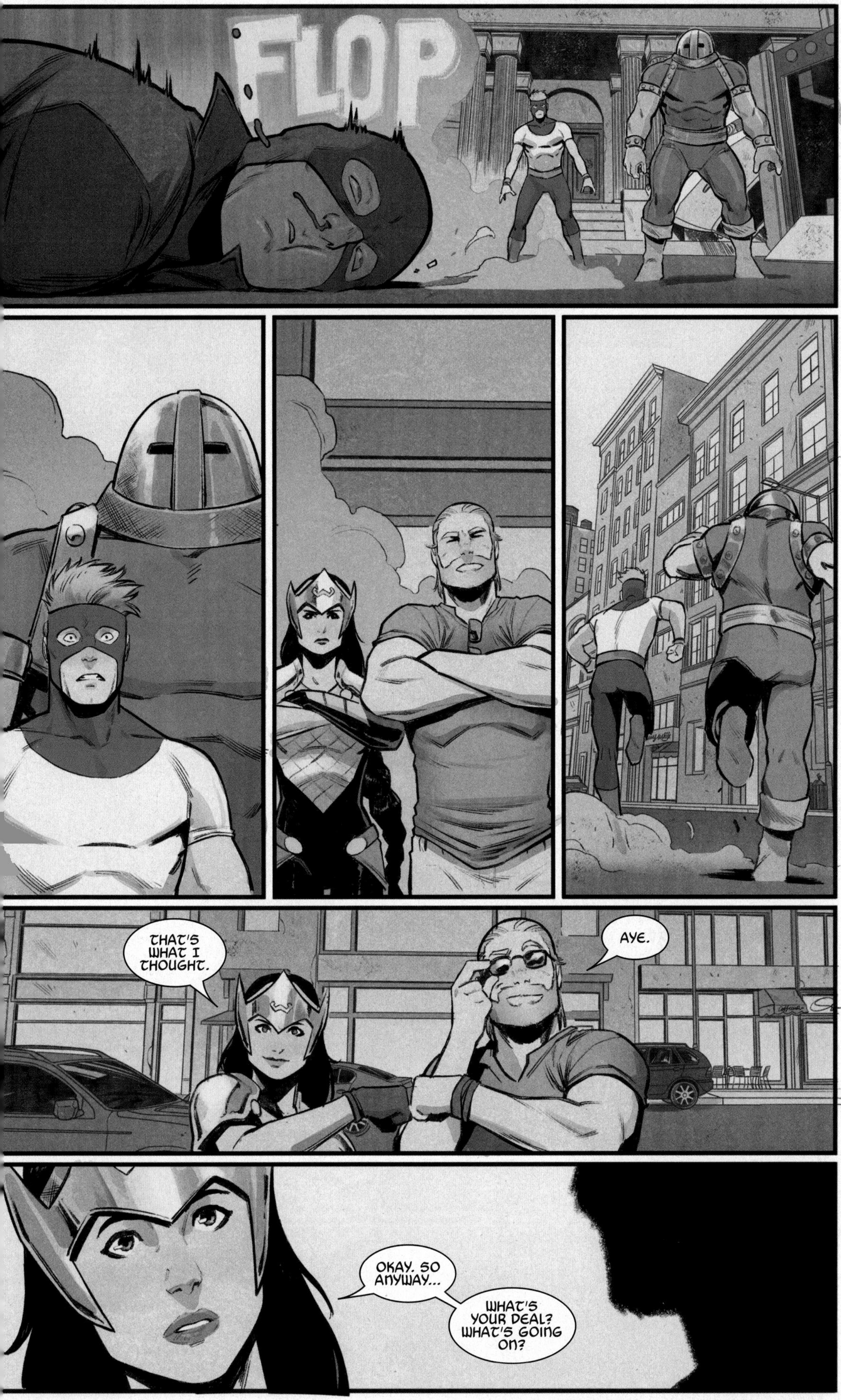
FLOP
THAT'S WHAT I THOUGHT.
AYE.
OKAY. SO ANYWAY...
WHAT'S YOUR DEAL? WHAT'S GOING ON?

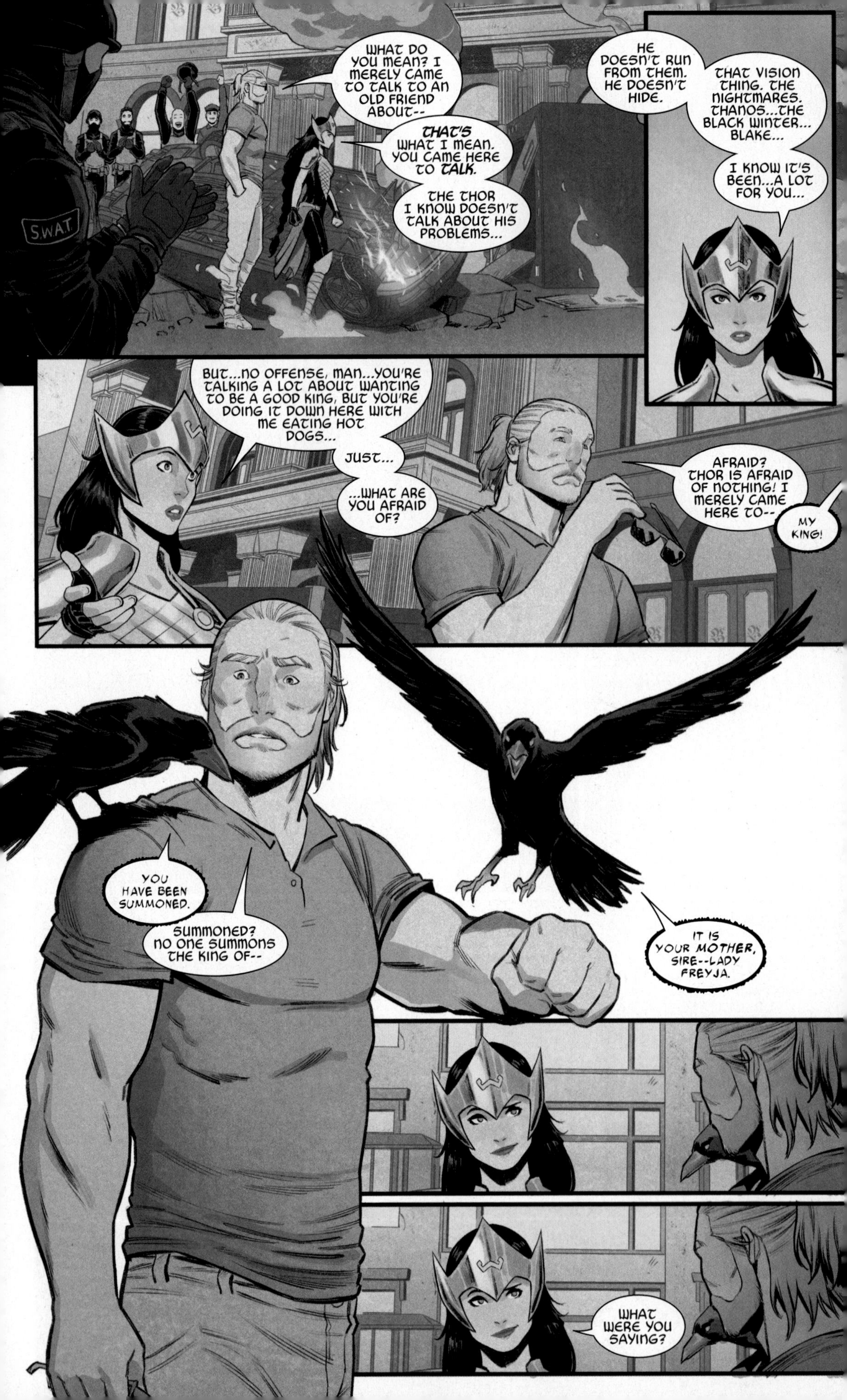
WHAT DO YOU MEAN? I MERELY CAME TO TALK TO AN OLD FRIEND ABOUT--
THAT'S WHAT I MEAN. YOU CAME HERE TO TALK.
THE THOR I KNOW DOESN'T TALK ABOUT HIS PROBLEMS...
HE DOESN'T RUN FROM THEM. HE DOESN'T HIDE.
THAT VISION THING. THE NIGHTMARES. THANOS...THE BLACK WINTER... BLAKE...
I KNOW IT'S BEEN...A LOT FOR YOU...
BUT...NO OFFENSE, MAN...YOU'RE TALKING A LOT ABOUT WANTING TO BE A GOOD KING, BUT YOU'RE DOING IT DOWN HERE WITH ME EATING HOT DOGS...
JUST...
...WHAT ARE YOU AFRAID OF?
AFRAID? THOR IS AFRAID OF NOTHING! I MERELY CAME HERE TO--
MY KING!
YOU HAVE BEEN SUMMONED.
SUMMONED? NO ONE SUMMONS THE KING OF--
IT IS YOUR MOTHER, SIRE--LADY FREYJA.
WHAT WERE YOU SAYING?

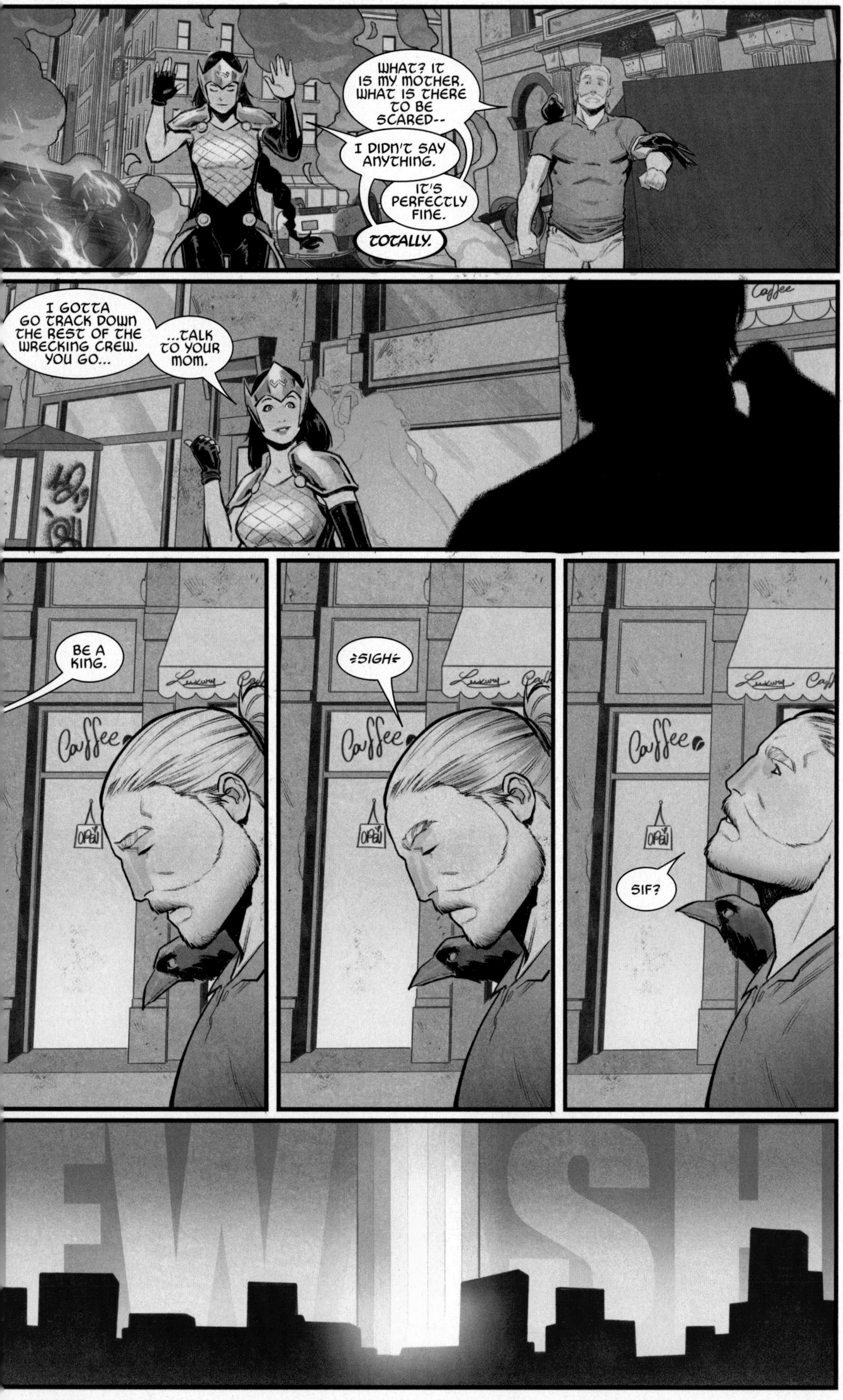
WHAT? IT IS MY MOTHER. WHAT IS THERE TO BE SCARED--
I DIDN'T SAY ANYTHING.
IT'S PERFECTLY FINE.
TOTALLY.
I GOTTA GO TRACK DOWN THE REST OF THE WRECKING CREW. YOU GO...
...TALK TO YOUR MOM.
BE A KING.
SIGH
SIF?

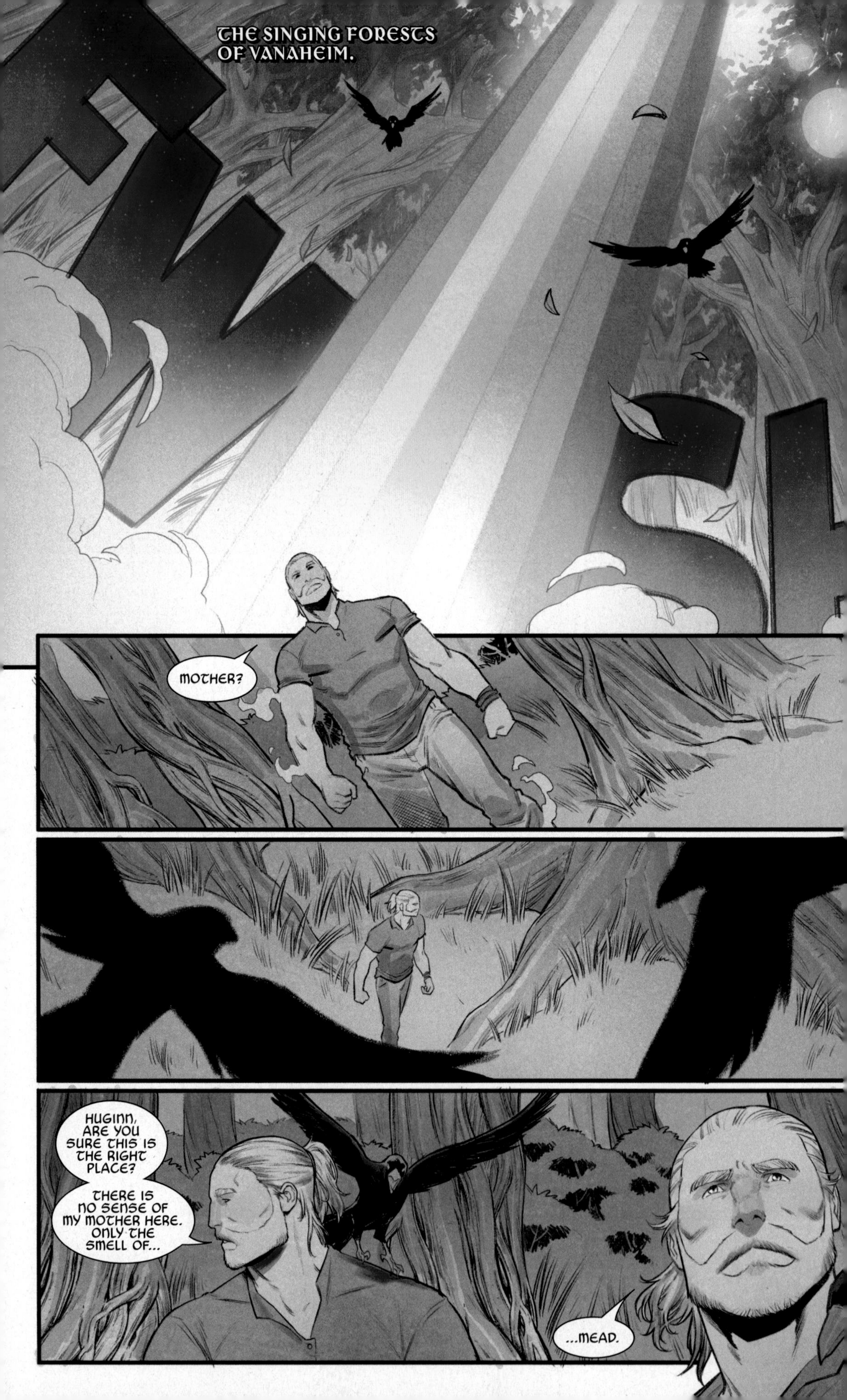
THE SINGING FORESTS OF VANAHEIM.
MOTHER?
HUGINN, ARE YOU SURE THIS IS THE RIGHT PLACE?
THERE IS NO SENSE OF MY MOTHER HERE. ONLY THE SMELL OF...
...MEAD.

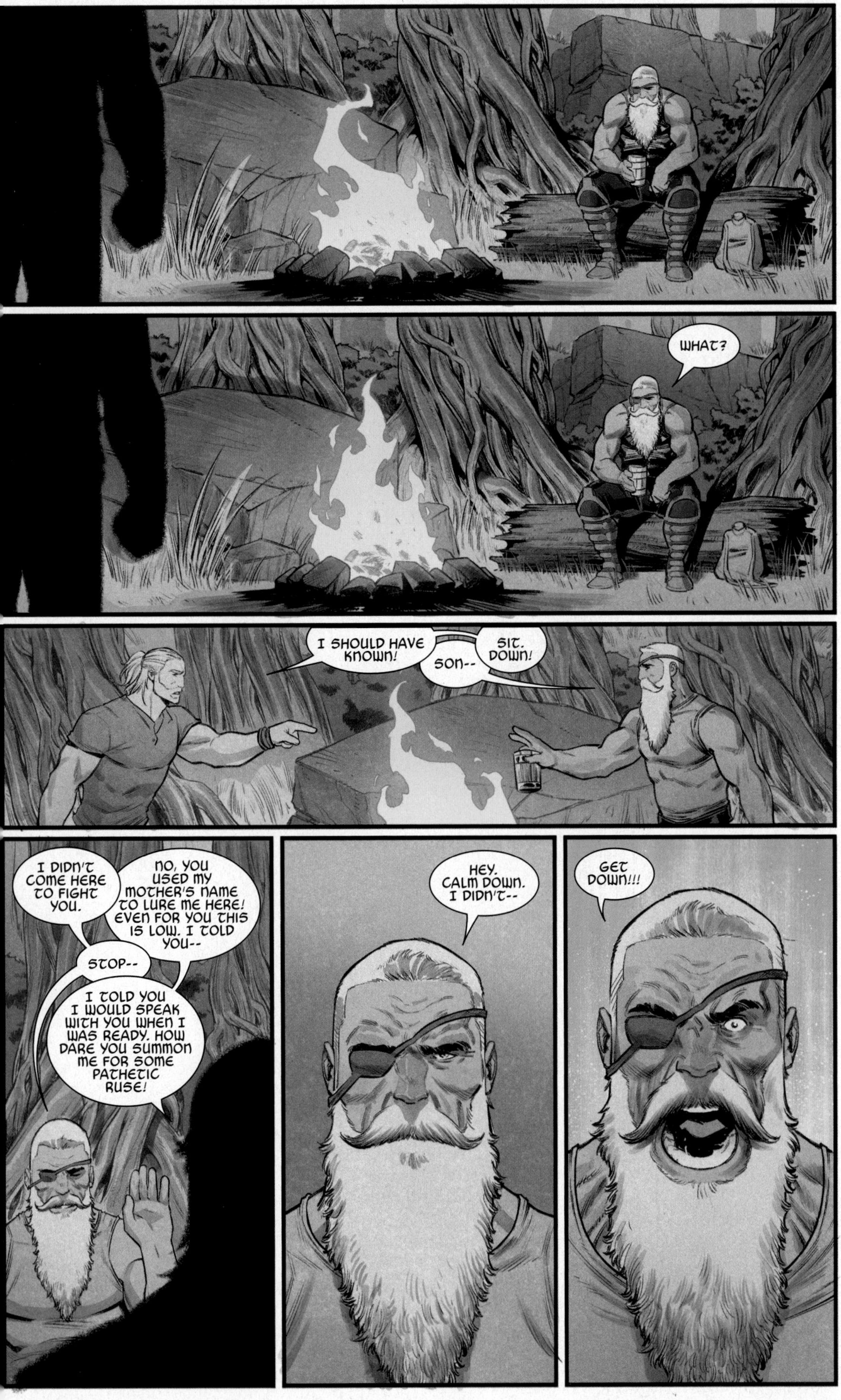
WHAT?
I SHOULD HAVE KNOWN!
SON--
SIT. DOWN!
I DIDN'T COME HERE TO FIGHT YOU.
NO, YOU USED MY MOTHER'S NAME TO LURE ME HERE! EVEN FOR YOU THIS IS LOW. I TOLD YOU--
STOP--
I TOLD YOU I WOULD SPEAK WITH YOU WHEN I WAS READY. HOW DARE YOU SUMMON ME FOR SOME PATHETIC RUSE!
HEY. CALM DOWN. I DIDN'T--
GET DOWN!!!

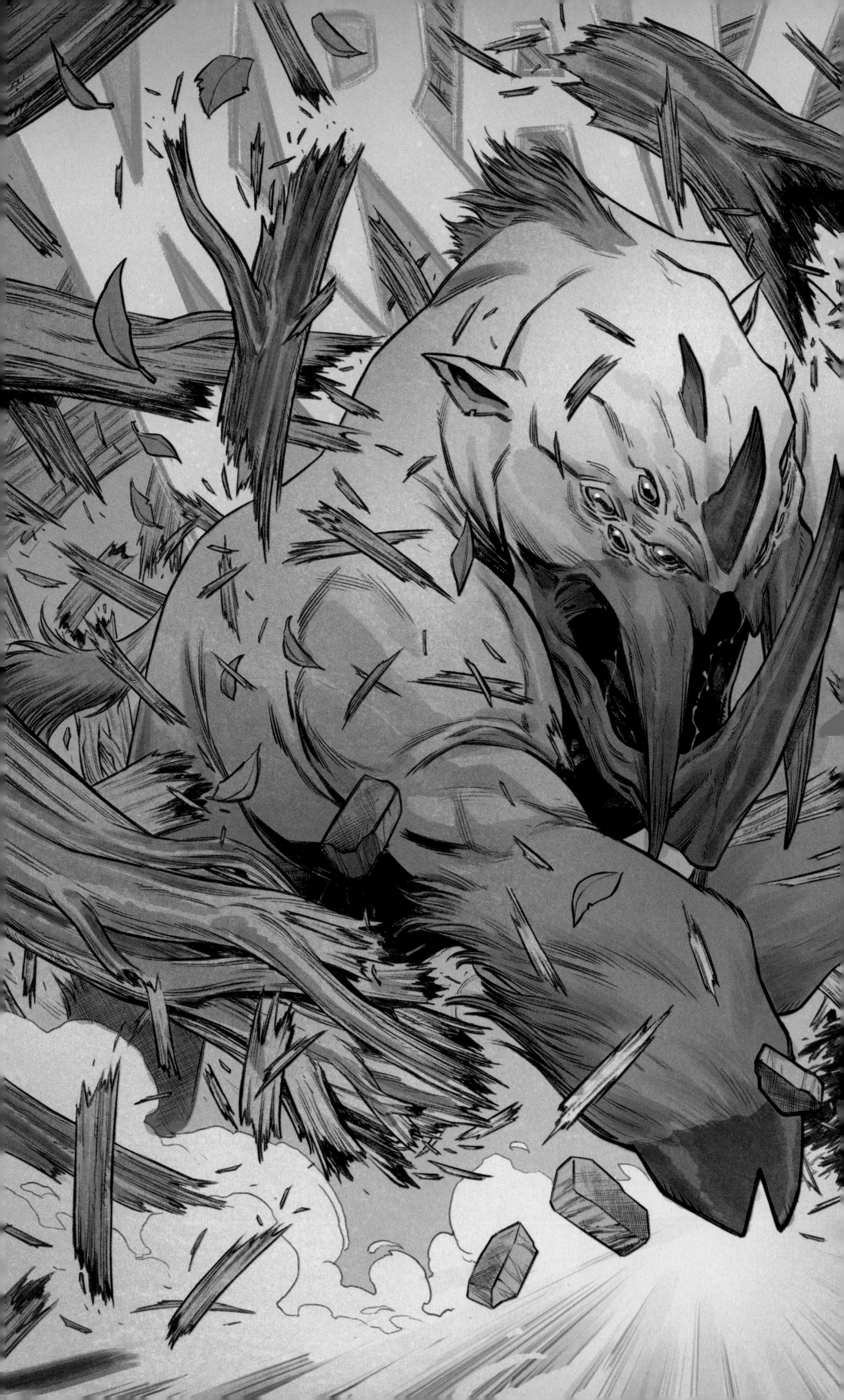

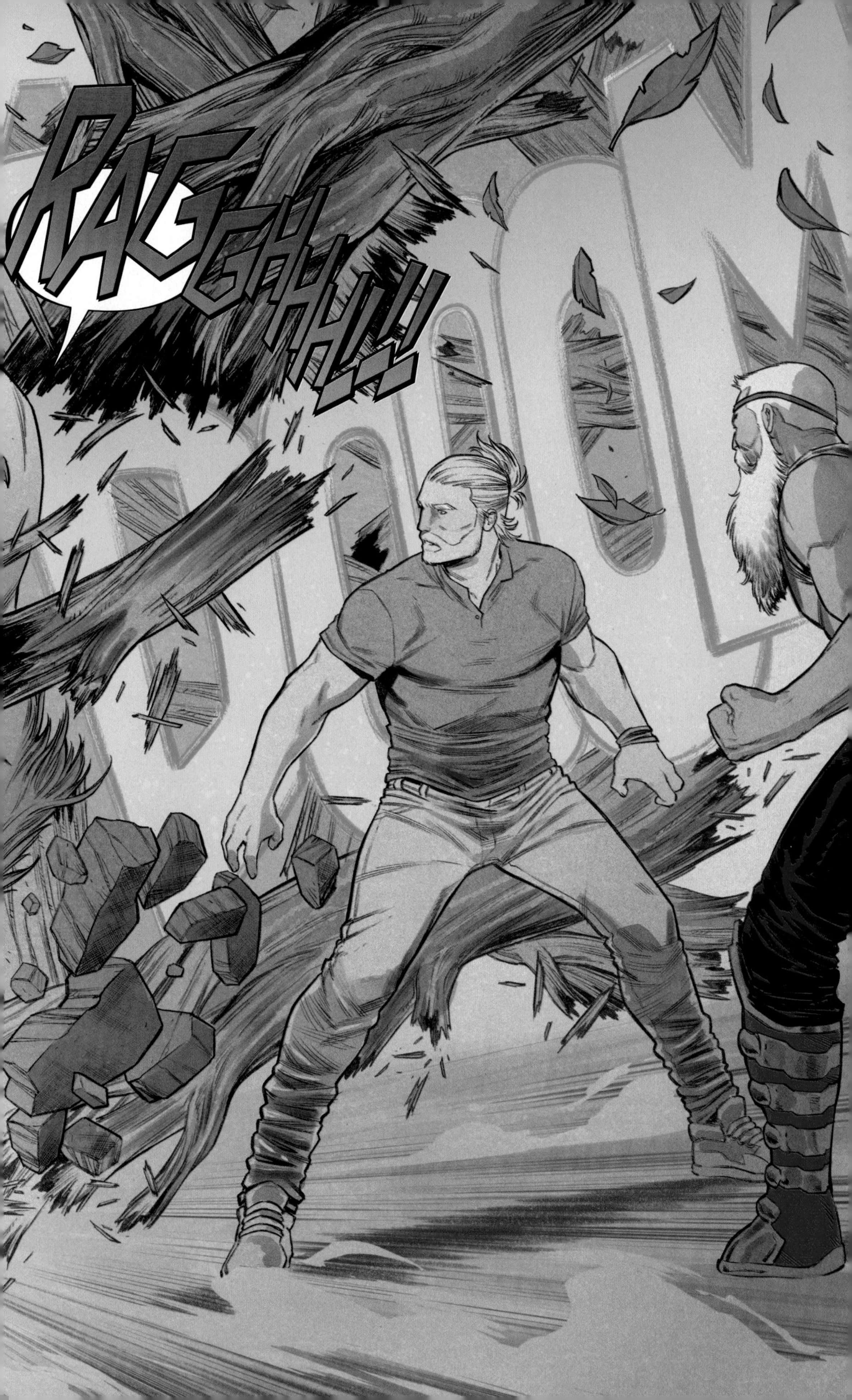
RAGGHH!!!

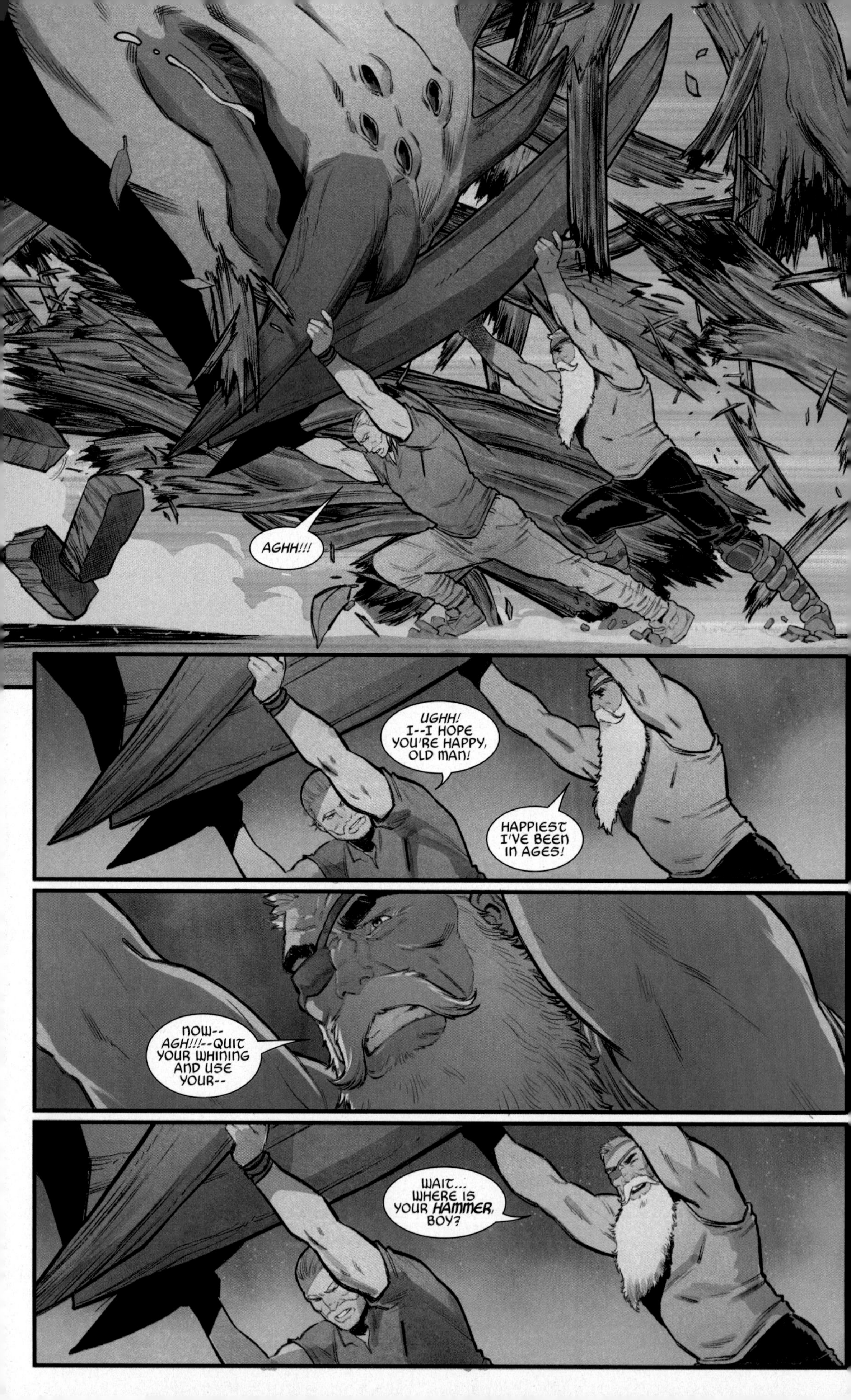
AGHH!!!
UGHH! I--I HOPE YOU'RE HAPPY, OLD MAN!
HAPPIEST I'VE BEEN IN AGES!
NOW-- AGH!!!--QUIT YOUR WHINING AND USE YOUR--
WAIT... WHERE IS YOUR HAMMER, BOY?

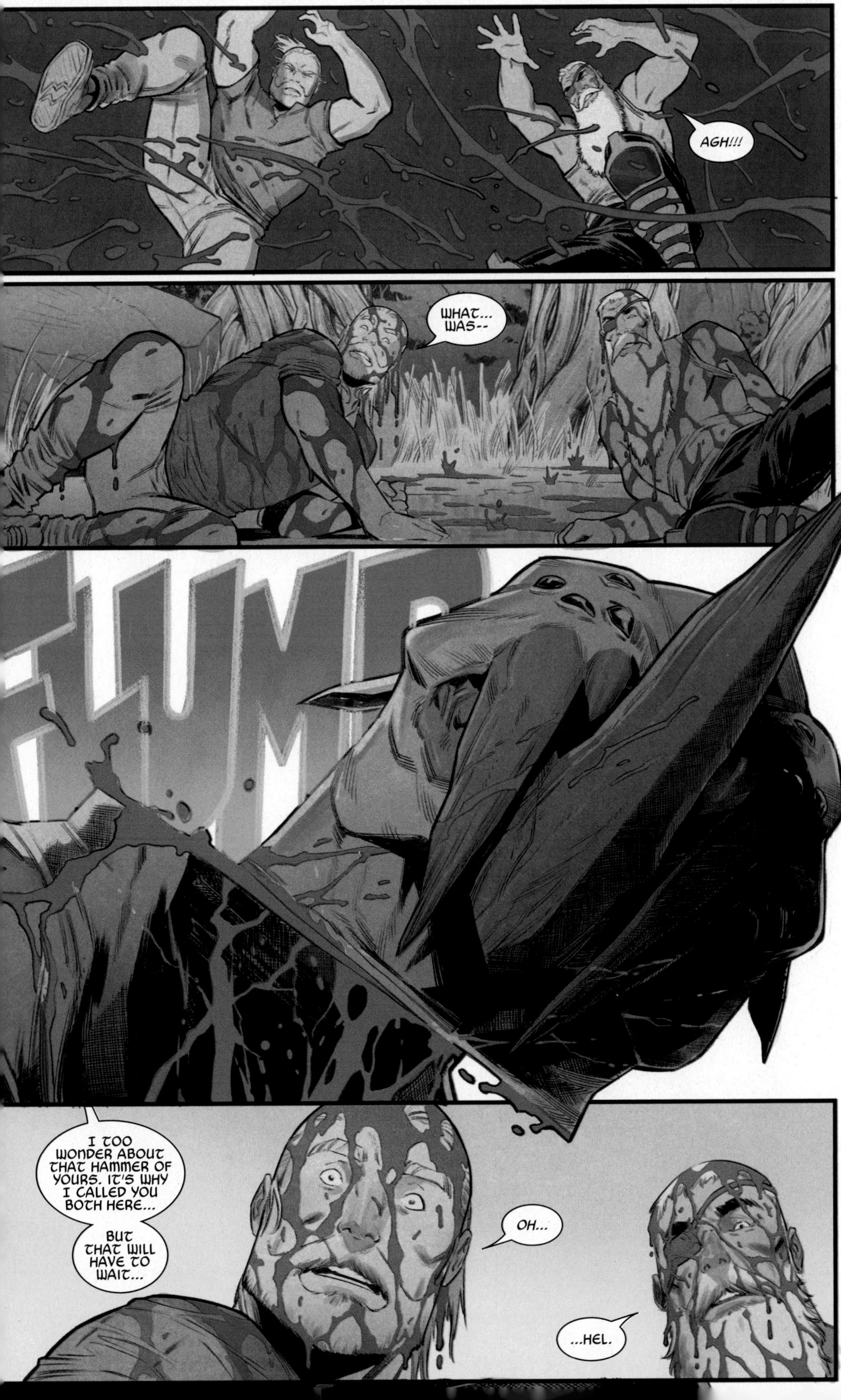
AGH!!!
WHAT... WAS--
I TOO WONDER ABOUT THAT HAMMER OF YOURS. IT'S WHY I CALLED YOU BOTH HERE...
BUT THAT WILL HAVE TO WAIT...
OH...
...HEL.

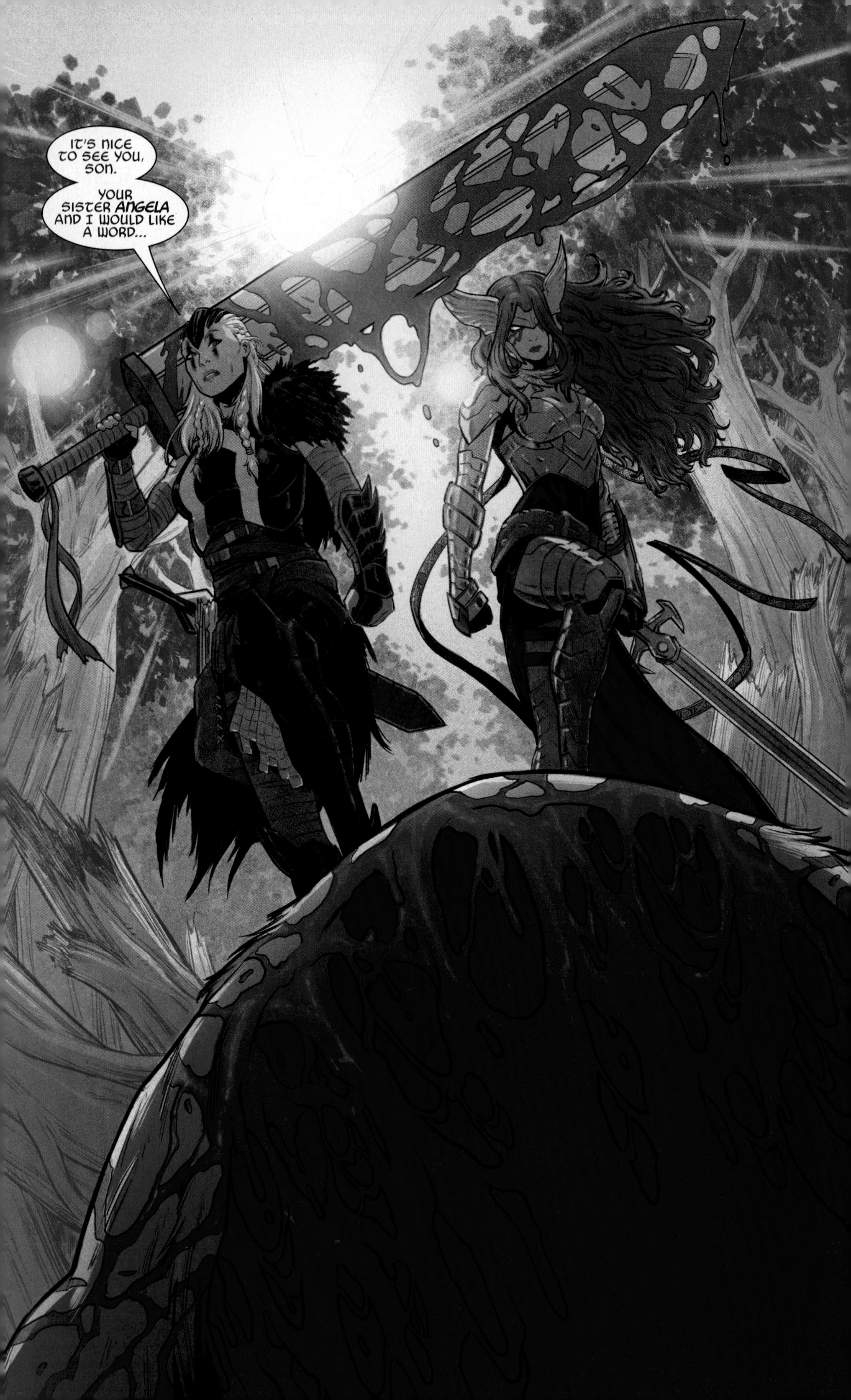
IT'S NICE TO SEE YOU, SON.
YOUR SISTER ANGELA AND I WOULD LIKE A WORD...

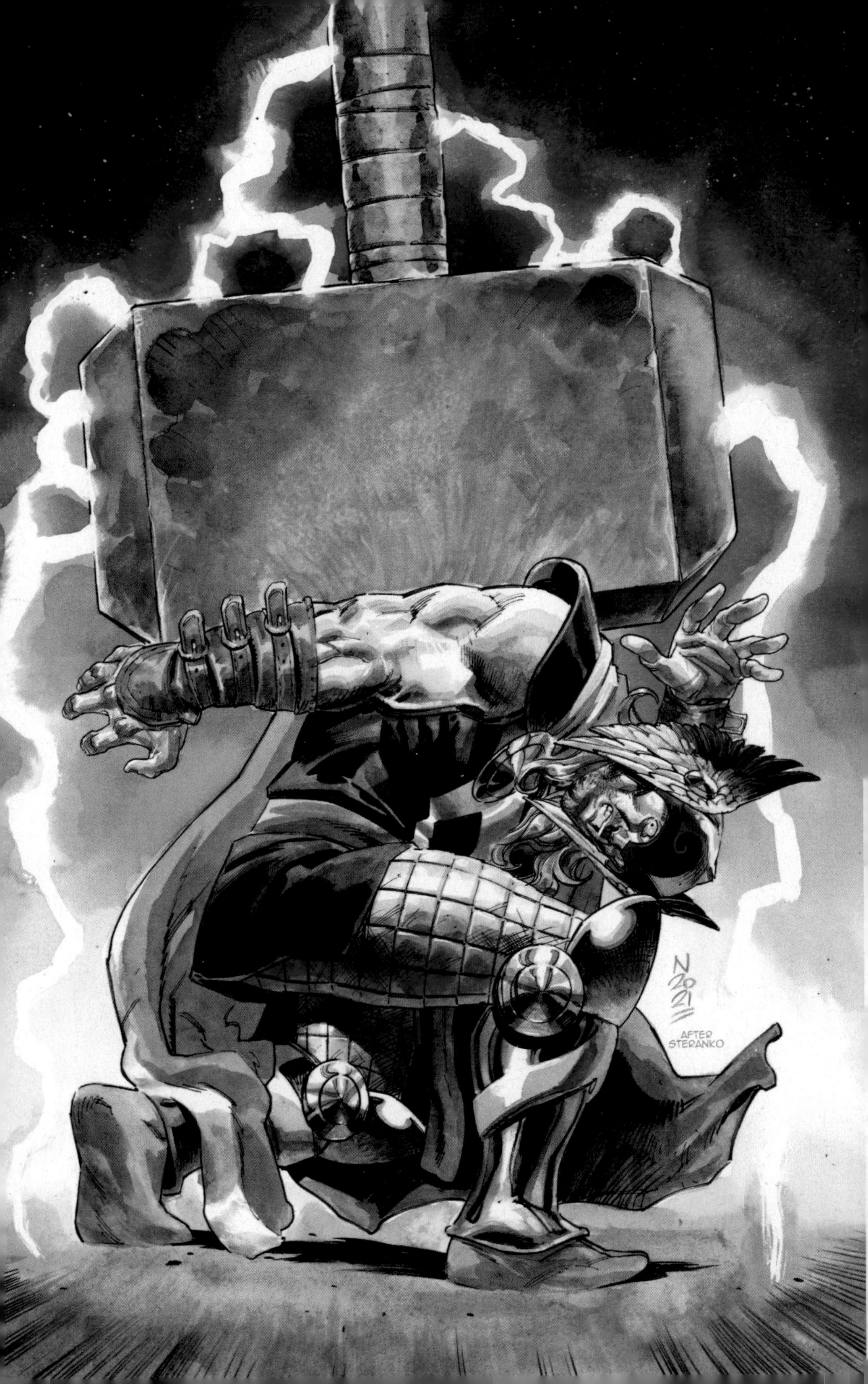
N 2021
AFTER
STERANKO

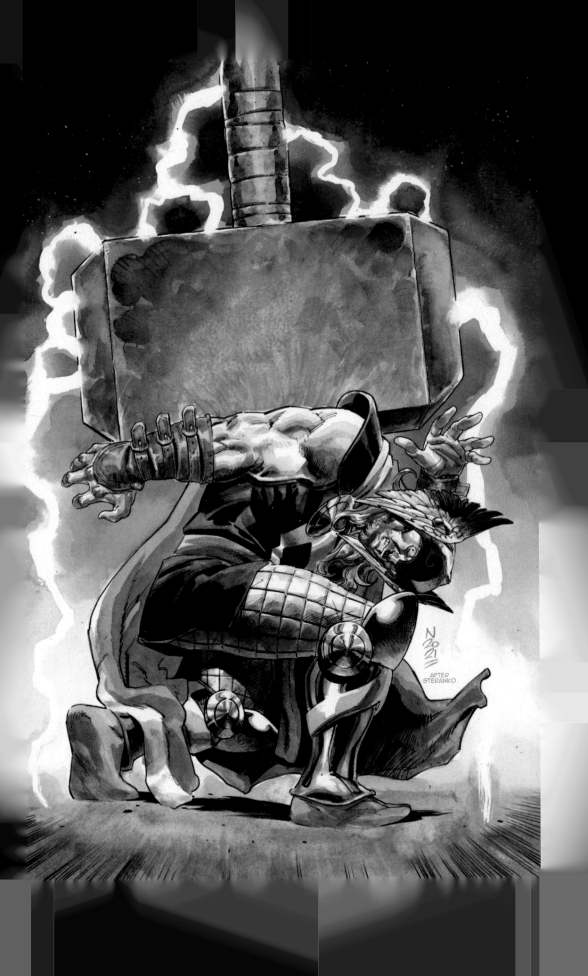

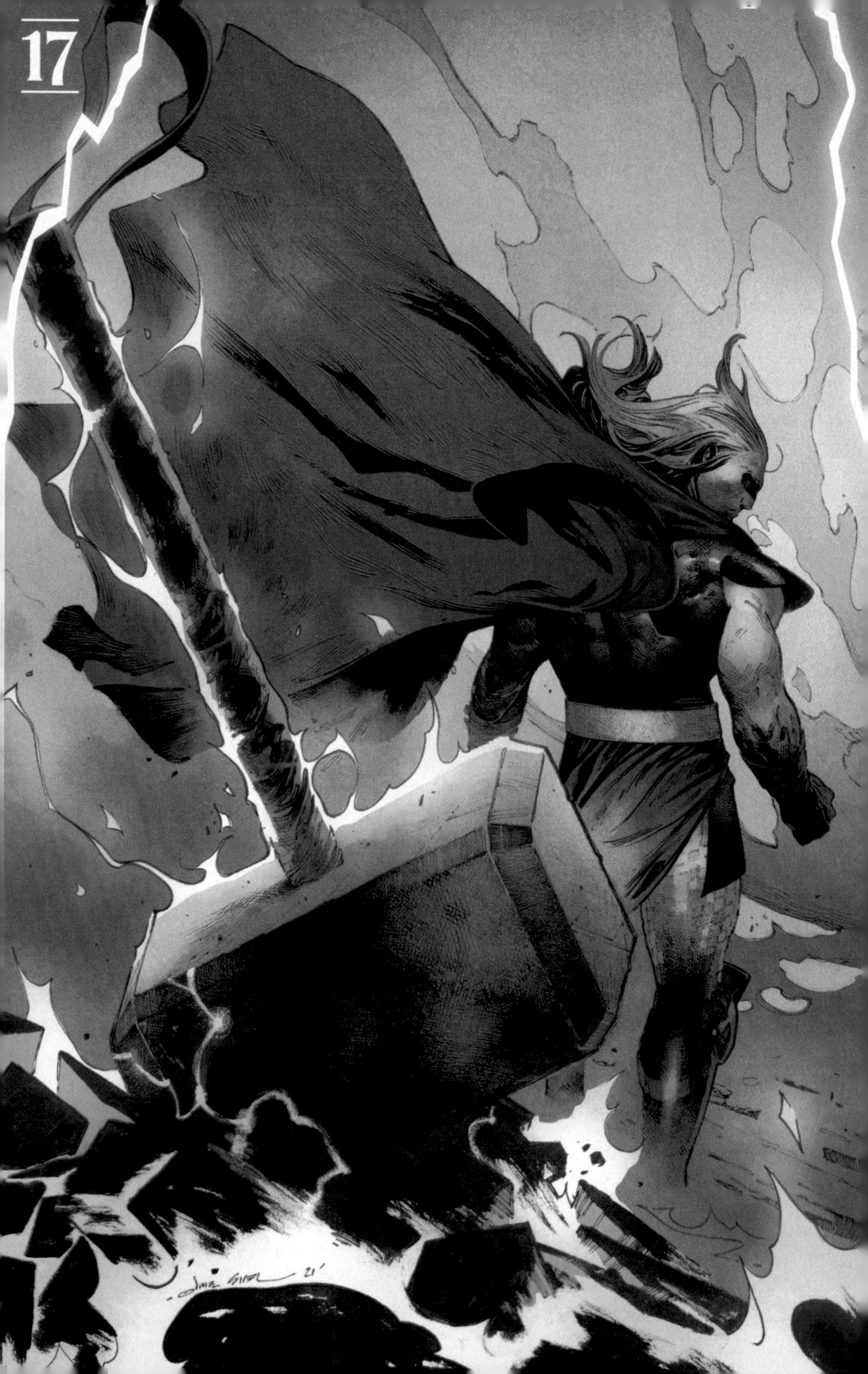
17

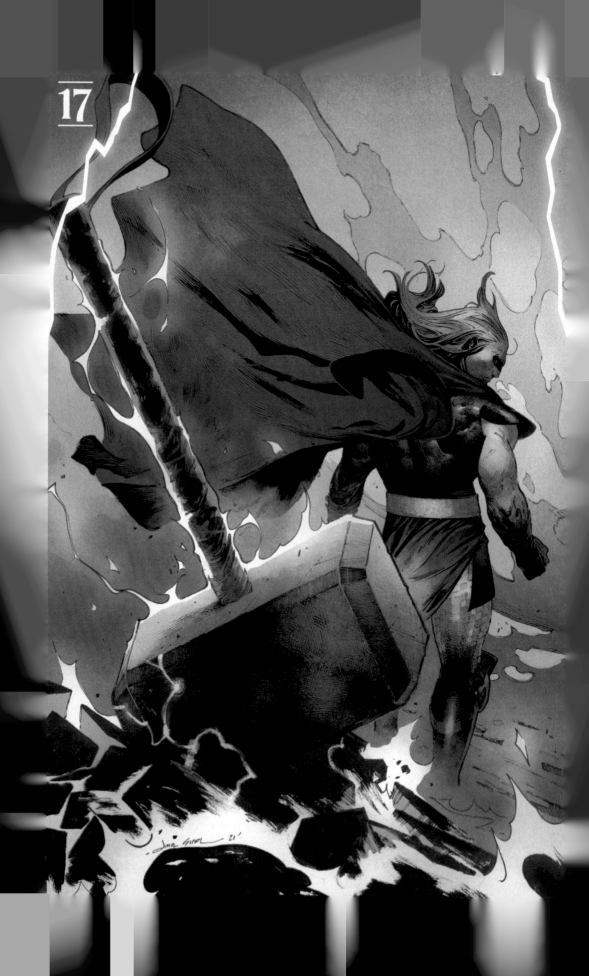

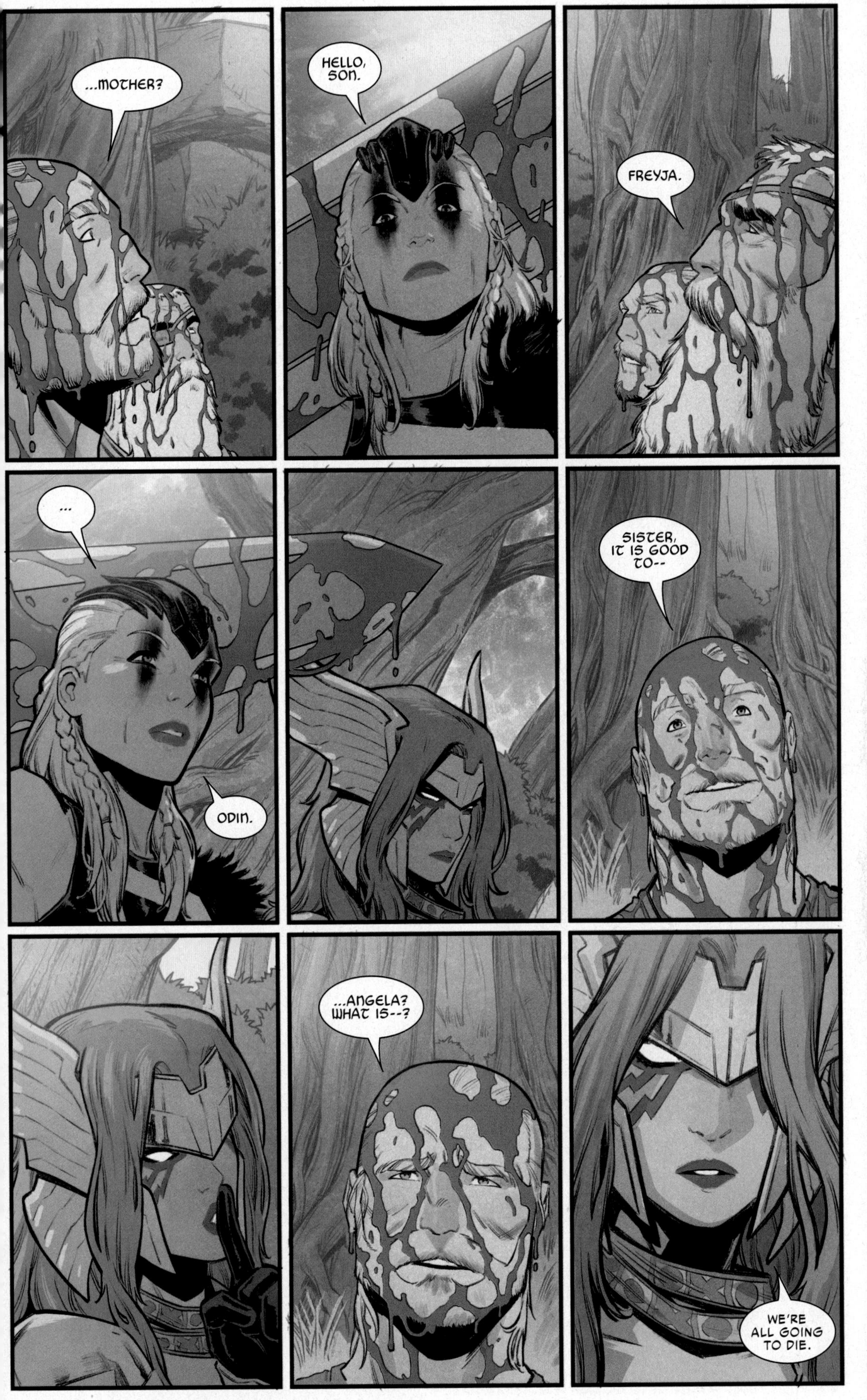
...MOTHER?
HELLO, SON.
FREYJA.
...
ODIN.
SISTER, IT IS GOOD TO--
...ANGELA? WHAT IS--?
WE'RE ALL GOING TO DIE.

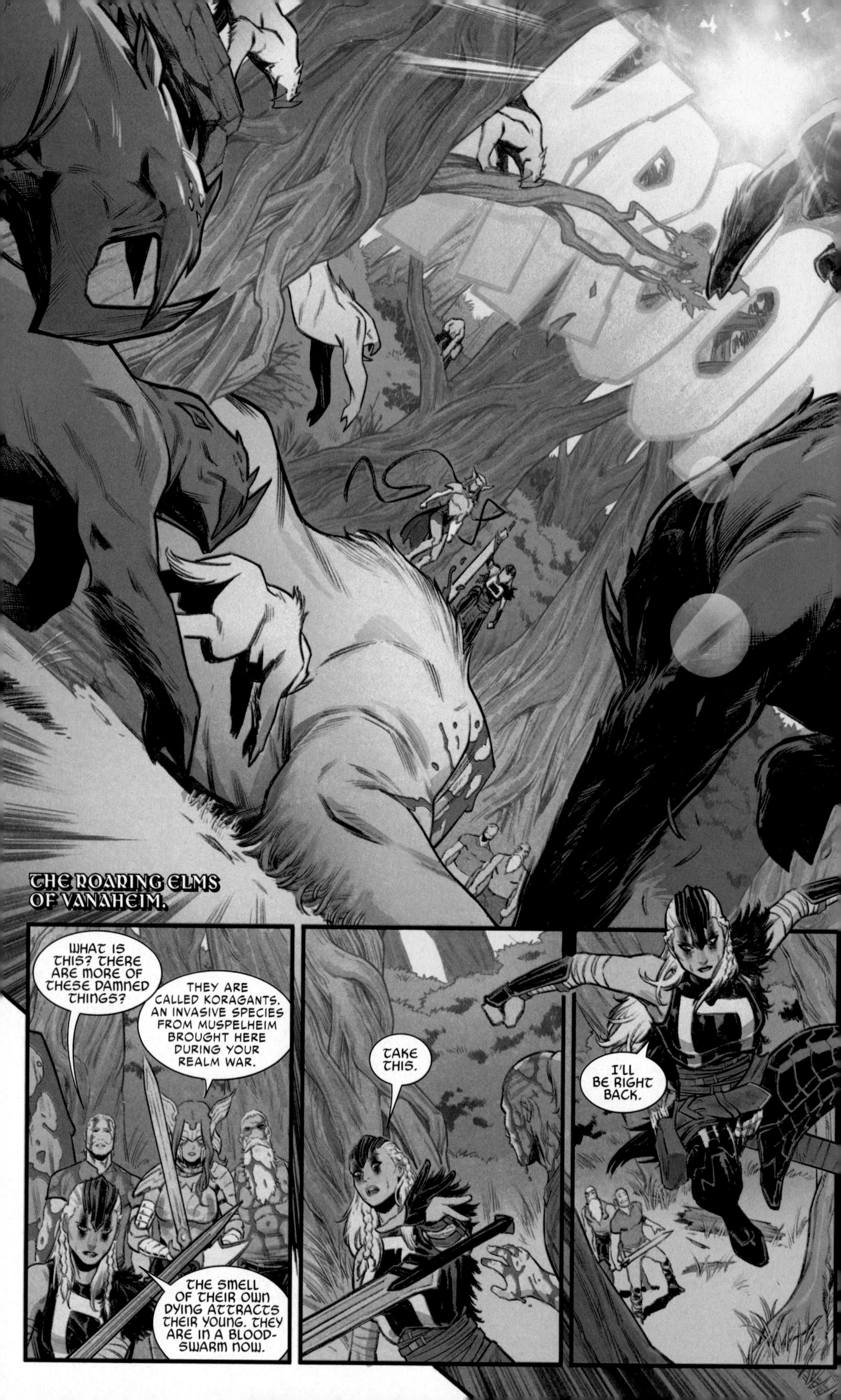
THE ROARING ELMS OF VANAHEIM.
WHAT IS THIS? THERE ARE MORE OF THESE DAMNED THINGS?
THEY ARE CALLED KORAGANTS. AN INVASIVE SPECIES FROM MUSPELHEIM BROUGHT HERE DURING YOUR REALM WAR.
THE SMELL OF THEIR OWN DYING ATTRACTS THEIR YOUNG. THEY ARE IN A BLOOD-SWARM NOW.
TAKE THIS.
I'LL BE RIGHT BACK.

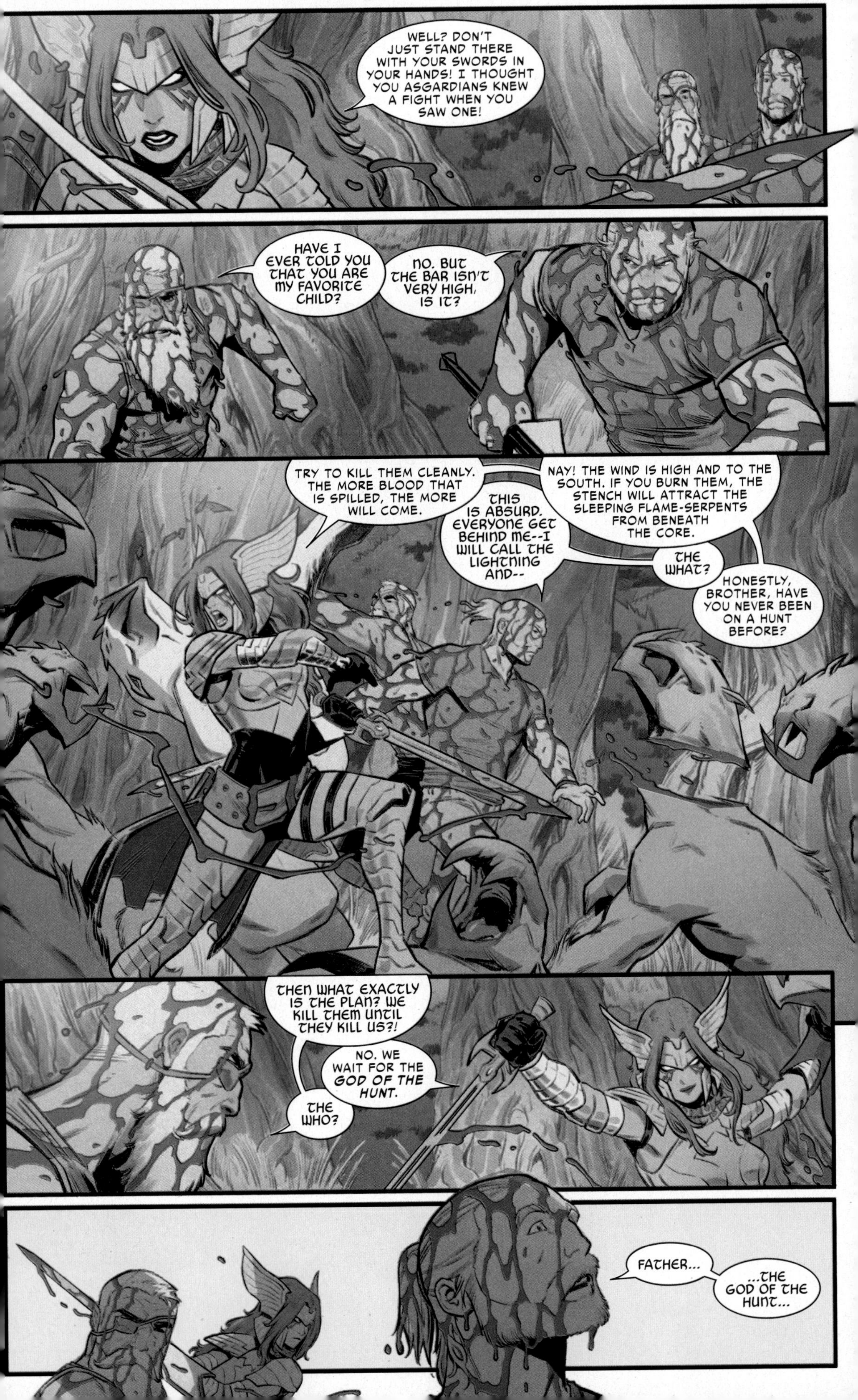
WELL? DON'T JUST STAND THERE WITH YOUR SWORDS IN YOUR HANDS! I THOUGHT YOU ASGARDIANS KNEW A FIGHT WHEN YOU SAW ONE!
HAVE I EVER TOLD YOU THAT YOU ARE MY FAVORITE CHILD?
NO. BUT THE BAR ISN'T VERY HIGH, IS IT?
TRY TO KILL THEM CLEANLY. THE MORE BLOOD THAT IS SPILLED, THE MORE WILL COME.
THIS IS ABSURD. EVERYONE GET BEHIND ME--I WILL CALL THE LIGHTNING AND--
NAY! THE WIND IS HIGH AND TO THE SOUTH. IF YOU BURN THEM, THE STENCH WILL ATTRACT THE SLEEPING FLAME-SERPENTS FROM BENEATH THE CORE.
THE WHAT?
HONESTLY, BROTHER, HAVE YOU NEVER BEEN ON A HUNT BEFORE?
THEN WHAT EXACTLY IS THE PLAN? WE KILL THEM UNTIL THEY KILL US?!
NO. WE WAIT FOR THE *GOD OF THE HUNT.*
THE WHO?
FATHER...
...THE GOD OF THE HUNT...

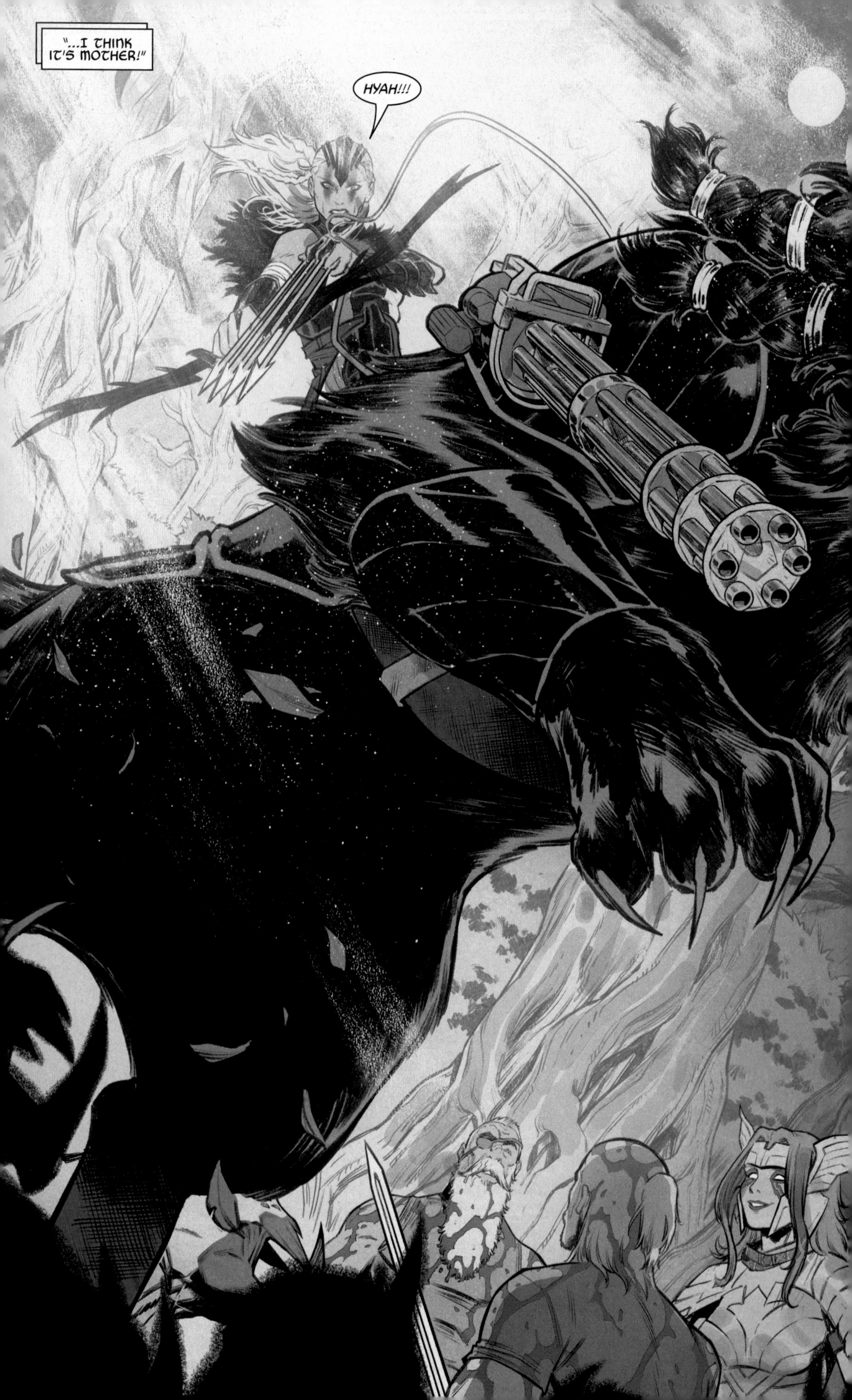
"...I THINK IT'S MOTHER!"
HYAH!!!

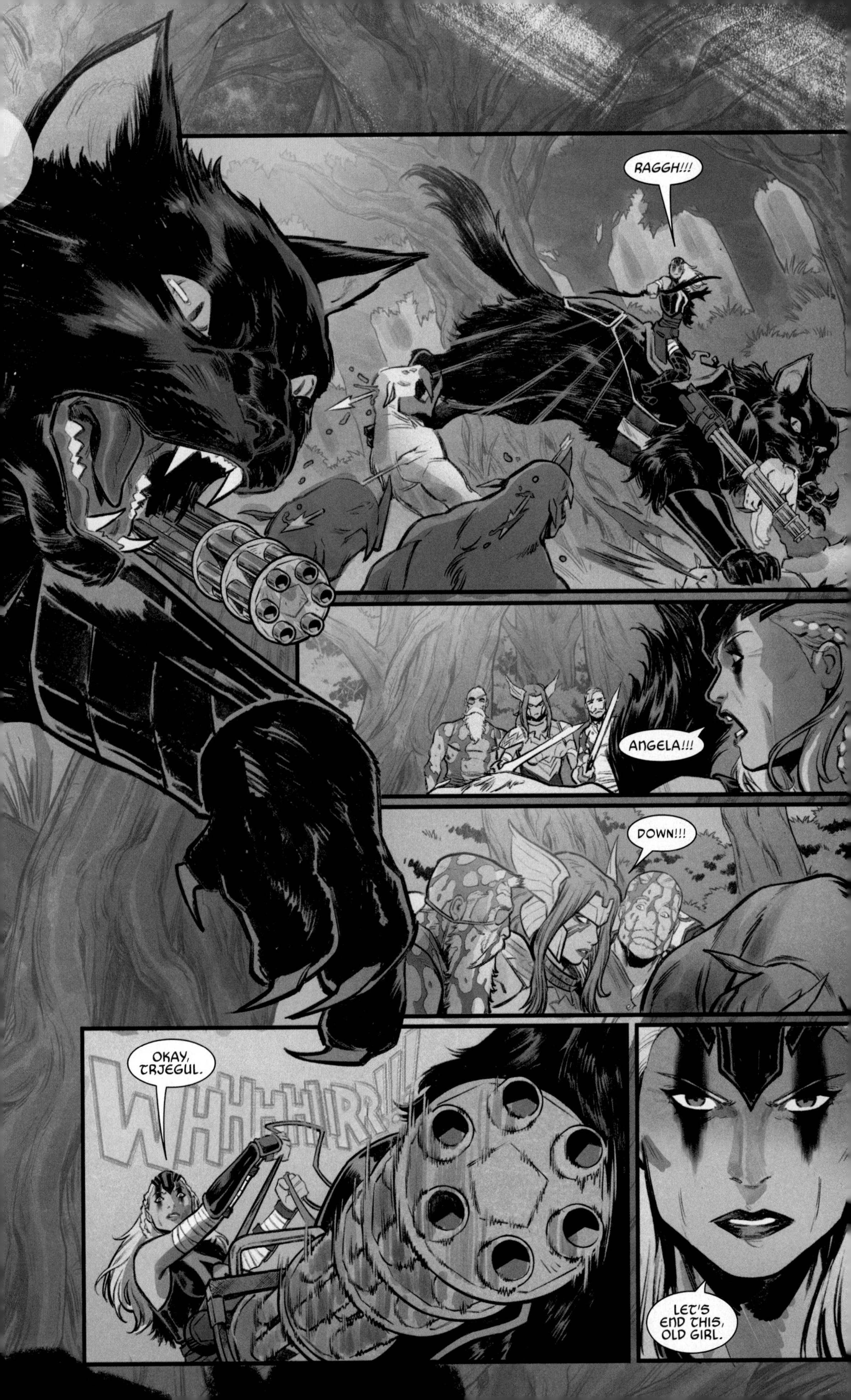

RAGGH!!!
ANGELA!!!
DOWN!!!
WHHHIRR!!
OKAY, TRJEGUL.
LET'S END THIS, OLD GIRL.

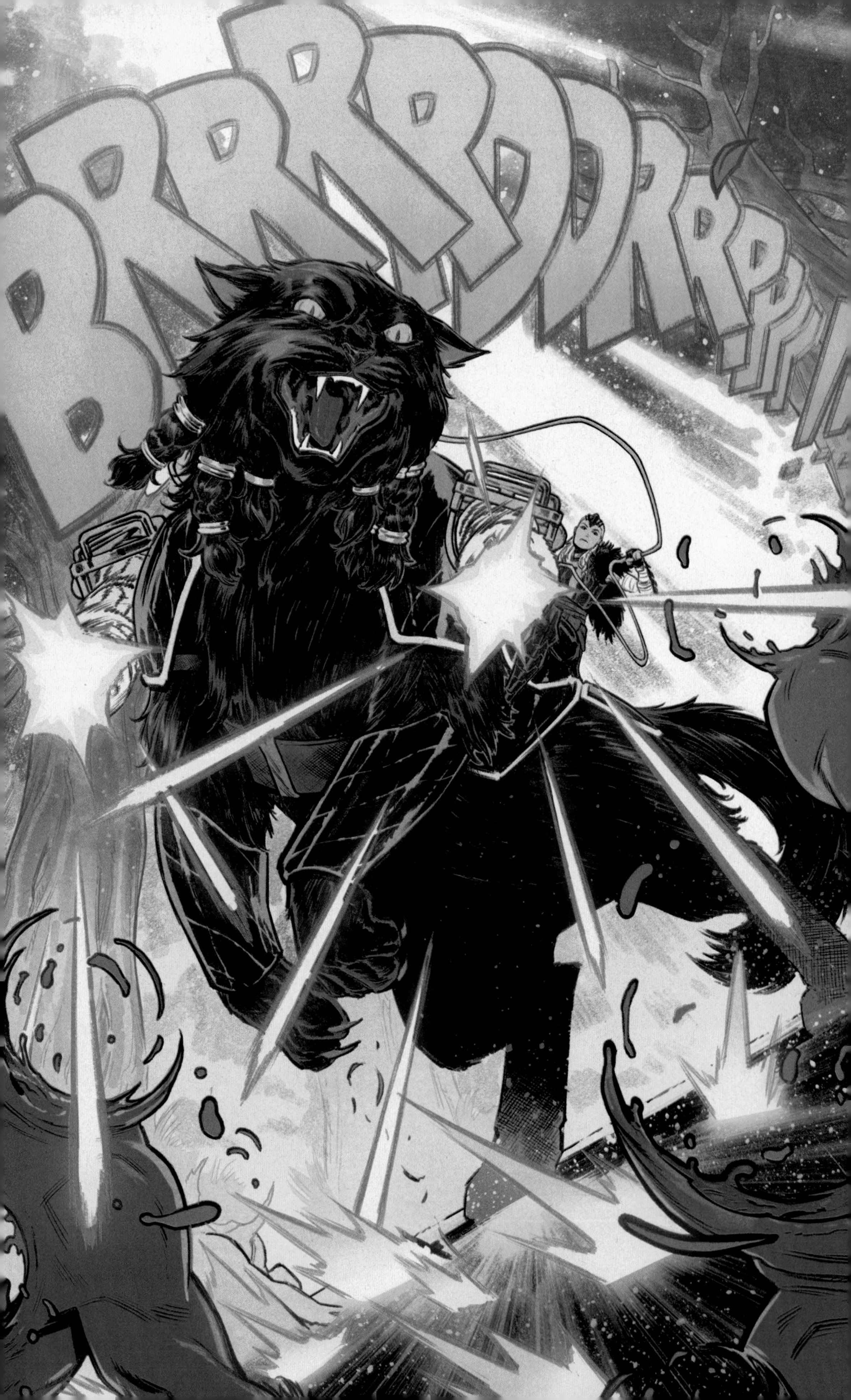

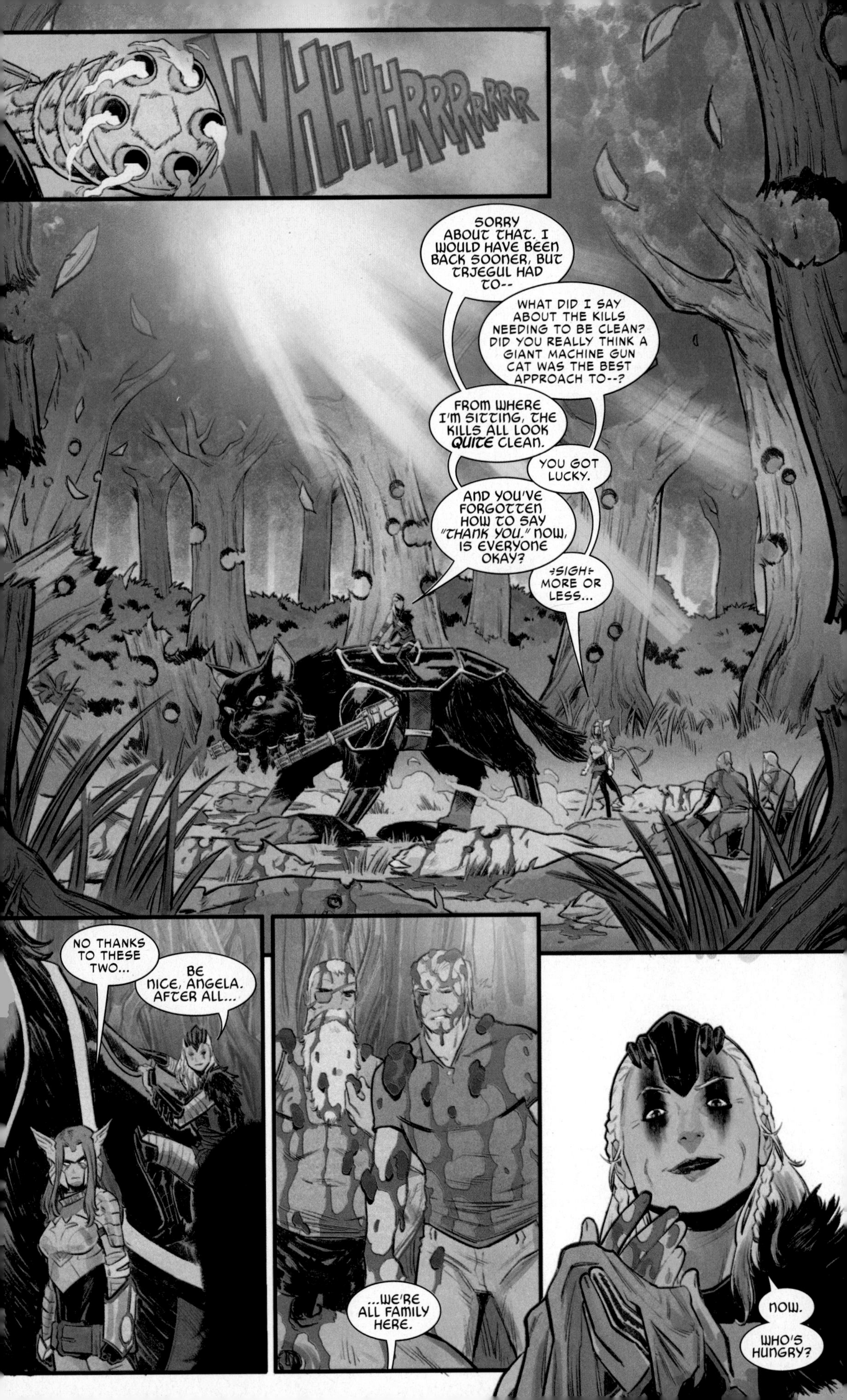
WHHHRRRRRRR
SORRY ABOUT THAT. I WOULD HAVE BEEN BACK SOONER, BUT TRJEGUL HAD TO--
WHAT DID I SAY ABOUT THE KILLS NEEDING TO BE CLEAN? DID YOU REALLY THINK A GIANT MACHINE GUN CAT WAS THE BEST APPROACH TO--?
FROM WHERE I'M SITTING, THE KILLS ALL LOOK QUITE CLEAN.
YOU GOT LUCKY.
AND YOU'VE FORGOTTEN HOW TO SAY "THANK YOU." NOW, IS EVERYONE OKAY?
÷SIGH÷ MORE OR LESS...
NO THANKS TO THESE TWO...
BE NICE, ANGELA. AFTER ALL...
...WE'RE ALL FAMILY HERE.
NOW.
WHO'S HUNGRY?

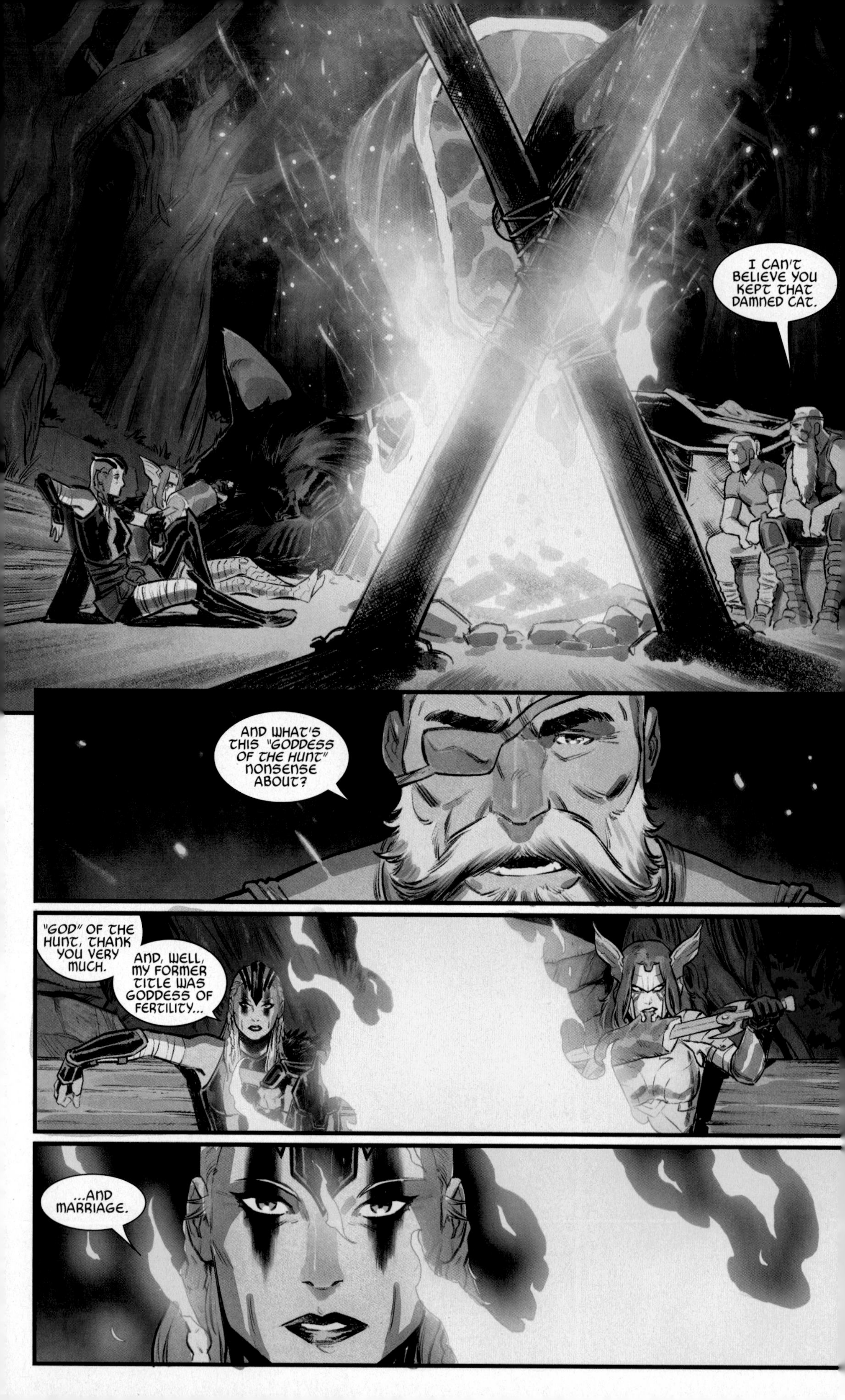
I CAN'T BELIEVE YOU KEPT THAT DAMNED CAT.
AND WHAT'S THIS "GODDESS OF THE HUNT" NONSENSE ABOUT?
"GOD" OF THE HUNT, THANK YOU VERY MUCH.
AND, WELL, MY FORMER TITLE WAS GODDESS OF FERTILITY...
...AND MARRIAGE.

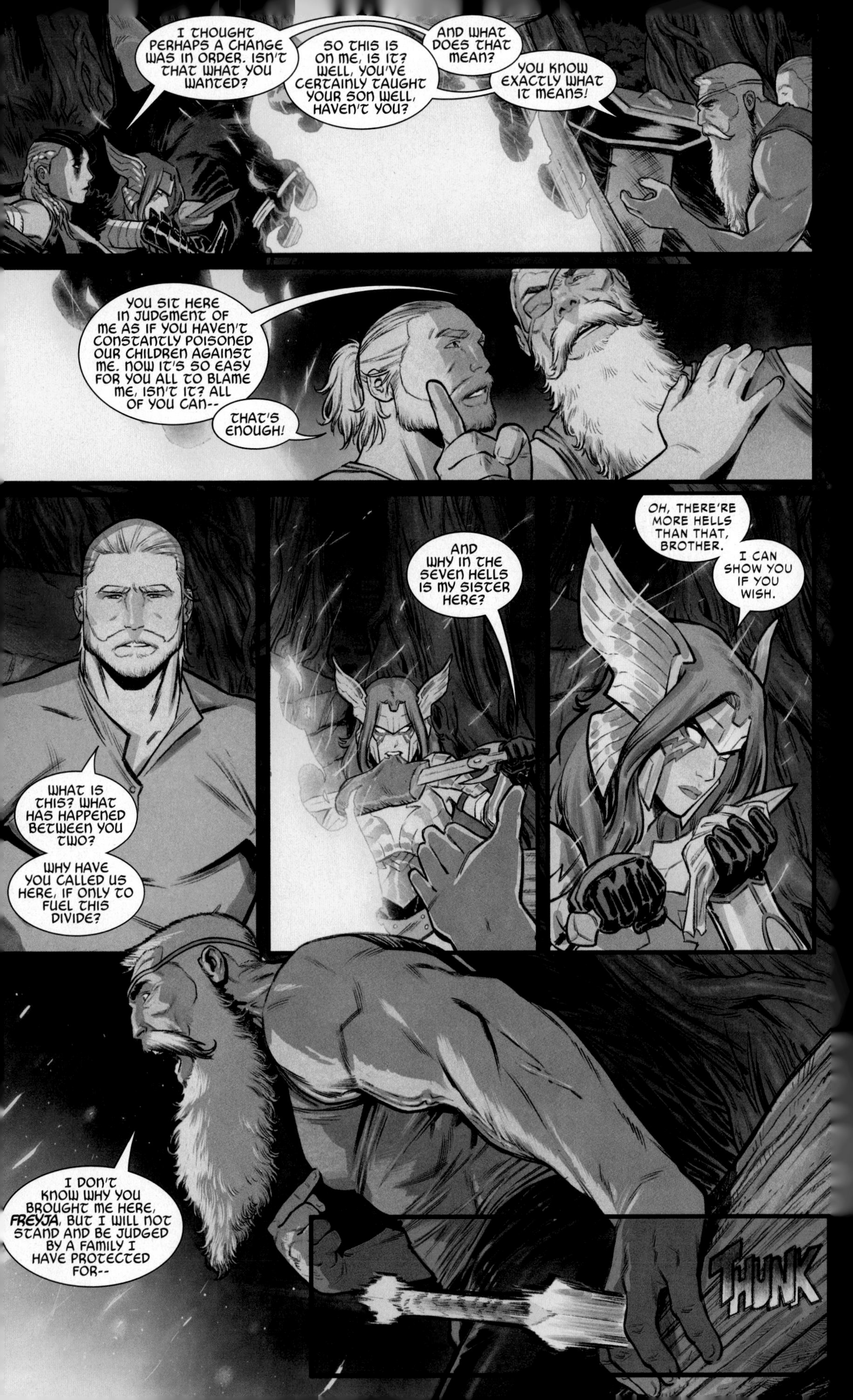

I THOUGHT PERHAPS A CHANGE WAS IN ORDER. ISN'T THAT WHAT YOU WANTED?
SO THIS IS ON ME, IS IT? WELL, YOU'VE CERTAINLY TAUGHT YOUR SON WELL, HAVEN'T YOU?
AND WHAT DOES THAT MEAN?
YOU KNOW EXACTLY WHAT IT MEANS!
YOU SIT HERE IN JUDGMENT OF ME AS IF YOU HAVEN'T CONSTANTLY POISONED OUR CHILDREN AGAINST ME. NOW IT'S SO EASY FOR YOU ALL TO BLAME ME, ISN'T IT? ALL OF YOU CAN--
THAT'S ENOUGH!
WHAT IS THIS? WHAT HAS HAPPENED BETWEEN YOU TWO?
WHY HAVE YOU CALLED US HERE, IF ONLY TO FUEL THIS DIVIDE?
AND WHY IN THE SEVEN HELLS IS MY SISTER HERE?
OH, THERE'RE MORE HELLS THAN THAT, BROTHER.
I CAN SHOW YOU IF YOU WISH.
I DON'T KNOW WHY YOU BROUGHT ME HERE, FREYJA, BUT I WILL NOT STAND AND BE JUDGED BY A FAMILY I HAVE PROTECTED FOR--
THUNK

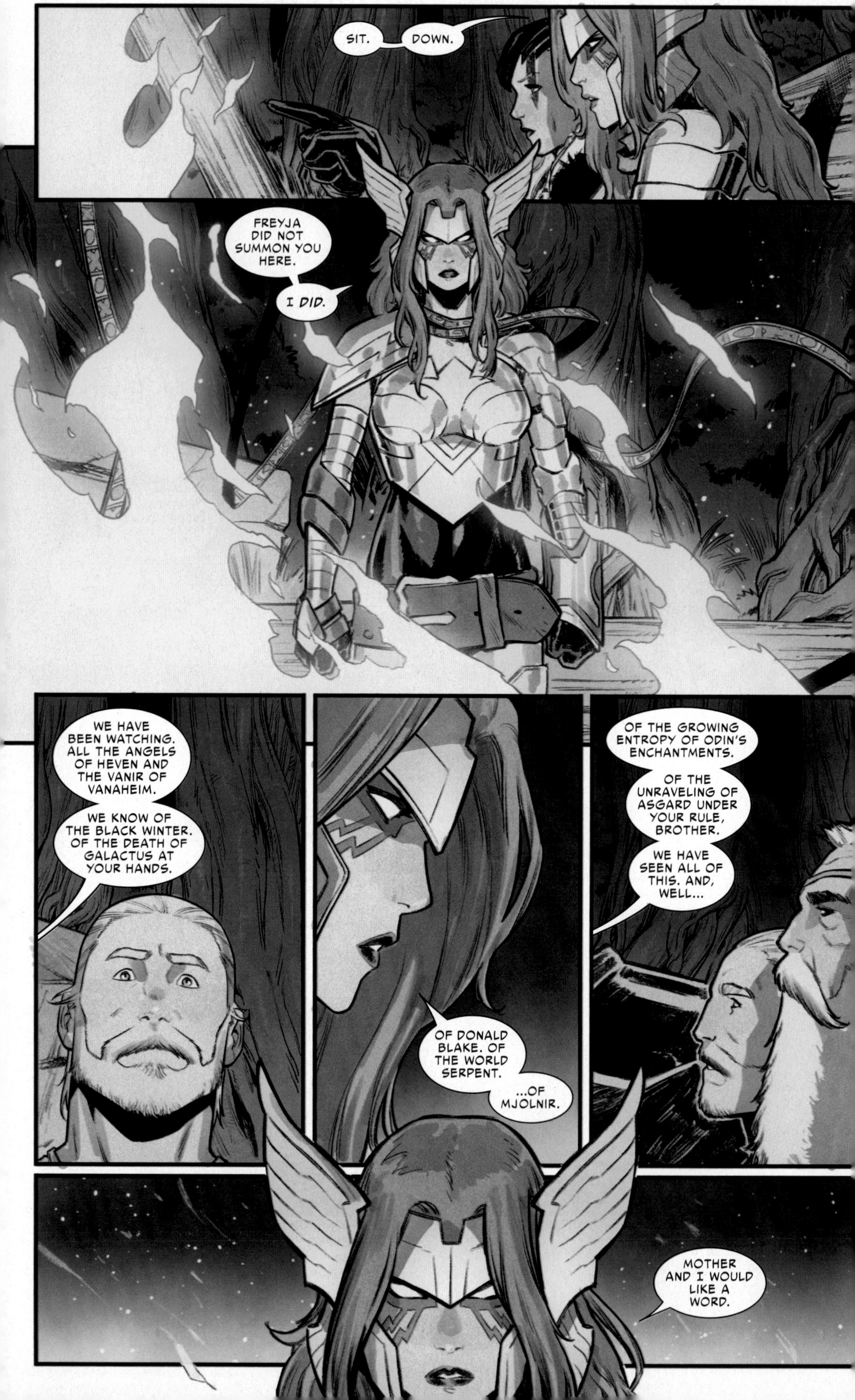

SIT.
DOWN.
FREYJA DID NOT SUMMON YOU HERE.
I DID.
WE HAVE BEEN WATCHING. ALL THE ANGELS OF HEVEN AND THE VANIR OF VANAHEIM.
WE KNOW OF THE BLACK WINTER. OF THE DEATH OF GALACTUS AT YOUR HANDS.
OF DONALD BLAKE. OF THE WORLD SERPENT.
...OF MJOLNIR.
OF THE GROWING ENTROPY OF ODIN'S ENCHANTMENTS.
OF THE UNRAVELING OF ASGARD UNDER YOUR RULE, BROTHER.
WE HAVE SEEN ALL OF THIS. AND, WELL...
MOTHER AND I WOULD LIKE A WORD.

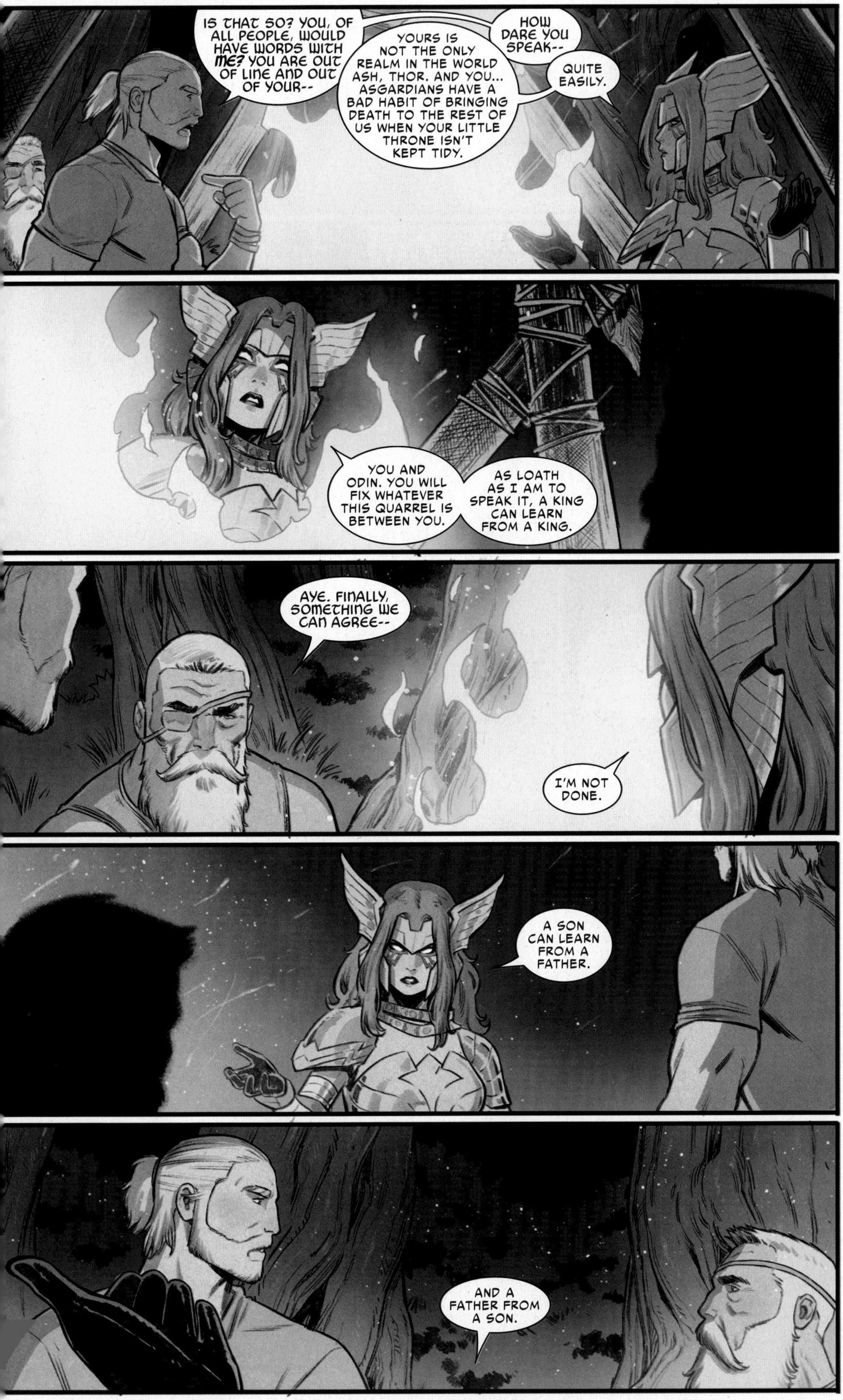
IS THAT SO? YOU, OF ALL PEOPLE, WOULD HAVE WORDS WITH ME? YOU ARE OUT OF LINE AND OUT OF YOUR--
HOW DARE YOU SPEAK--
QUITE EASILY.
YOURS IS NOT THE ONLY REALM IN THE WORLD ASH, THOR. AND YOU... ASGARDIANS HAVE A BAD HABIT OF BRINGING DEATH TO THE REST OF US WHEN YOUR LITTLE THRONE ISN'T KEPT TIDY.
YOU AND ODIN. YOU WILL FIX WHATEVER THIS QUARREL IS BETWEEN YOU.
AS LOATH AS I AM TO SPEAK IT, A KING CAN LEARN FROM A KING.
AYE. FINALLY, SOMETHING WE CAN AGREE--
I'M NOT DONE.
A SON CAN LEARN FROM A FATHER.
AND A FATHER FROM A SON.

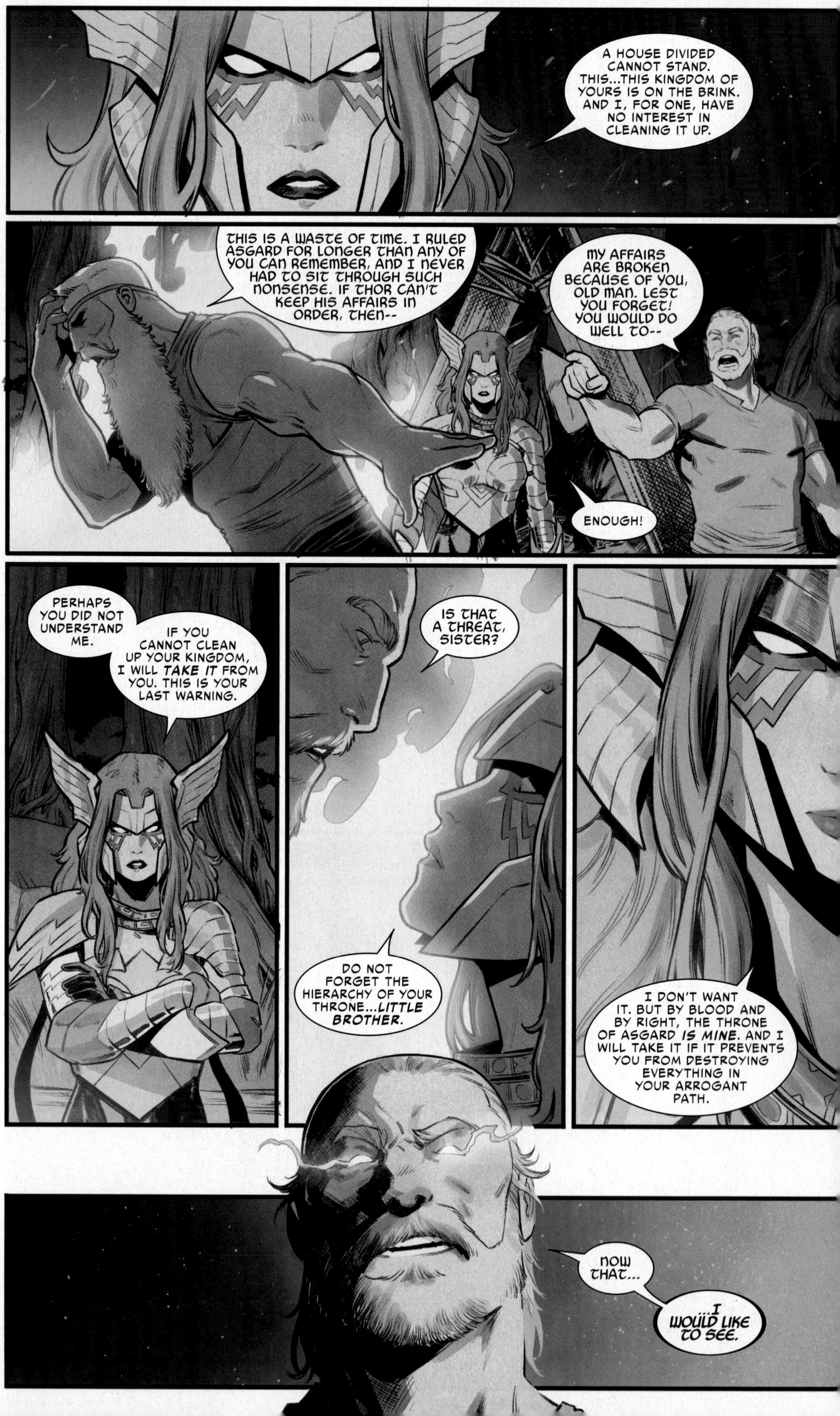
A HOUSE DIVIDED CANNOT STAND. THIS...THIS KINGDOM OF YOURS IS ON THE BRINK. AND I, FOR ONE, HAVE NO INTEREST IN CLEANING IT UP.
THIS IS A WASTE OF TIME. I RULED ASGARD FOR LONGER THAN ANY OF YOU CAN REMEMBER, AND I NEVER HAD TO SIT THROUGH SUCH NONSENSE. IF THOR CAN'T KEEP HIS AFFAIRS IN ORDER, THEN--
MY AFFAIRS ARE BROKEN BECAUSE OF YOU, OLD MAN. LEST YOU FORGET! YOU WOULD DO WELL TO--
ENOUGH!
PERHAPS YOU DID NOT UNDERSTAND ME.
IF YOU CANNOT CLEAN UP YOUR KINGDOM, I WILL TAKE IT FROM YOU. THIS IS YOUR LAST WARNING.
IS THAT A THREAT, SISTER?
DO NOT FORGET THE HIERARCHY OF YOUR THRONE...LITTLE BROTHER.
I DON'T WANT IT. BUT BY BLOOD AND BY RIGHT, THE THRONE OF ASGARD IS MINE. AND I WILL TAKE IT IF IT PREVENTS YOU FROM DESTROYING EVERYTHING IN YOUR ARROGANT PATH.
NOW THAT...
...I WOULD LIKE TO SEE.

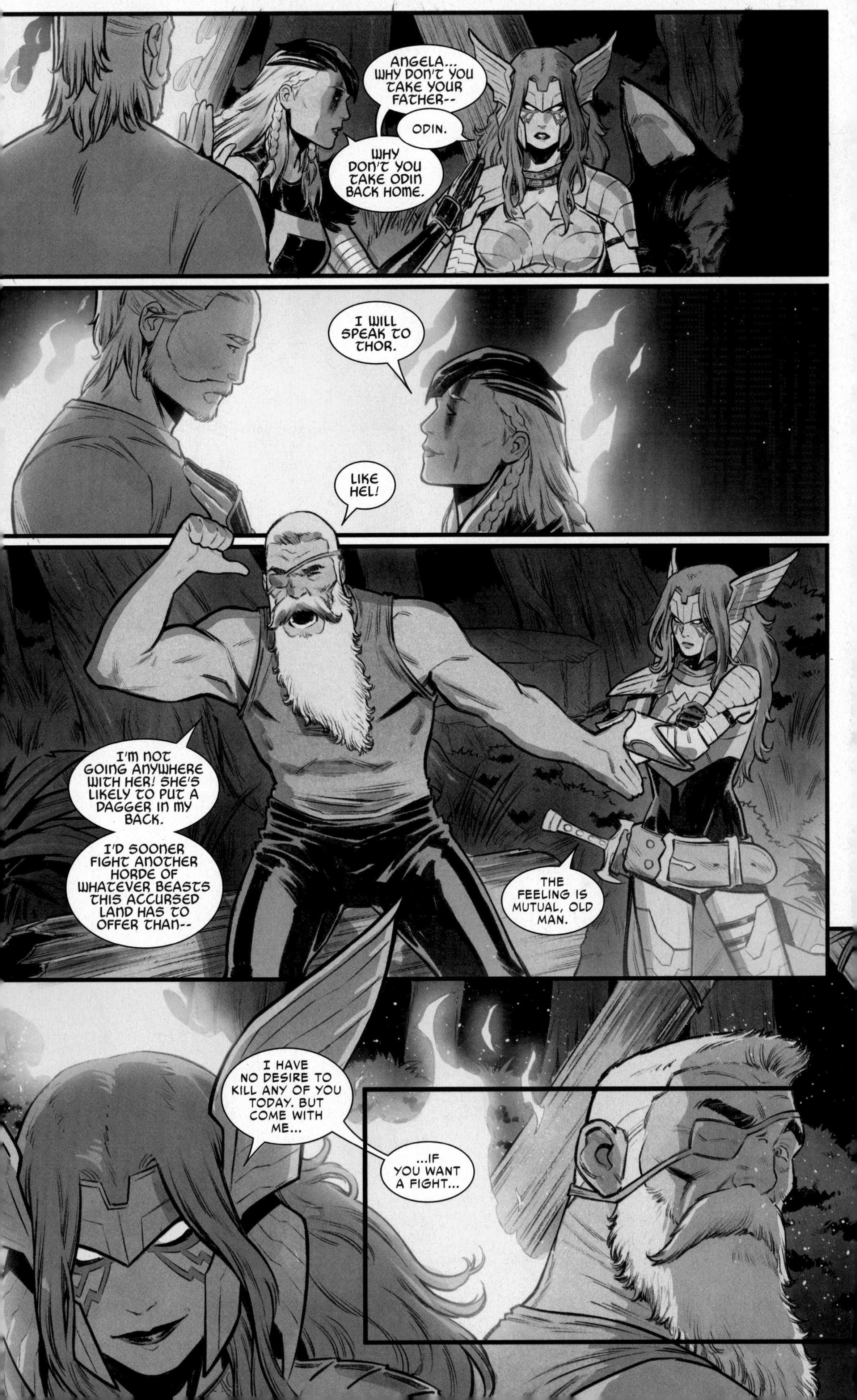
ANGELA... WHY DON'T YOU TAKE YOUR FATHER--
ODIN.
WHY DON'T YOU TAKE ODIN BACK HOME.
I WILL SPEAK TO THOR.
LIKE HEL!
I'M NOT GOING ANYWHERE WITH HER! SHE'S LIKELY TO PUT A DAGGER IN MY BACK.
I'D SOONER FIGHT ANOTHER HORDE OF WHATEVER BEASTS THIS ACCURSED LAND HAS TO OFFER THAN--
THE FEELING IS MUTUAL, OLD MAN.
I HAVE NO DESIRE TO KILL ANY OF YOU TODAY. BUT COME WITH ME...
...IF YOU WANT A FIGHT...

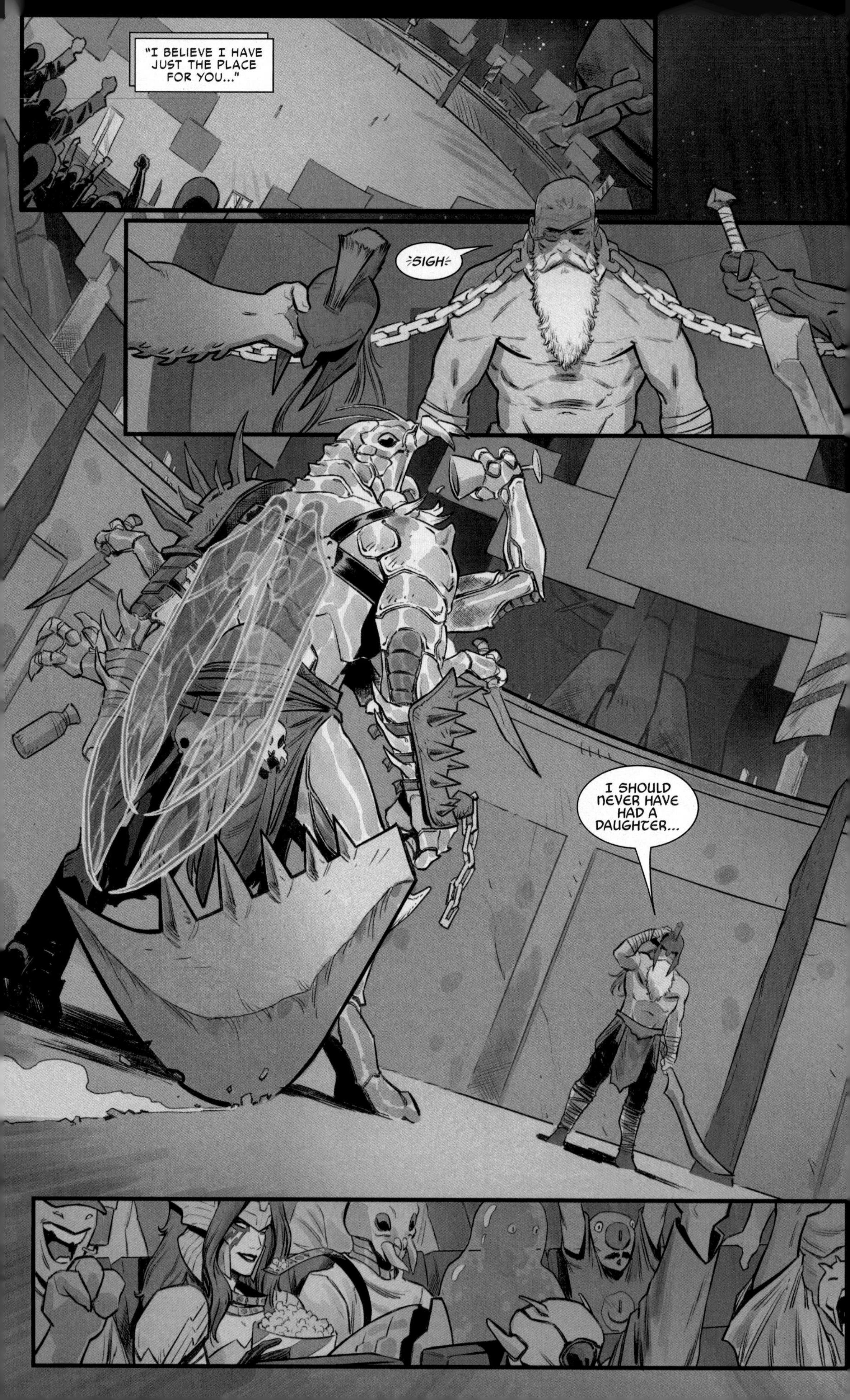
"I BELIEVE I HAVE JUST THE PLACE FOR YOU..."
SIGH
I SHOULD NEVER HAVE HAD A DAUGHTER...

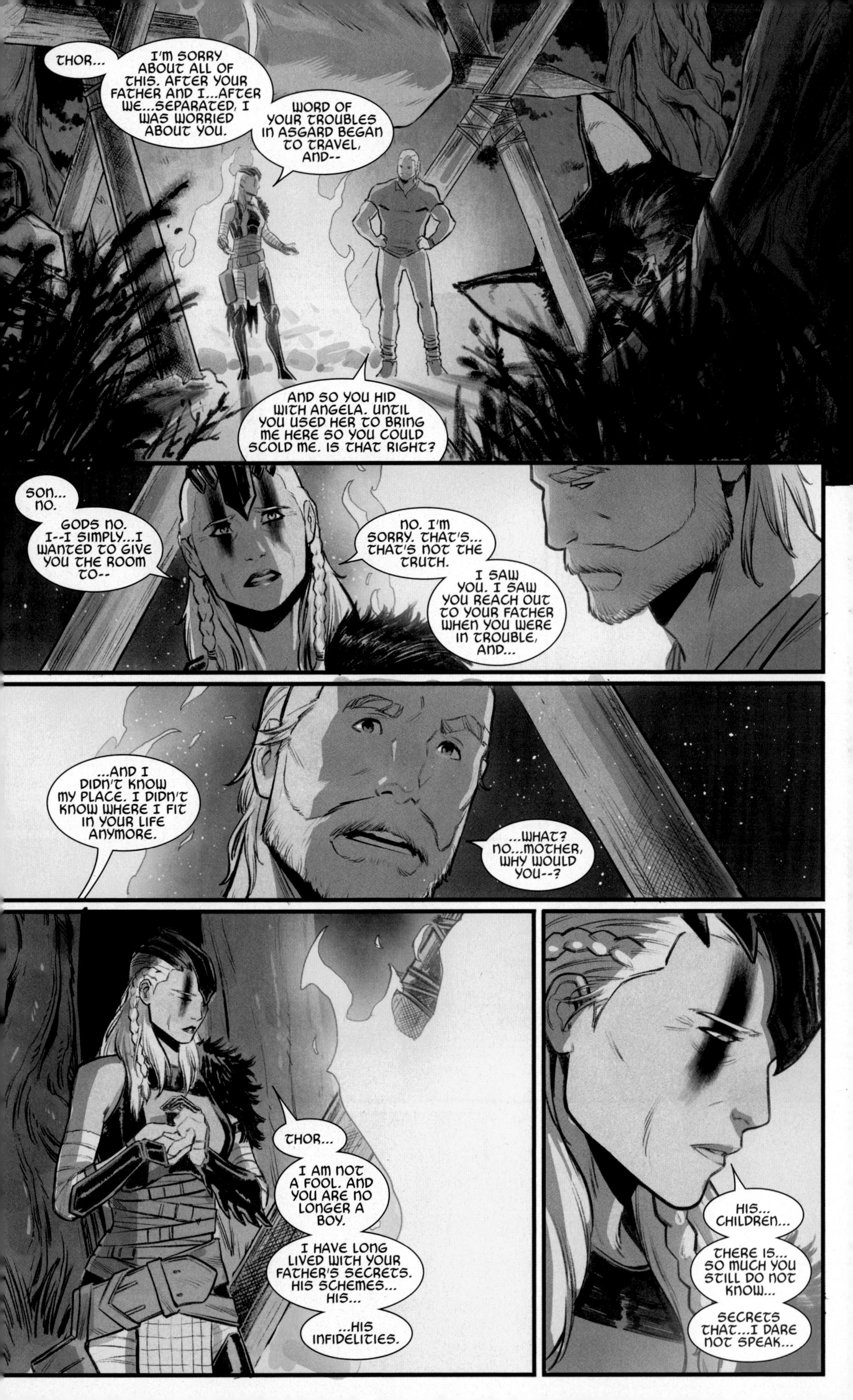
THOR...
I'M SORRY ABOUT ALL OF THIS. AFTER YOUR FATHER AND I...AFTER WE...SEPARATED, I WAS WORRIED ABOUT YOU.
WORD OF YOUR TROUBLES IN ASGARD BEGAN TO TRAVEL, AND--
AND SO YOU HID WITH ANGELA. UNTIL YOU USED HER TO BRING ME HERE SO YOU COULD SCOLD ME. IS THAT RIGHT?
SON... NO.
GODS NO. I--I SIMPLY...I WANTED TO GIVE YOU THE ROOM TO--
NO. I'M SORRY. THAT'S... THAT'S NOT THE TRUTH.
I SAW YOU. I SAW YOU REACH OUT TO YOUR FATHER WHEN YOU WERE IN TROUBLE, AND...
...AND I DIDN'T KNOW MY PLACE. I DIDN'T KNOW WHERE I FIT IN YOUR LIFE ANYMORE.
...WHAT? NO...MOTHER, WHY WOULD YOU--?
THOR...
I AM NOT A FOOL. AND YOU ARE NO LONGER A BOY.
I HAVE LONG LIVED WITH YOUR FATHER'S SECRETS. HIS SCHEMES... HIS...
...HIS INFIDELITIES.
HIS... CHILDREN...
THERE IS... SO MUCH YOU STILL DO NOT KNOW...
SECRETS THAT...I DARE NOT SPEAK...

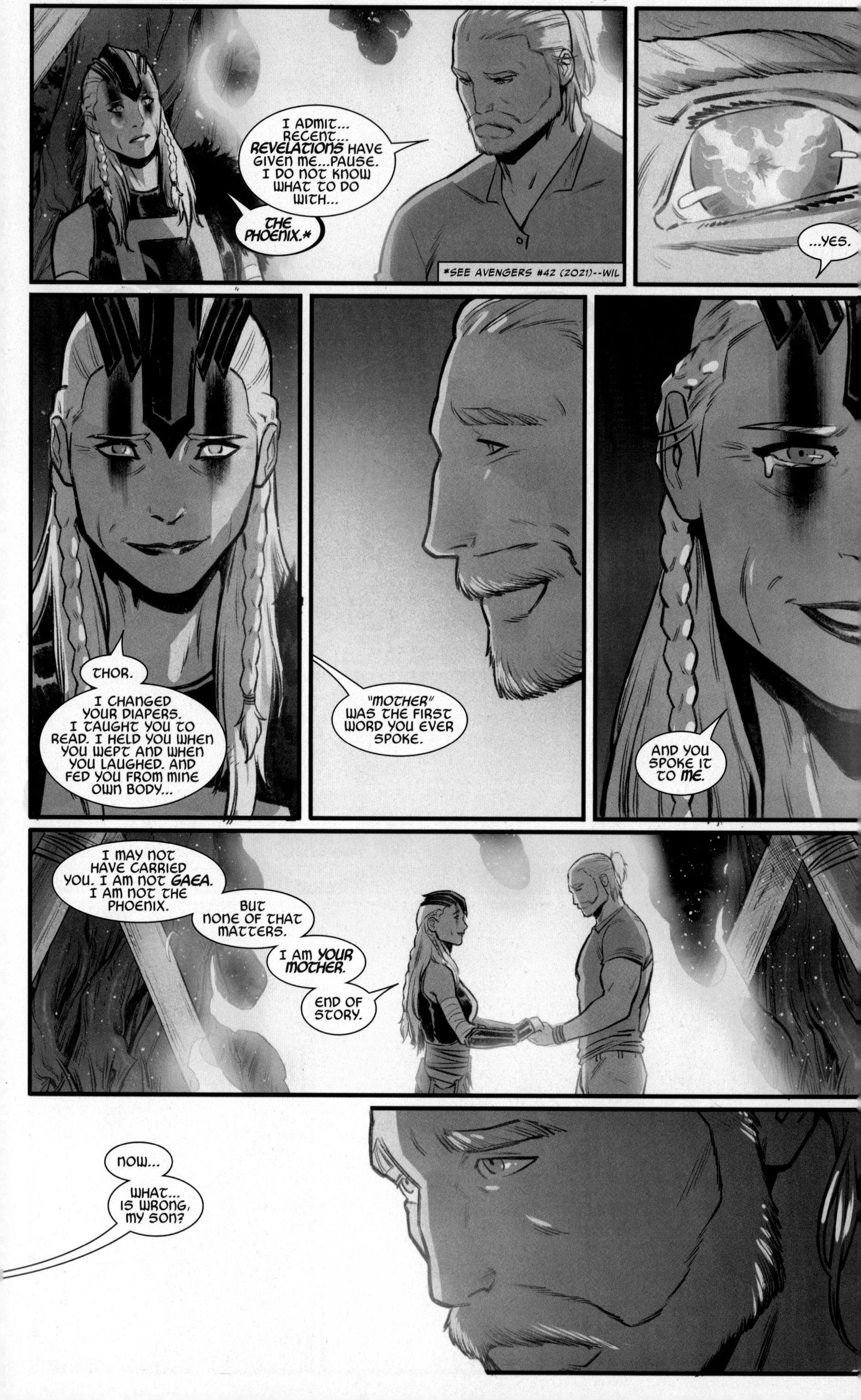
I ADMIT... RECENT... REVELATIONS HAVE GIVEN ME...PAUSE. I DO NOT KNOW WHAT TO DO WITH...
THE PHOENIX.*
*SEE AVENGERS #42 (2021)--WIL
...YES.
THOR.
I CHANGED YOUR DIAPERS. I TAUGHT YOU TO READ. I HELD YOU WHEN YOU WEPT AND WHEN YOU LAUGHED. AND FED YOU FROM MINE OWN BODY...
"MOTHER" WAS THE FIRST WORD YOU EVER SPOKE.
AND YOU SPOKE IT TO ME.
I MAY NOT HAVE CARRIED YOU. I AM NOT GAEA. I AM NOT THE PHOENIX.
BUT NONE OF THAT MATTERS.
I AM YOUR MOTHER.
END OF STORY.
NOW...
WHAT... IS WRONG, MY SON?

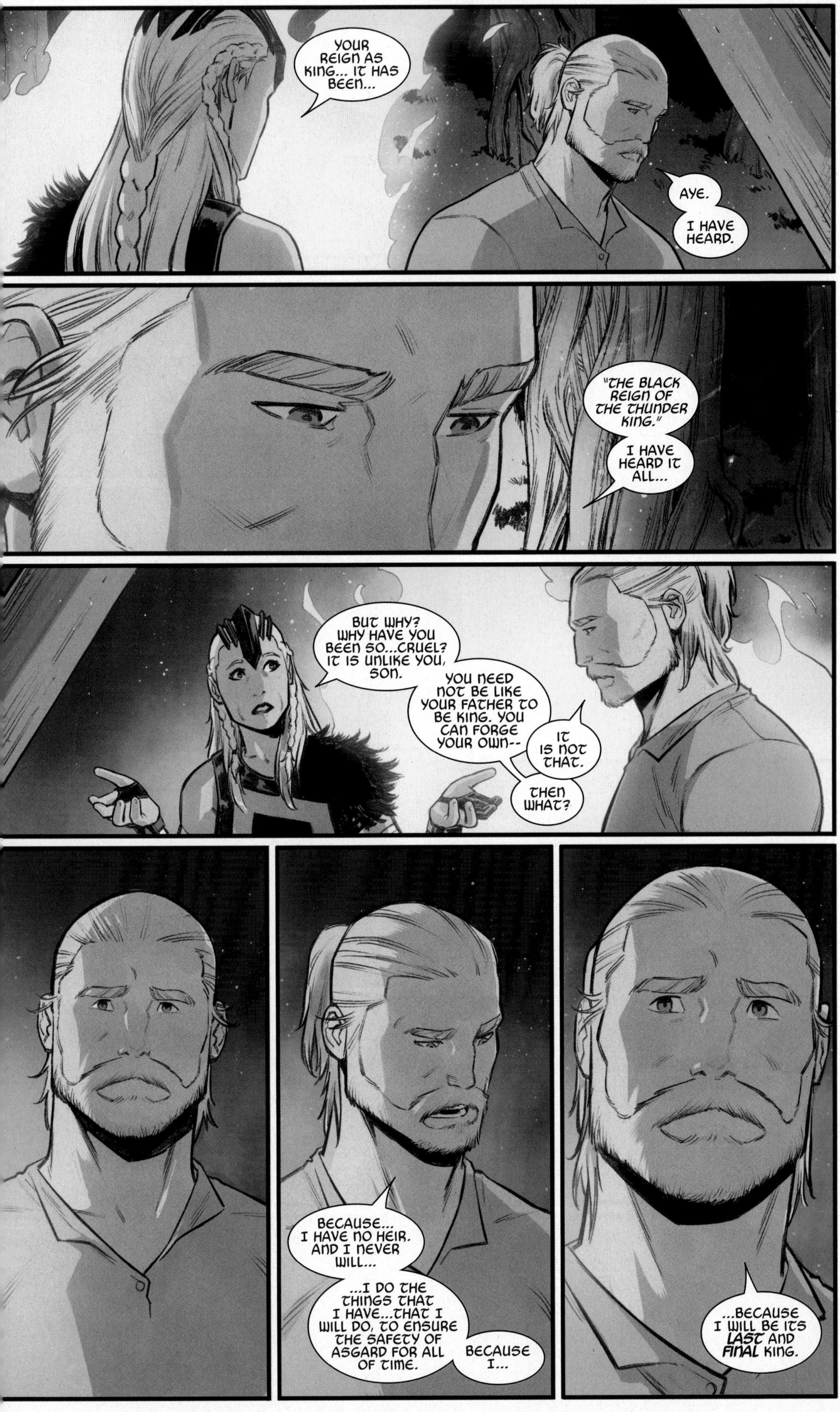

YOUR REIGN AS KING... IT HAS BEEN...
AYE.
I HAVE HEARD.
"THE BLACK REIGN OF THE THUNDER KING."
I HAVE HEARD IT ALL...
BUT WHY? WHY HAVE YOU BEEN SO...CRUEL? IT IS UNLIKE YOU, SON.
YOU NEED NOT BE LIKE YOUR FATHER TO BE KING. YOU CAN FORGE YOUR OWN--
IT IS NOT THAT.
THEN WHAT?
BECAUSE... I HAVE NO HEIR. AND I NEVER WILL...
...I DO THE THINGS THAT I HAVE...THAT I WILL DO, TO ENSURE THE SAFETY OF ASGARD FOR ALL OF TIME.
BECAUSE I...
...BECAUSE I WILL BE ITS LAST AND FINAL KING.

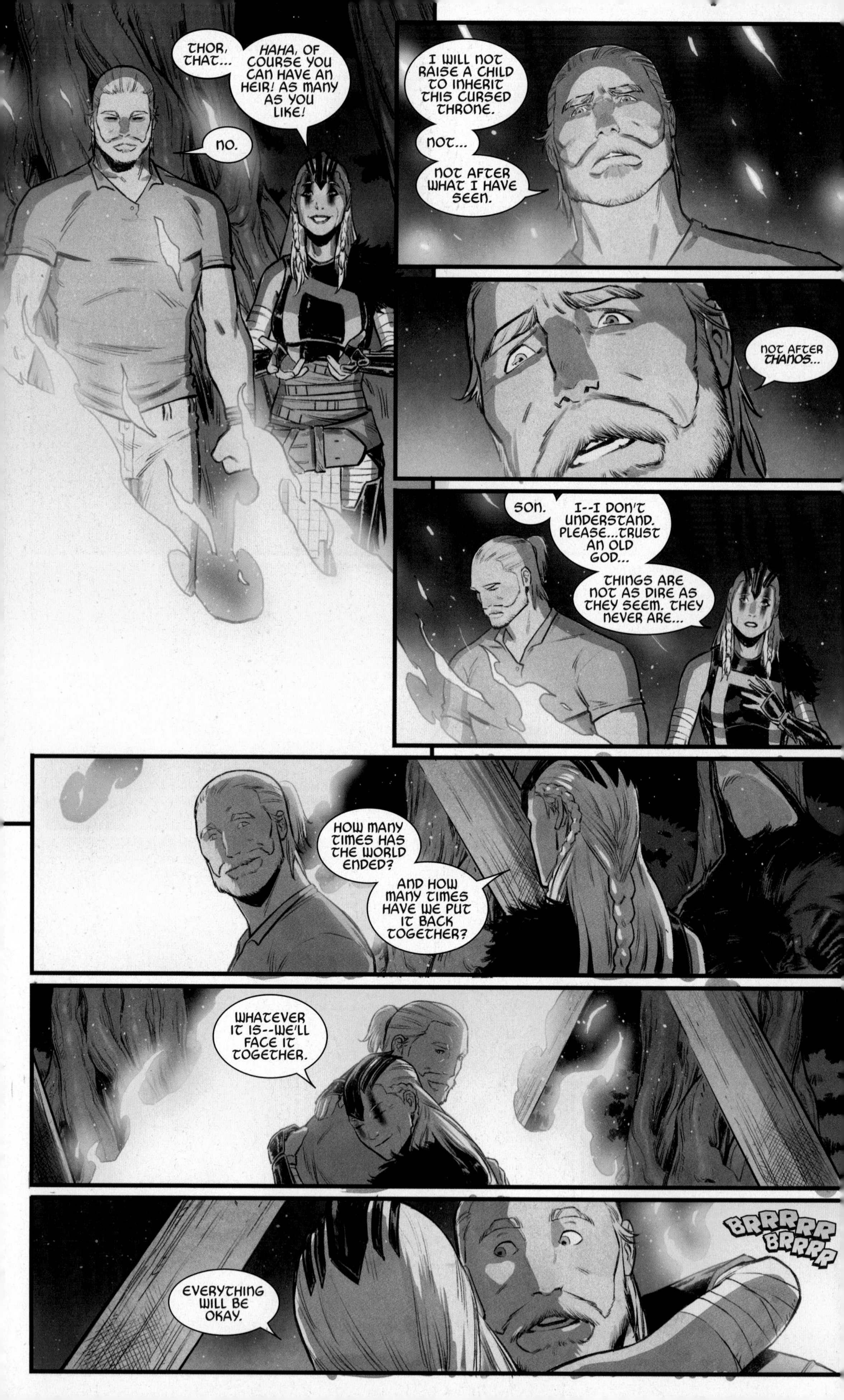
THOR, THAT...
HAHA, OF COURSE YOU CAN HAVE AN HEIR! AS MANY AS YOU LIKE!
NO.
I WILL NOT RAISE A CHILD TO INHERIT THIS CURSED THRONE.
NOT...
NOT AFTER WHAT I HAVE SEEN.
NOT AFTER THANOS...
SON.
I--I DON'T UNDERSTAND. PLEASE...TRUST AN OLD GOD...
THINGS ARE NOT AS DIRE AS THEY SEEM. THEY NEVER ARE...
HOW MANY TIMES HAS THE WORLD ENDED?
AND HOW MANY TIMES HAVE WE PUT IT BACK TOGETHER?
WHATEVER IT IS--WE'LL FACE IT TOGETHER.
BRRRRR BRRRR
EVERYTHING WILL BE OKAY.

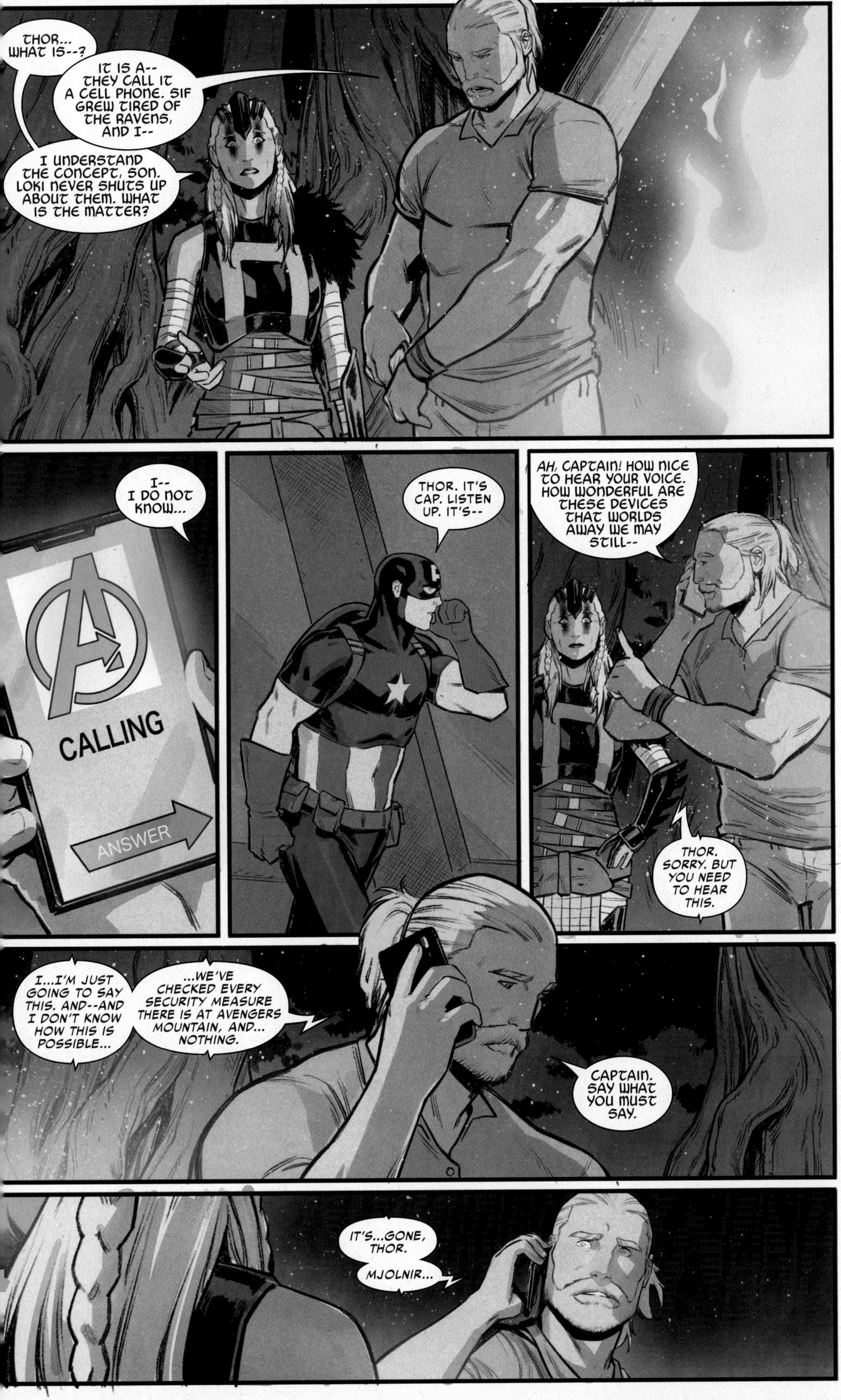
THOR... WHAT IS--?
IT IS A-- THEY CALL IT A CELL PHONE. SIF GREW TIRED OF THE RAVENS, AND I--
I UNDERSTAND THE CONCEPT, SON. LOKI NEVER SHUTS UP ABOUT THEM. WHAT IS THE MATTER?
I-- I DO NOT KNOW...
CALLING
ANSWER
THOR. IT'S CAP. LISTEN UP. IT'S--
AH, CAPTAIN! HOW NICE TO HEAR YOUR VOICE. HOW WONDERFUL ARE THESE DEVICES THAT WORLDS AWAY WE MAY STILL--
THOR. SORRY. BUT YOU NEED TO HEAR THIS.
I...I'M JUST GOING TO SAY THIS. AND--AND I DON'T KNOW HOW THIS IS POSSIBLE...
...WE'VE CHECKED EVERY SECURITY MEASURE THERE IS AT AVENGERS MOUNTAIN, AND... NOTHING.
CAPTAIN. SAY WHAT YOU MUST SAY.
IT'S...GONE, THOR.
MJOLNIR...

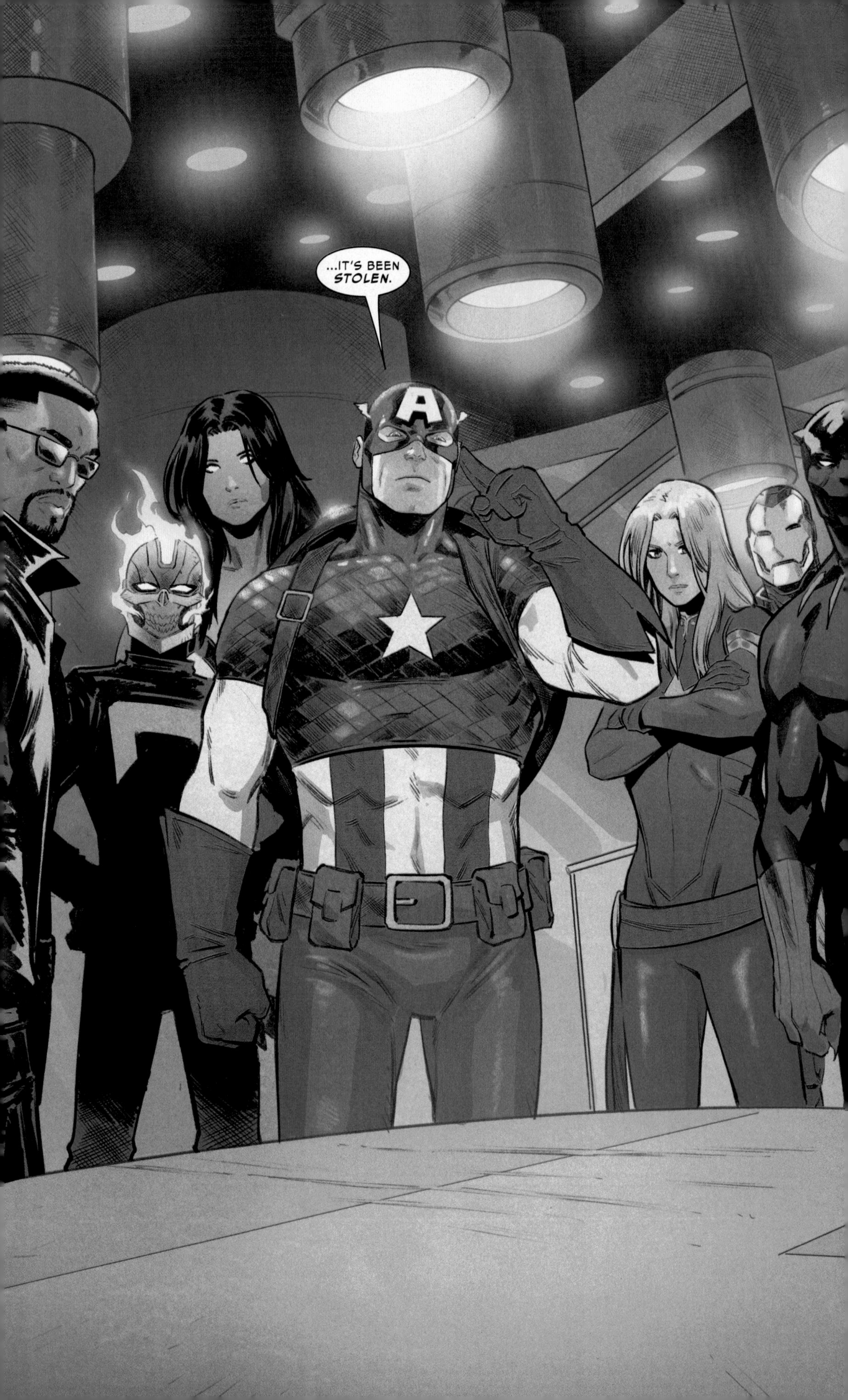
...IT'S BEEN STOLEN.

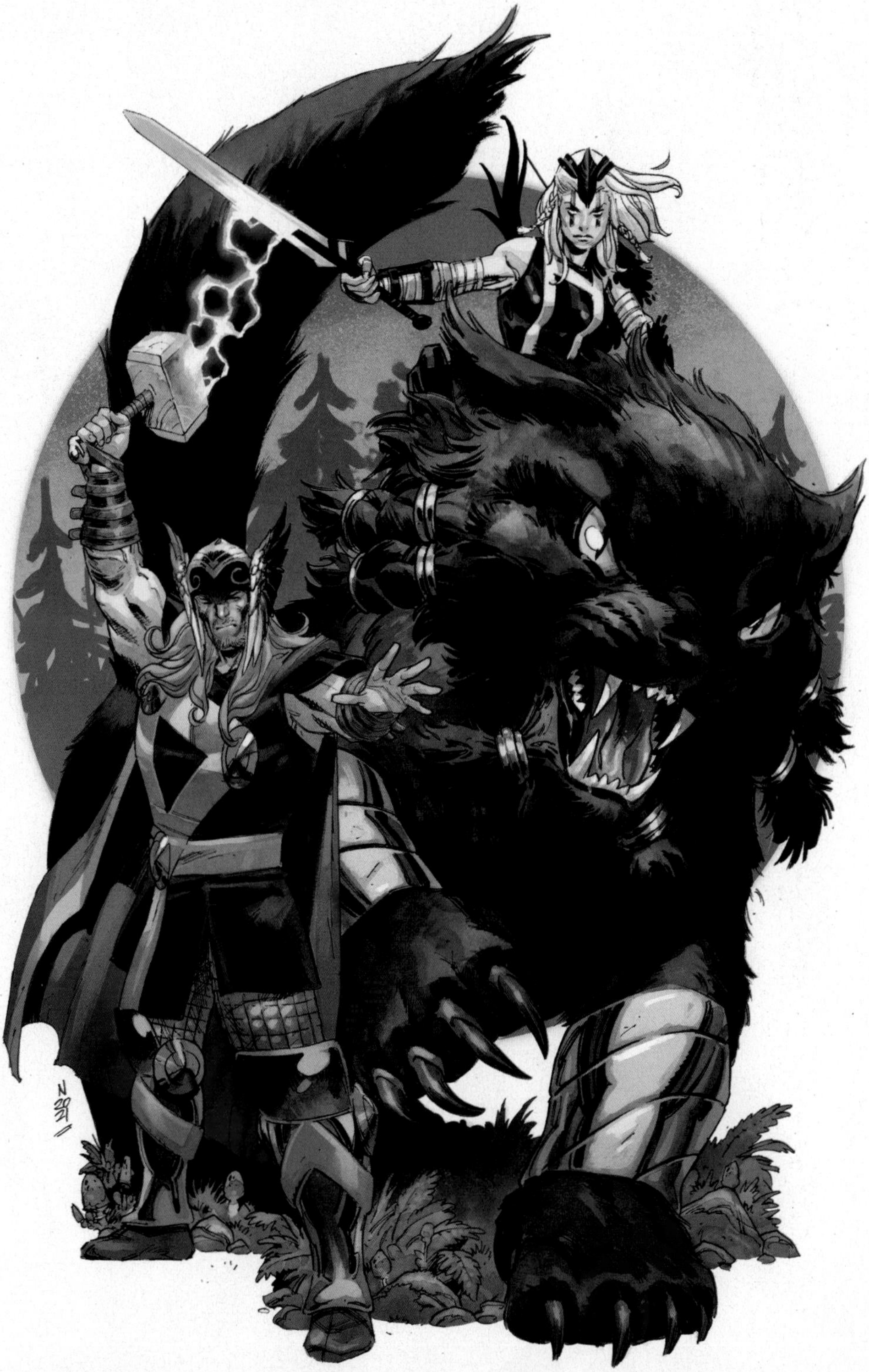

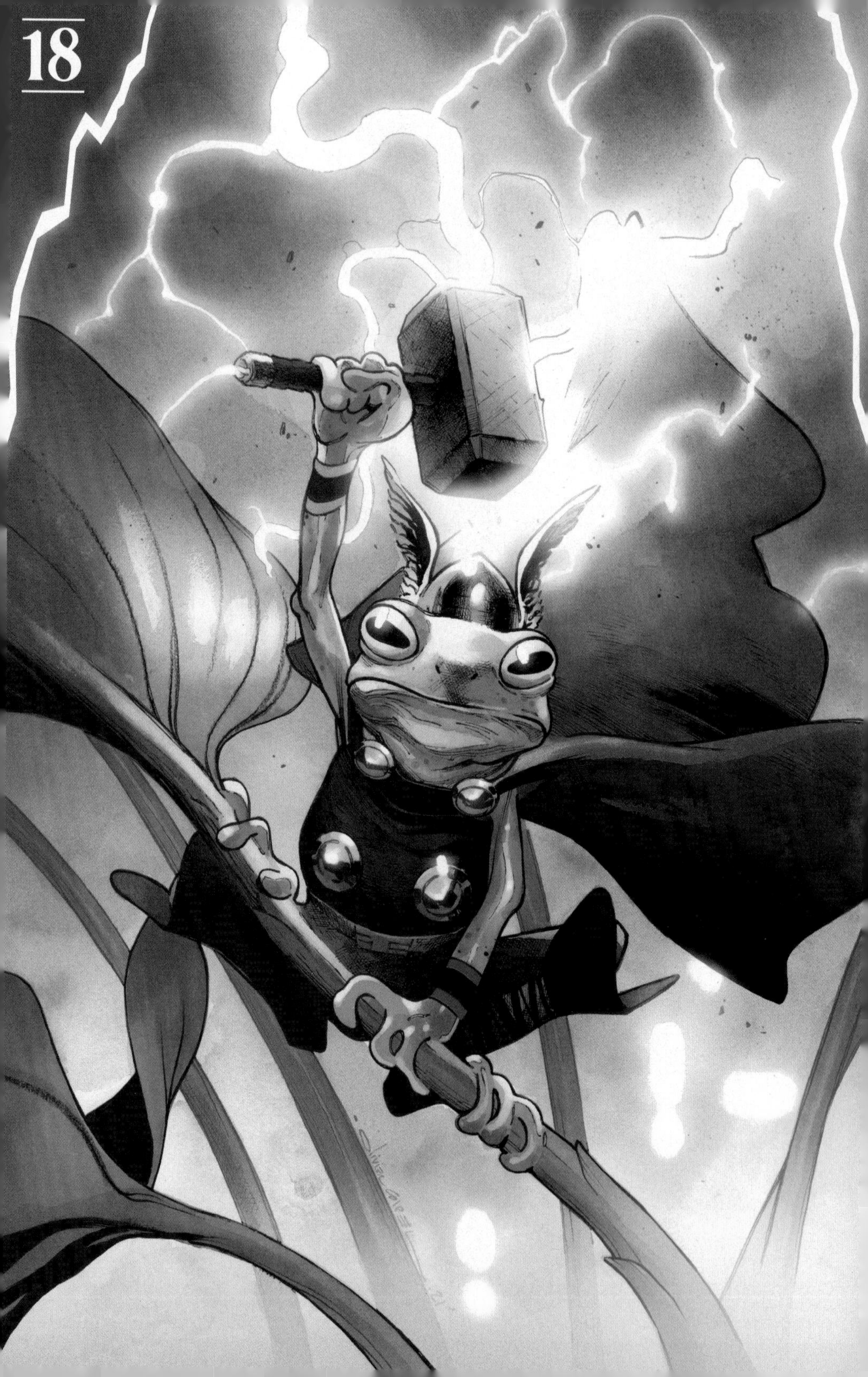
18

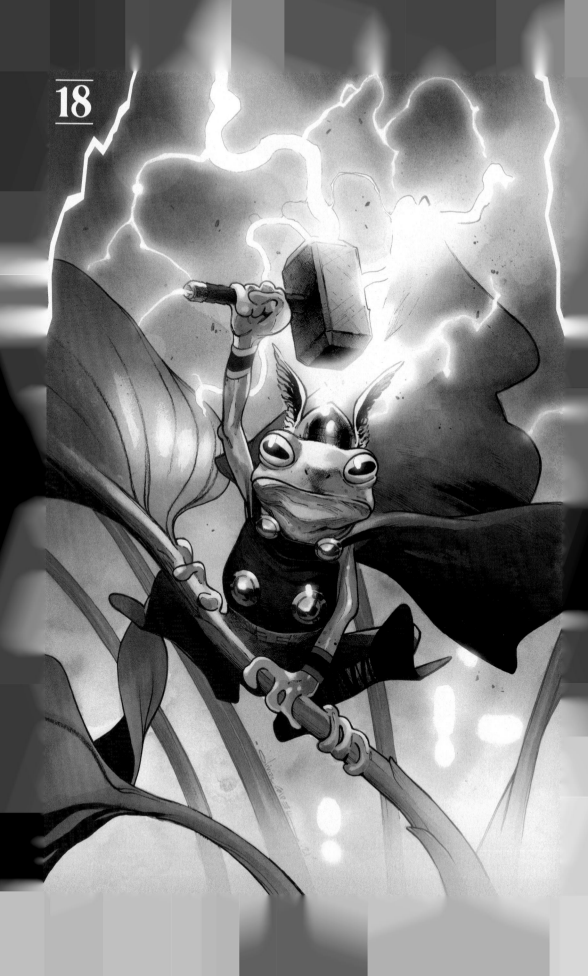

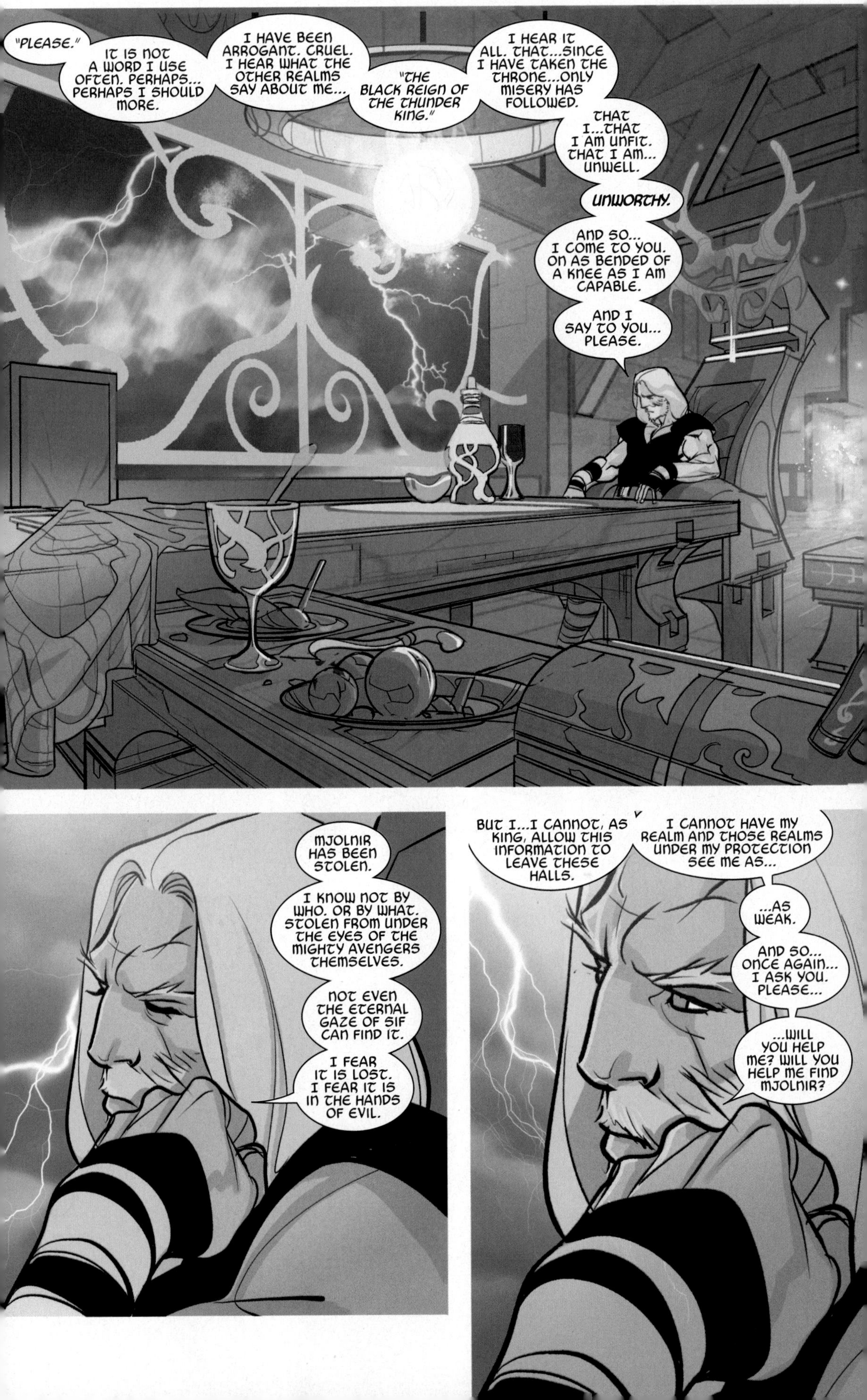
"PLEASE."
IT IS NOT A WORD I USE OFTEN. PERHAPS... PERHAPS I SHOULD MORE.
I HAVE BEEN ARROGANT. CRUEL. I HEAR WHAT THE OTHER REALMS SAY ABOUT ME...
"THE BLACK REIGN OF THE THUNDER KING."
I HEAR IT ALL. THAT...SINCE I HAVE TAKEN THE THRONE...ONLY MISERY HAS FOLLOWED.
THAT I...THAT I AM UNFIT. THAT I AM... UNWELL.
UNWORTHY.
AND SO... I COME TO YOU. ON AS BENDED OF A KNEE AS I AM CAPABLE.
AND I SAY TO YOU... PLEASE.
MJOLNIR HAS BEEN STOLEN.
I KNOW NOT BY WHO. OR BY WHAT. STOLEN FROM UNDER THE EYES OF THE MIGHTY AVENGERS THEMSELVES.
NOT EVEN THE ETERNAL GAZE OF SIF CAN FIND IT.
I FEAR IT IS LOST. I FEAR IT IS IN THE HANDS OF EVIL.
BUT I...I CANNOT, AS KING, ALLOW THIS INFORMATION TO LEAVE THESE HALLS.
I CANNOT HAVE MY REALM AND THOSE REALMS UNDER MY PROTECTION SEE ME AS...
...AS WEAK.
AND SO... ONCE AGAIN... I ASK YOU. PLEASE...
...WILL YOU HELP ME? WILL YOU HELP ME FIND MJOLNIR?

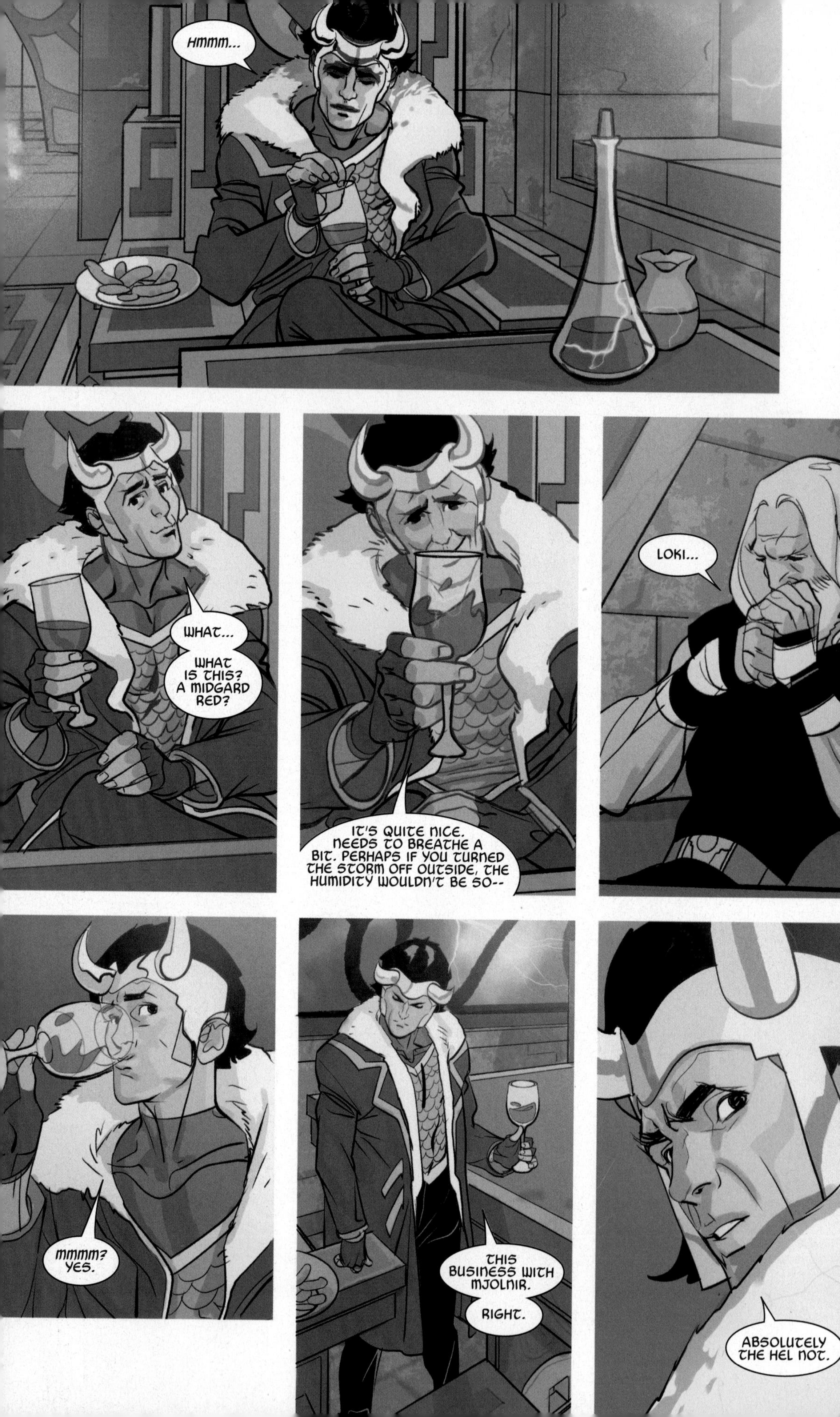
HMMM...
WHAT...
WHAT IS THIS? A MIDGARD RED?
IT'S QUITE NICE. NEEDS TO BREATHE A BIT. PERHAPS IF YOU TURNED THE STORM OFF OUTSIDE, THE HUMIDITY WOULDN'T BE SO--
LOKI...
MMMM? YES.
THIS BUSINESS WITH MJOLNIR.
RIGHT.
ABSOLUTELY THE HEL NOT.

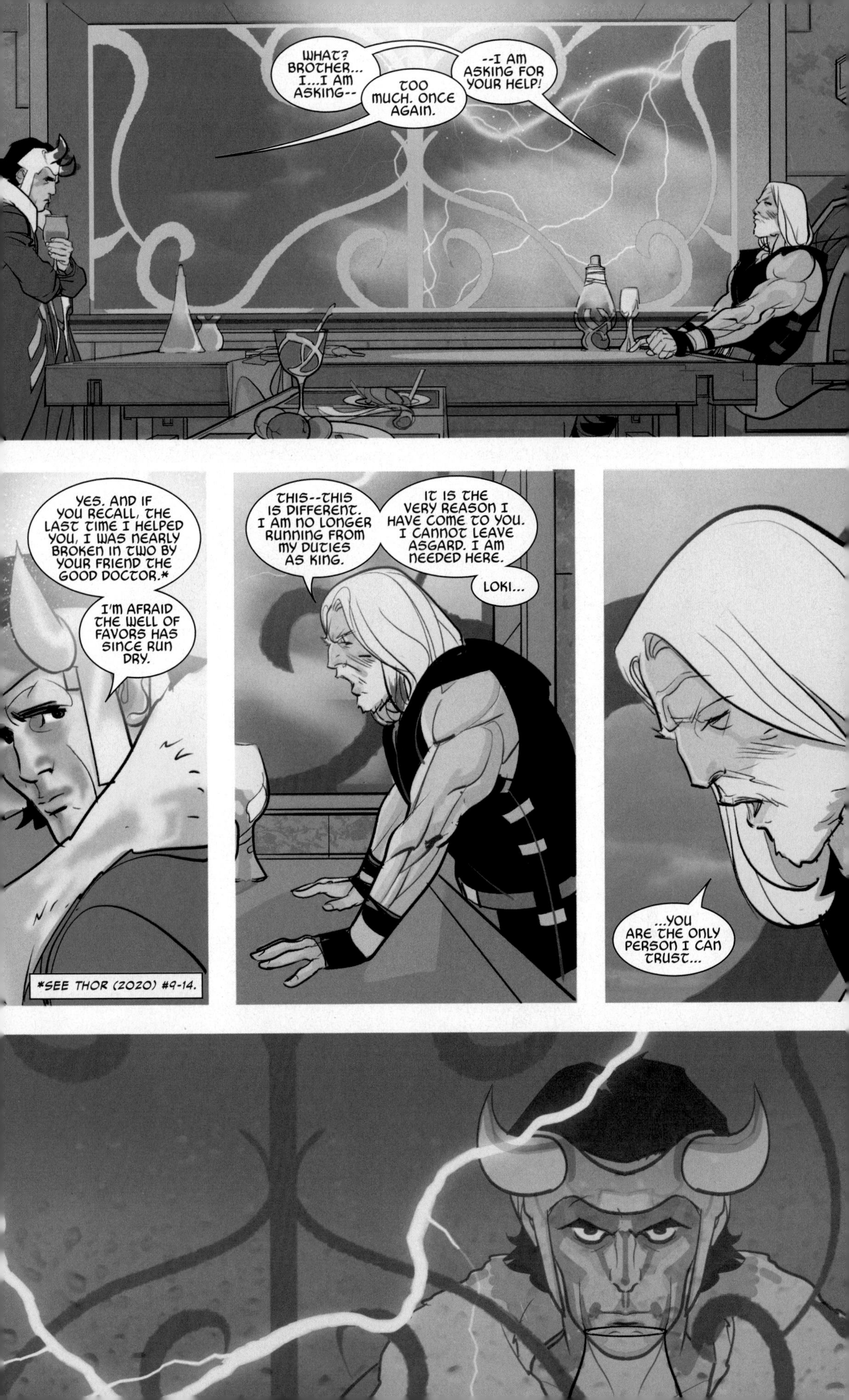
WHAT? BROTHER... I...I AM ASKING--
TOO MUCH. ONCE AGAIN.
--I AM ASKING FOR YOUR HELP!
YES. AND IF YOU RECALL, THE LAST TIME I HELPED YOU, I WAS NEARLY BROKEN IN TWO BY YOUR FRIEND THE GOOD DOCTOR.*
I'M AFRAID THE WELL OF FAVORS HAS SINCE RUN DRY.
*SEE THOR (2020) #9-14.
THIS--THIS IS DIFFERENT. I AM NO LONGER RUNNING FROM MY DUTIES AS KING.
IT IS THE VERY REASON I HAVE COME TO YOU. I CANNOT LEAVE ASGARD. I AM NEEDED HERE.
LOKI...
...YOU ARE THE ONLY PERSON I CAN TRUST...

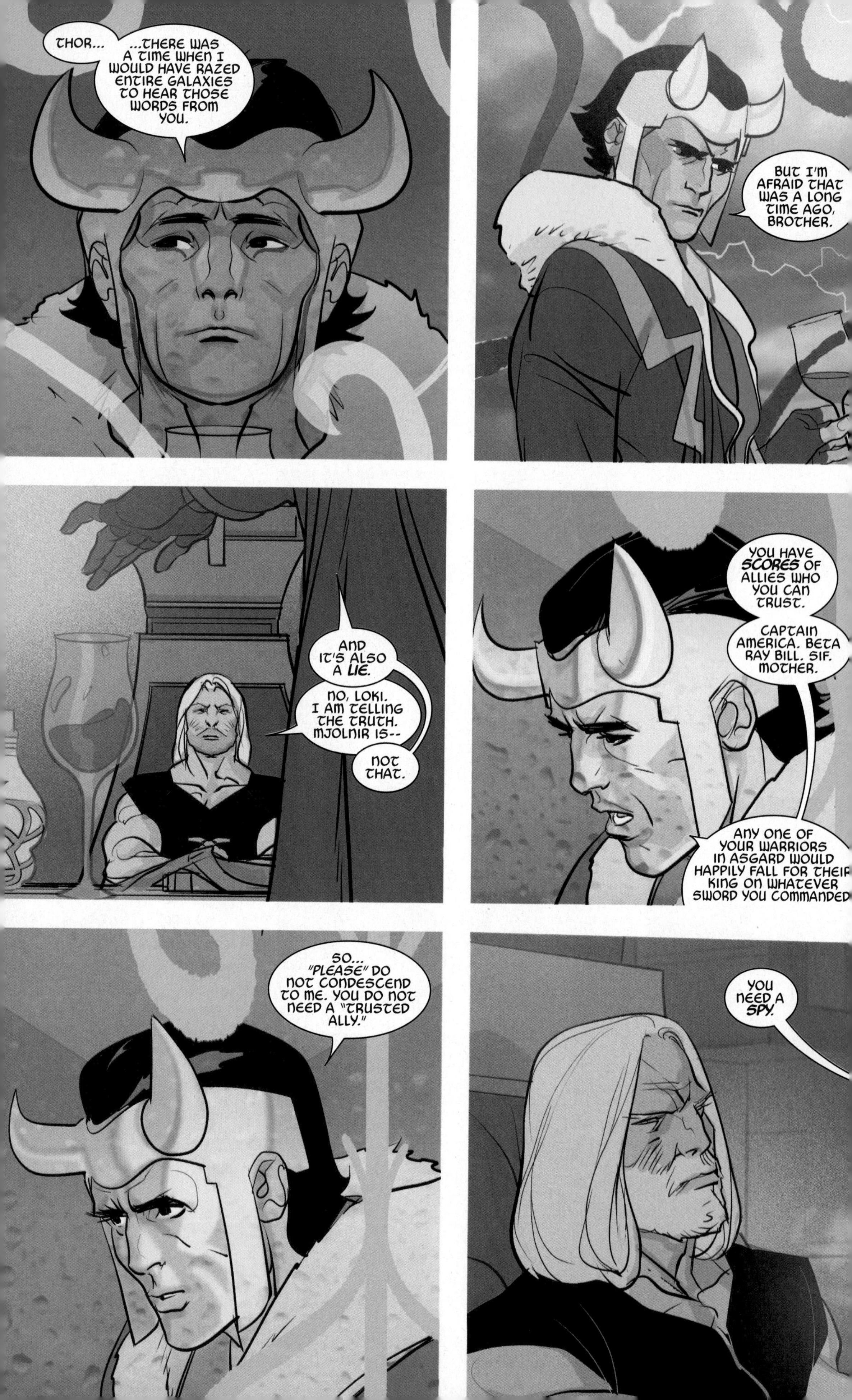
THOR...
...THERE WAS A TIME WHEN I WOULD HAVE RAZED ENTIRE GALAXIES TO HEAR THOSE WORDS FROM YOU.
BUT I'M AFRAID THAT WAS A LONG TIME AGO, BROTHER.
AND IT'S ALSO A LIE.
NO, LOKI. I AM TELLING THE TRUTH. MJOLNIR IS--
NOT THAT.
YOU HAVE SCORES OF ALLIES WHO YOU CAN TRUST.
CAPTAIN AMERICA. BETA RAY BILL. SIF. MOTHER.
ANY ONE OF YOUR WARRIORS IN ASGARD WOULD HAPPILY FALL FOR THEIR KING ON WHATEVER SWORD YOU COMMANDED.
SO... "PLEASE" DO NOT CONDESCEND TO ME. YOU DO NOT NEED A "TRUSTED ALLY."
YOU NEED A SPY.

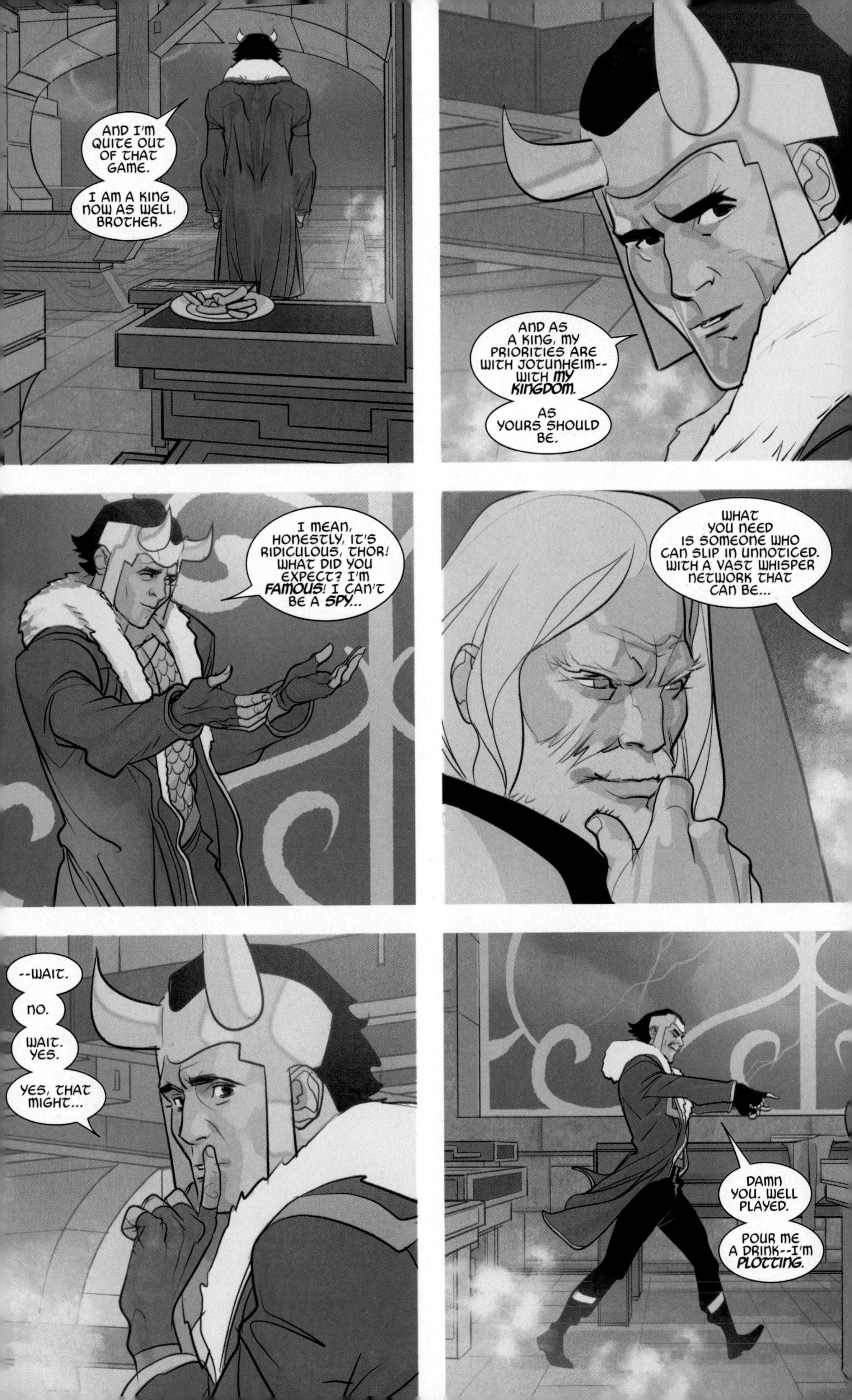
AND I'M QUITE OUT OF THAT GAME.
I AM A KING NOW AS WELL, BROTHER.
AND AS A KING, MY PRIORITIES ARE WITH JOTUNHEIM--WITH MY KINGDOM.
AS YOURS SHOULD BE.
I MEAN, HONESTLY, IT'S RIDICULOUS, THOR! WHAT DID YOU EXPECT? I'M FAMOUS! I CAN'T BE A SPY...
WHAT YOU NEED IS SOMEONE WHO CAN SLIP IN UNNOTICED. WITH A VAST WHISPER NETWORK THAT CAN BE...
--WAIT.
NO.
WAIT. YES.
YES, THAT MIGHT...
DAMN YOU. WELL PLAYED.
POUR ME A DRINK--I'M PLOTTING.

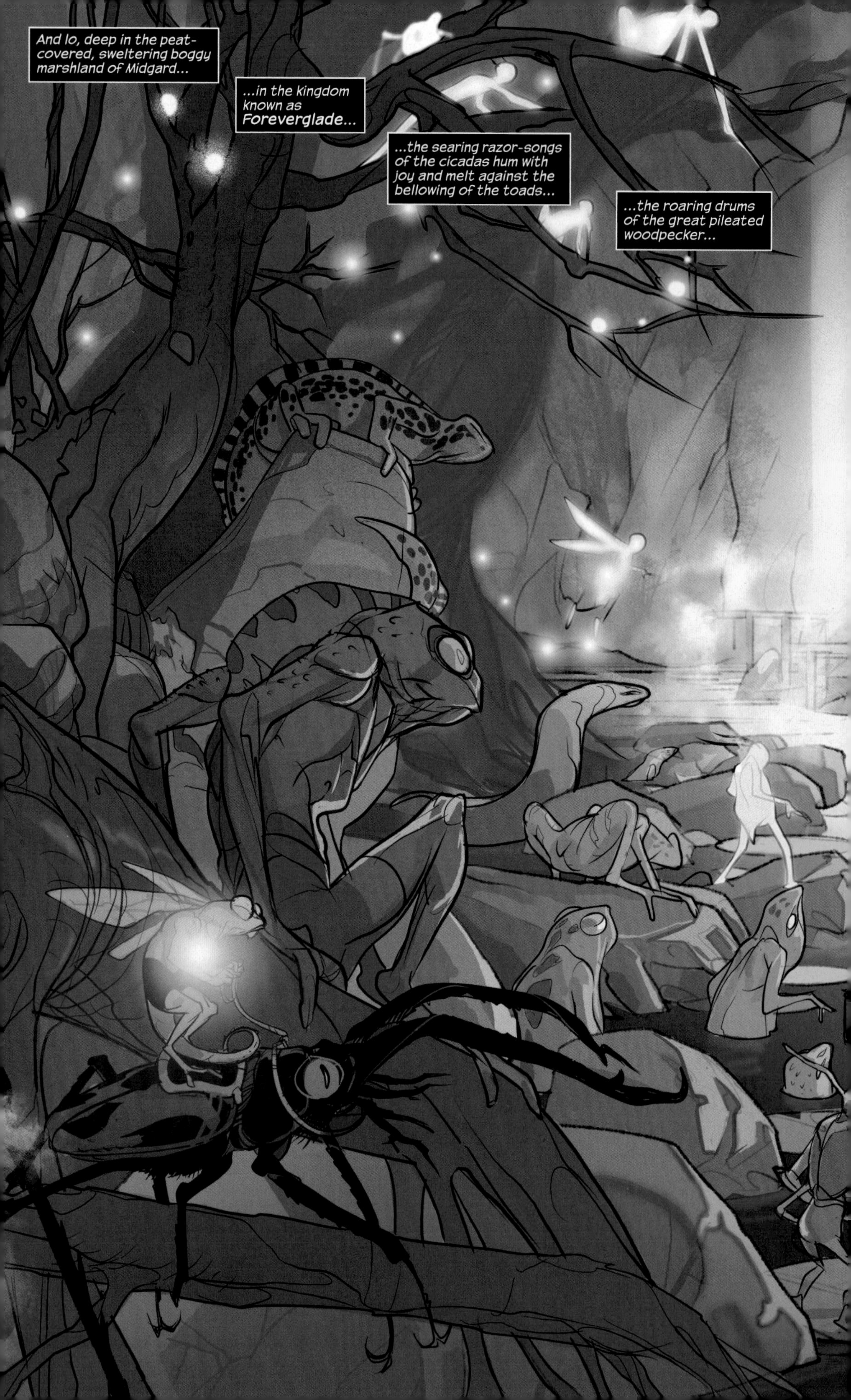
And lo, deep in the peat-covered, sweltering boggy marshland of Midgard...
...in the kingdom known as Foreverglade...
...the searing razor-songs of the cicadas hum with joy and melt against the bellowing of the toads...
...the roaring drums of the great pileated woodpecker...

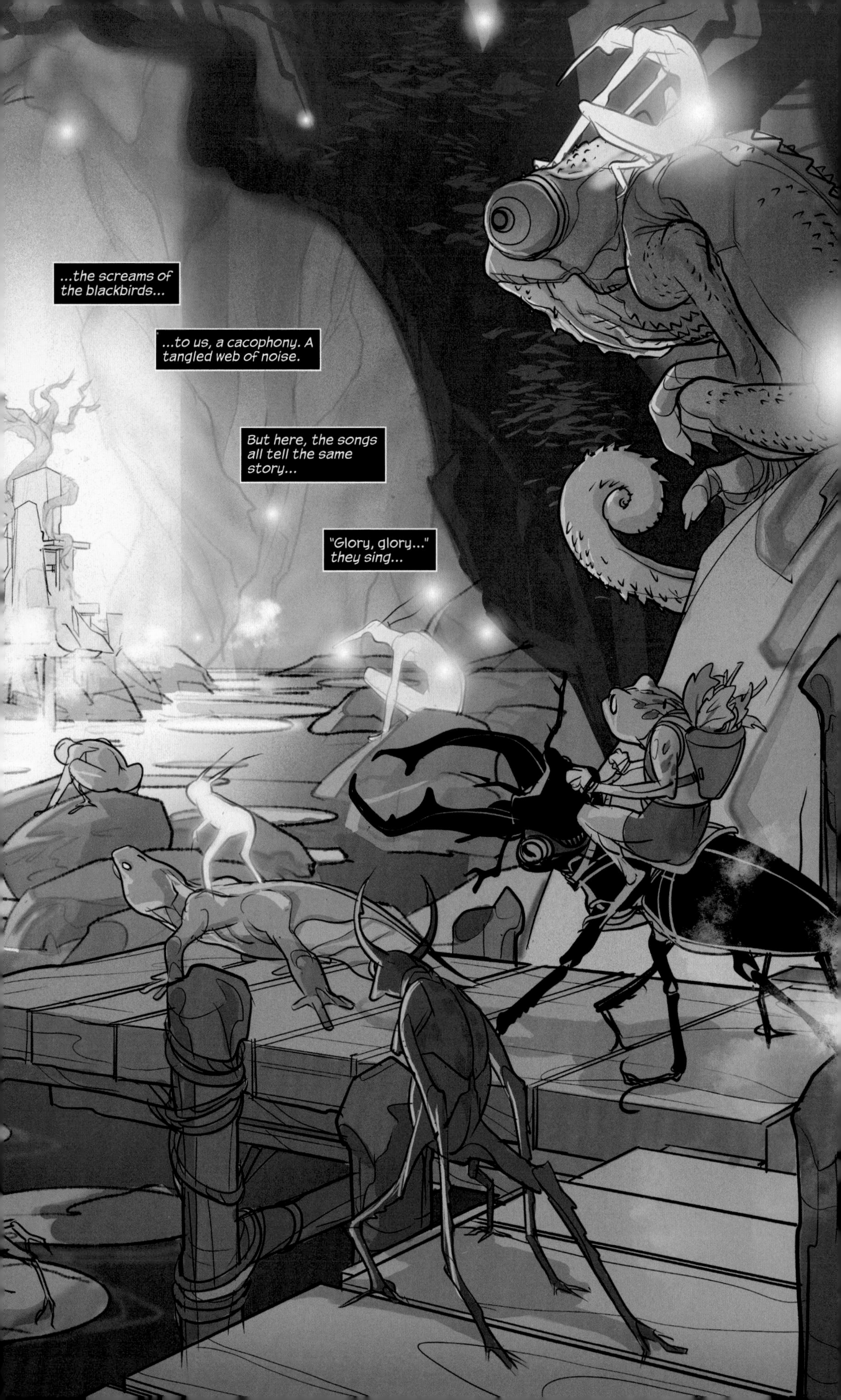
...the screams of the blackbirds...
...to us, a cacophony. A tangled web of noise.
But here, the songs all tell the same story...
"Glory, glory..." they sing...

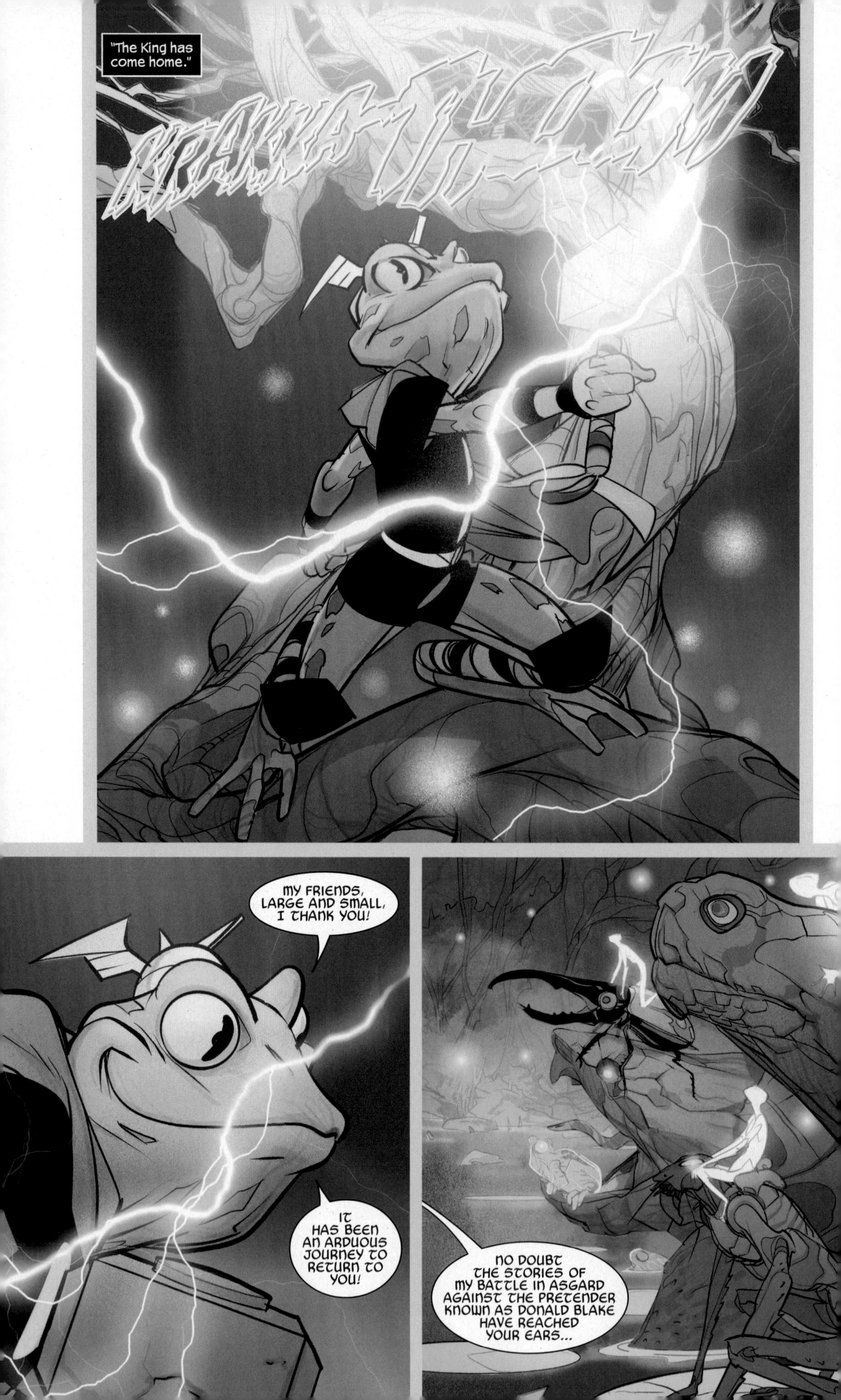
"The King has come home."
MY FRIENDS, LARGE AND SMALL, I THANK YOU!
IT HAS BEEN AN ARDUOUS JOURNEY TO RETURN TO YOU!
NO DOUBT THE STORIES OF MY BATTLE IN ASGARD AGAINST THE PRETENDER KNOWN AS DONALD BLAKE HAVE REACHED YOUR EARS...

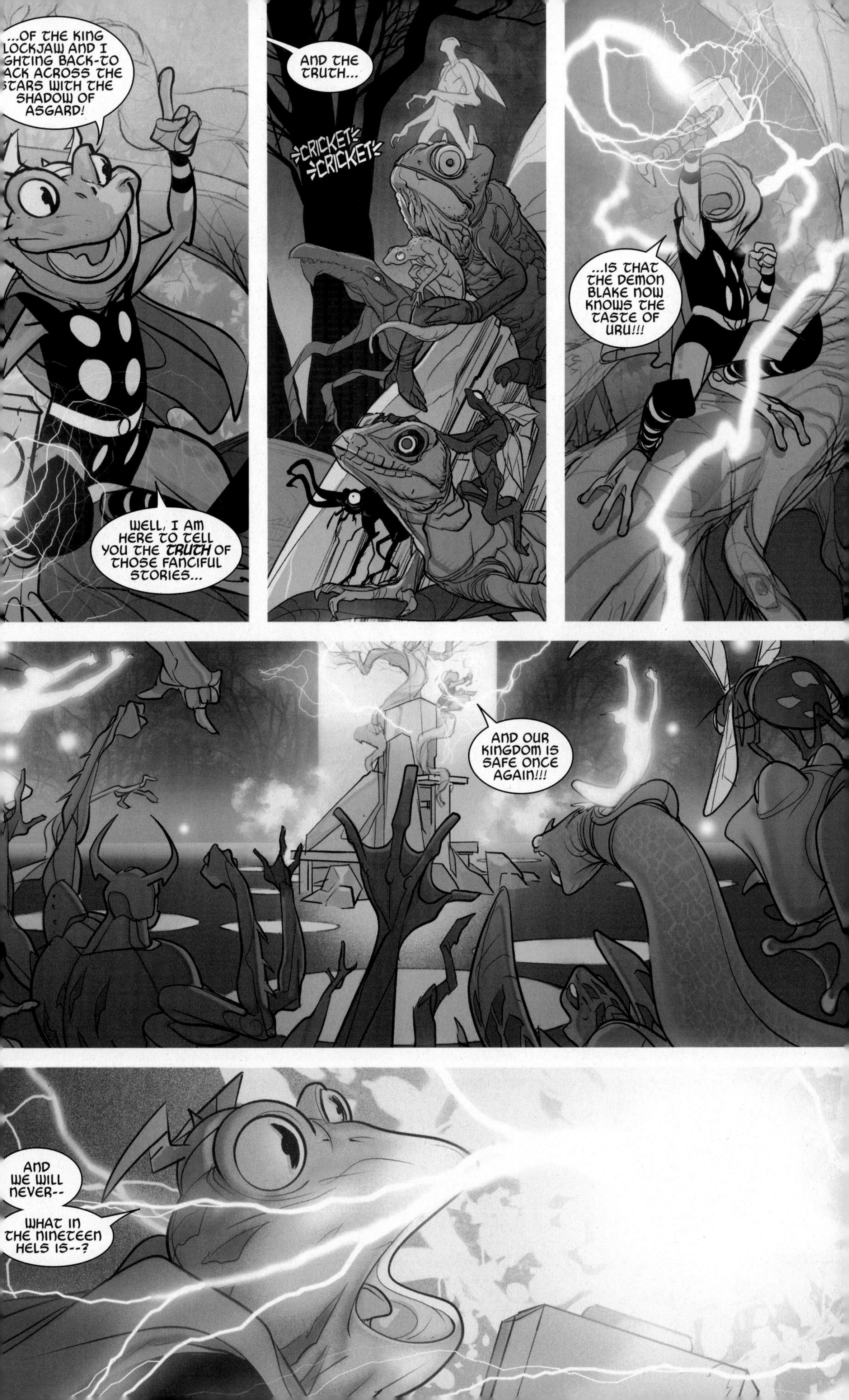
...OF THE KING
LOCKJAW AND I
IGHTING BACK-TO
ACK ACROSS THE
STARS WITH THE
SHADOW OF
ASGARD!
WELL, I AM
HERE TO TELL
YOU THE TRUTH OF
THOSE FANCIFUL
STORIES...
AND THE
TRUTH...
CRICKET CRICKET
...IS THAT
THE DEMON
BLAKE NOW
KNOWS THE
TASTE OF
URU!!!
AND OUR
KINGDOM IS
SAFE ONCE
AGAIN!!!
AND
WE WILL
NEVER--
WHAT IN
THE NINETEEN
HELS IS--?

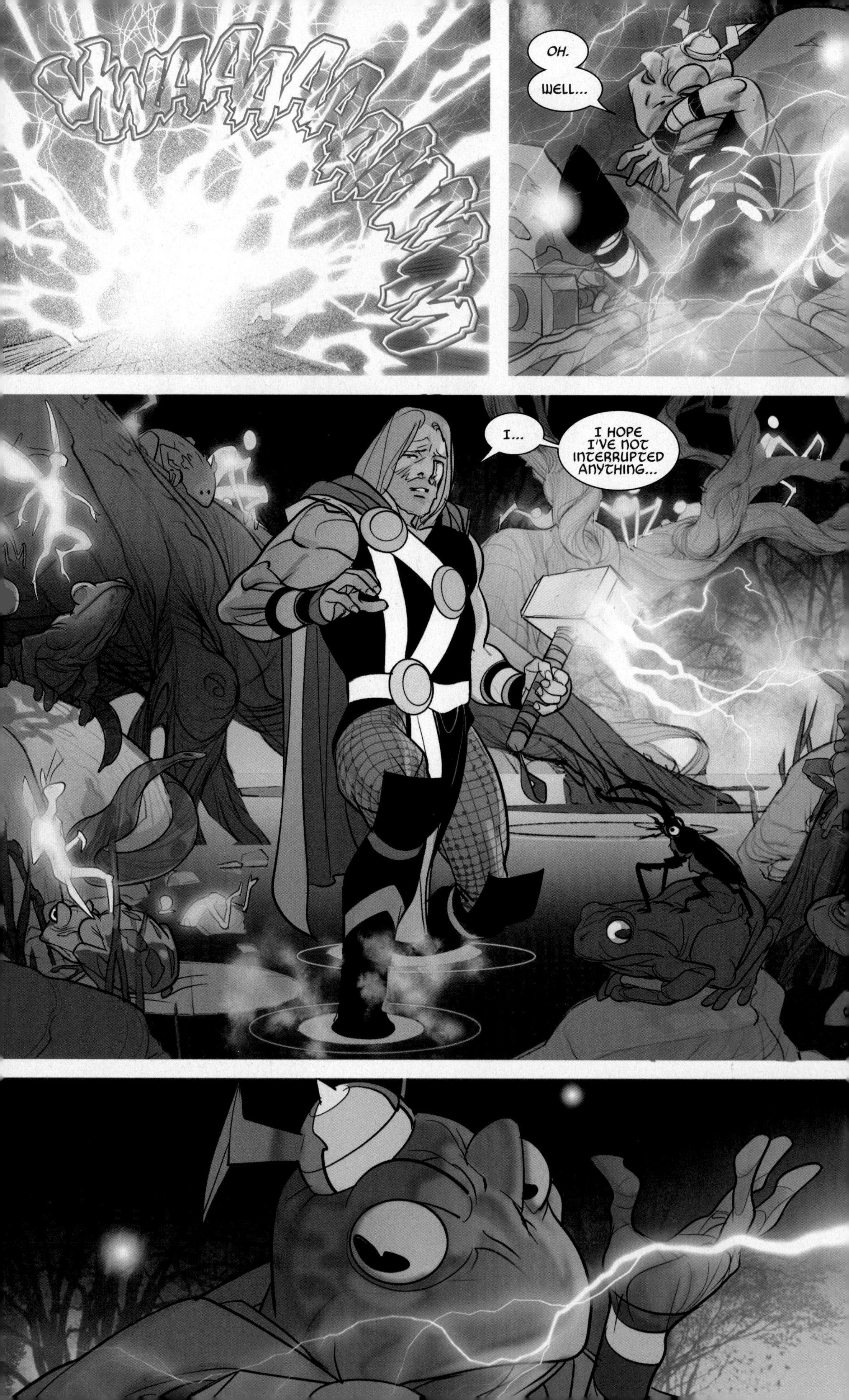

KWAAAAMMMM
OH.
WELL...
I...
I HOPE I'VE NOT INTERRUPTED ANYTHING...

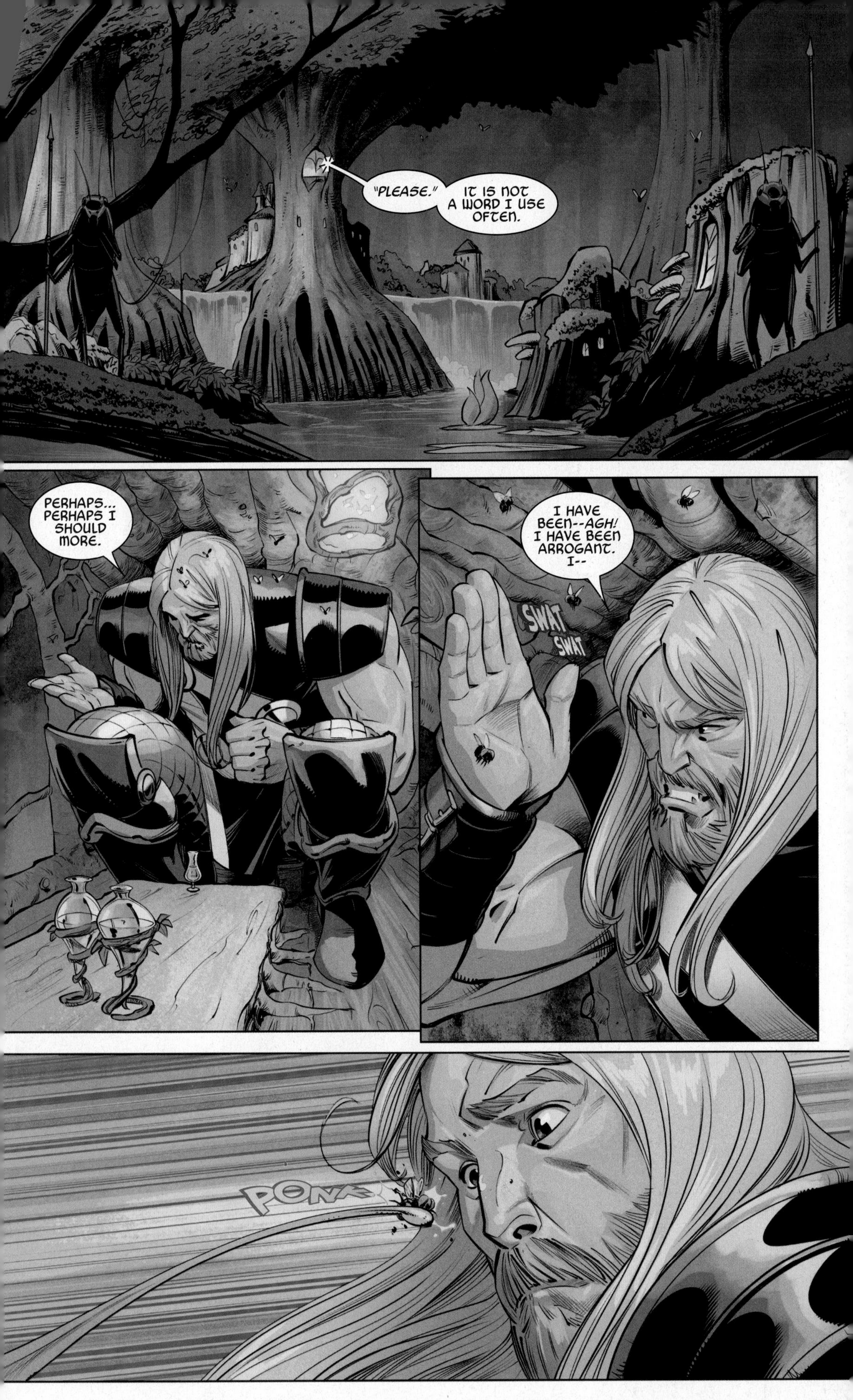
"PLEASE."
IT IS NOT A WORD I USE OFTEN.
PERHAPS... PERHAPS I SHOULD MORE.
I HAVE BEEN--AGH! I HAVE BEEN ARROGANT. I--
SWAT
SWAT
PONK

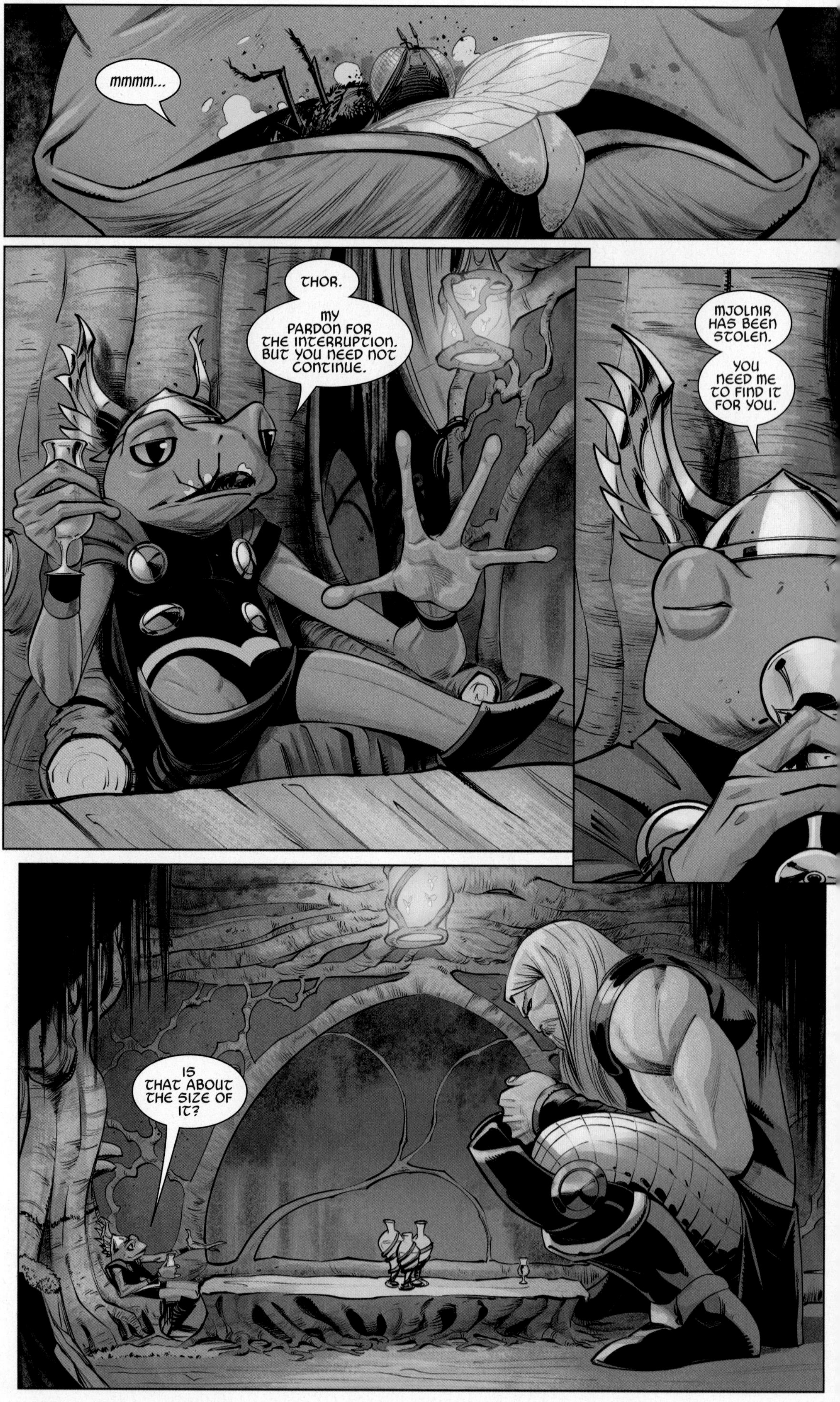
mmmm...
THOR.
MY PARDON FOR THE INTERRUPTION. BUT YOU NEED NOT CONTINUE.
MJOLNIR HAS BEEN STOLEN.
YOU NEED ME TO FIND IT FOR YOU.
IS THAT ABOUT THE SIZE OF IT?

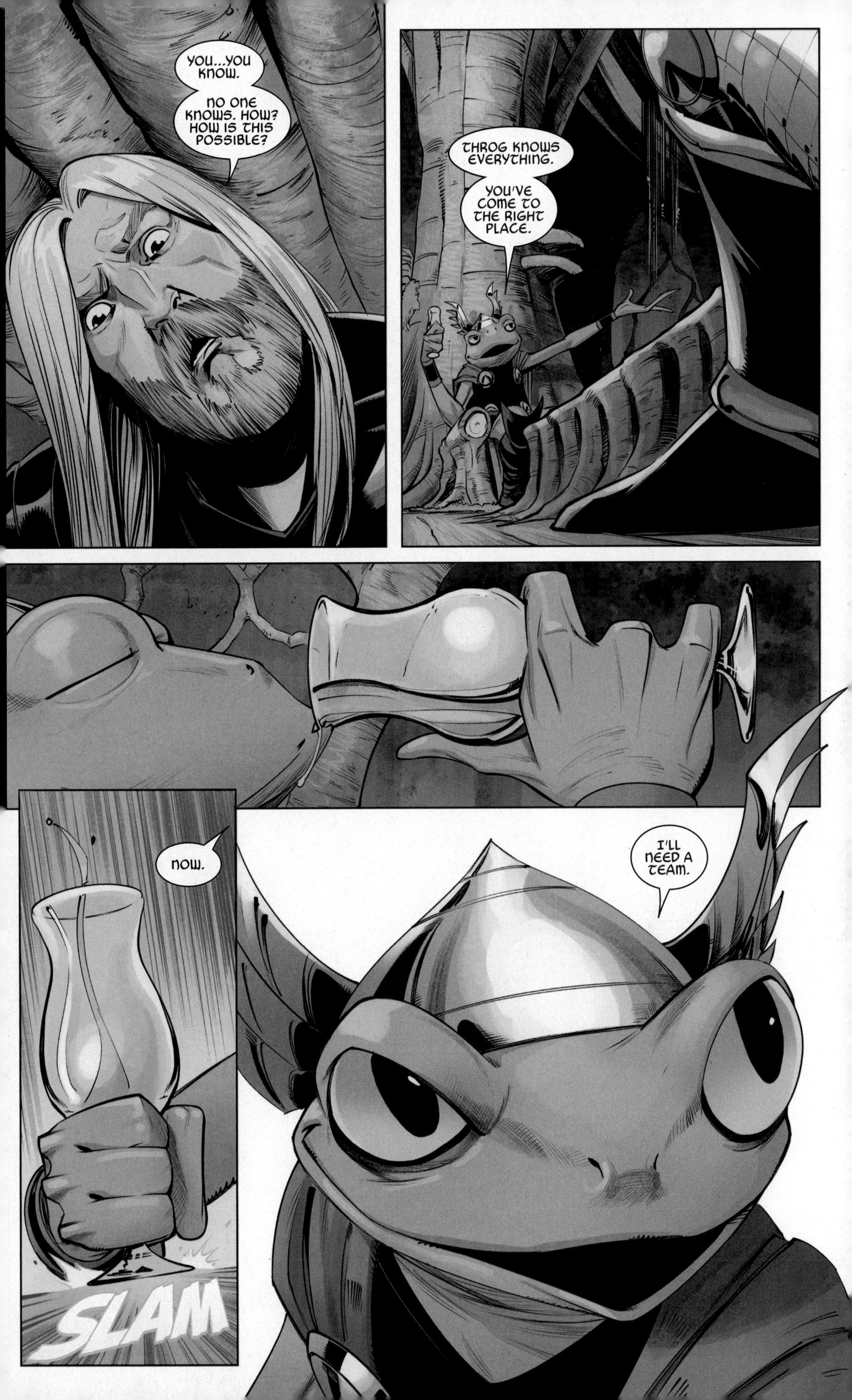
YOU...YOU KNOW.
NO ONE KNOWS. HOW? HOW IS THIS POSSIBLE?
THROG KNOWS EVERYTHING.
YOU'VE COME TO THE RIGHT PLACE.
NOW.
SLAM
I'LL NEED A TEAM.

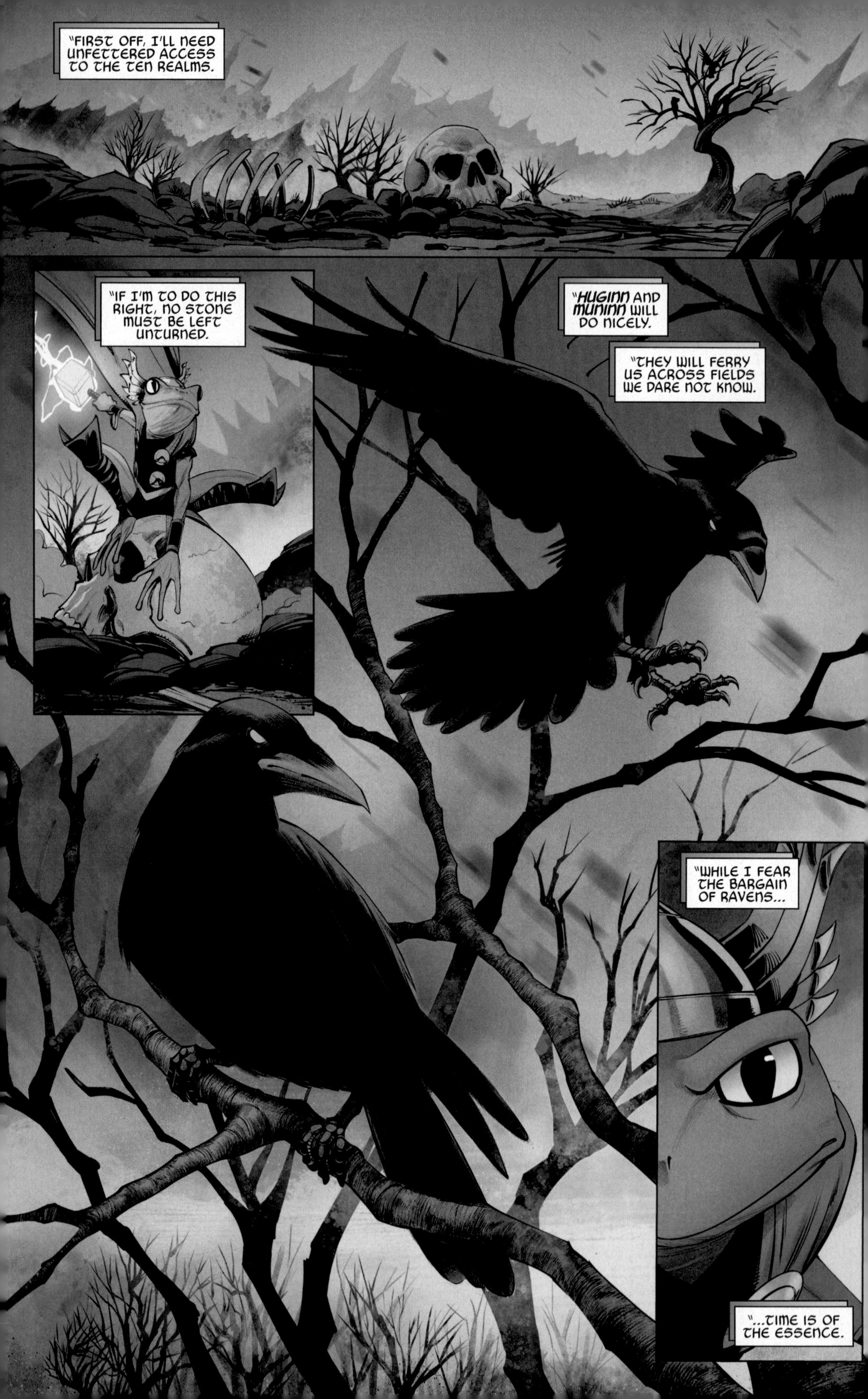
"FIRST OFF, I'LL NEED UNFETTERED ACCESS TO THE TEN REALMS.
"IF I'M TO DO THIS RIGHT, NO STONE MUST BE LEFT UNTURNED.
"HUGINN AND MUNINN WILL DO NICELY.
"THEY WILL FERRY US ACROSS FIELDS WE DARE NOT KNOW.
"WHILE I FEAR THE BARGAIN OF RAVENS...
"...TIME IS OF THE ESSENCE.

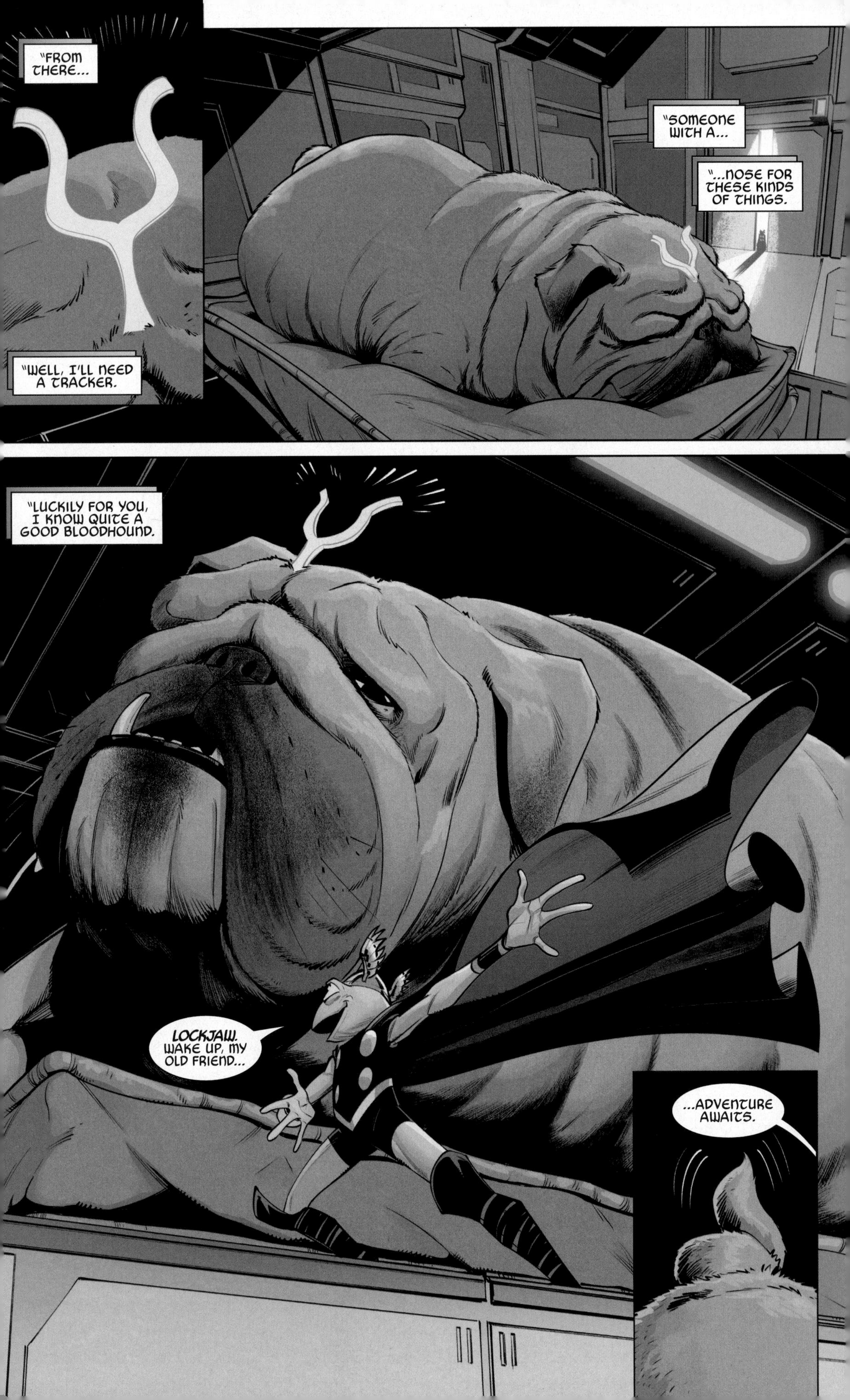
"FROM THERE...
"WELL, I'LL NEED A TRACKER.
"SOMEONE WITH A...
"...NOSE FOR THESE KINDS OF THINGS.
"LUCKILY FOR YOU, I KNOW QUITE A GOOD BLOODHOUND.
LOCKJAW. WAKE UP, MY OLD FRIEND...
...ADVENTURE AWAITS.

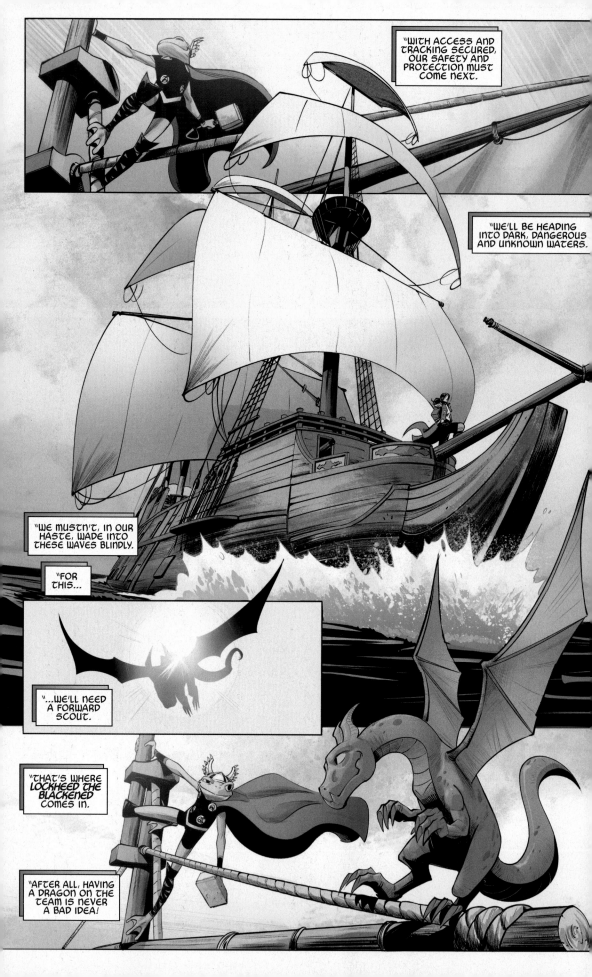

"WITH ACCESS AND TRACKING SECURED, OUR SAFETY AND PROTECTION MUST COME NEXT.

"WE'LL BE HEADING INTO DARK, DANGEROUS AND UNKNOWN WATERS.

"WE MUSTN'T, IN OUR HASTE, WADE INTO THESE WAVES BLINDLY.

"FOR THIS...

"...WE'LL NEED A FORWARD SCOUT.

"THAT'S WHERE LOCKHEED THE BLACKENED COMES IN.

"AFTER ALL, HAVING A DRAGON ON THE TEAM IS NEVER A BAD IDEA!

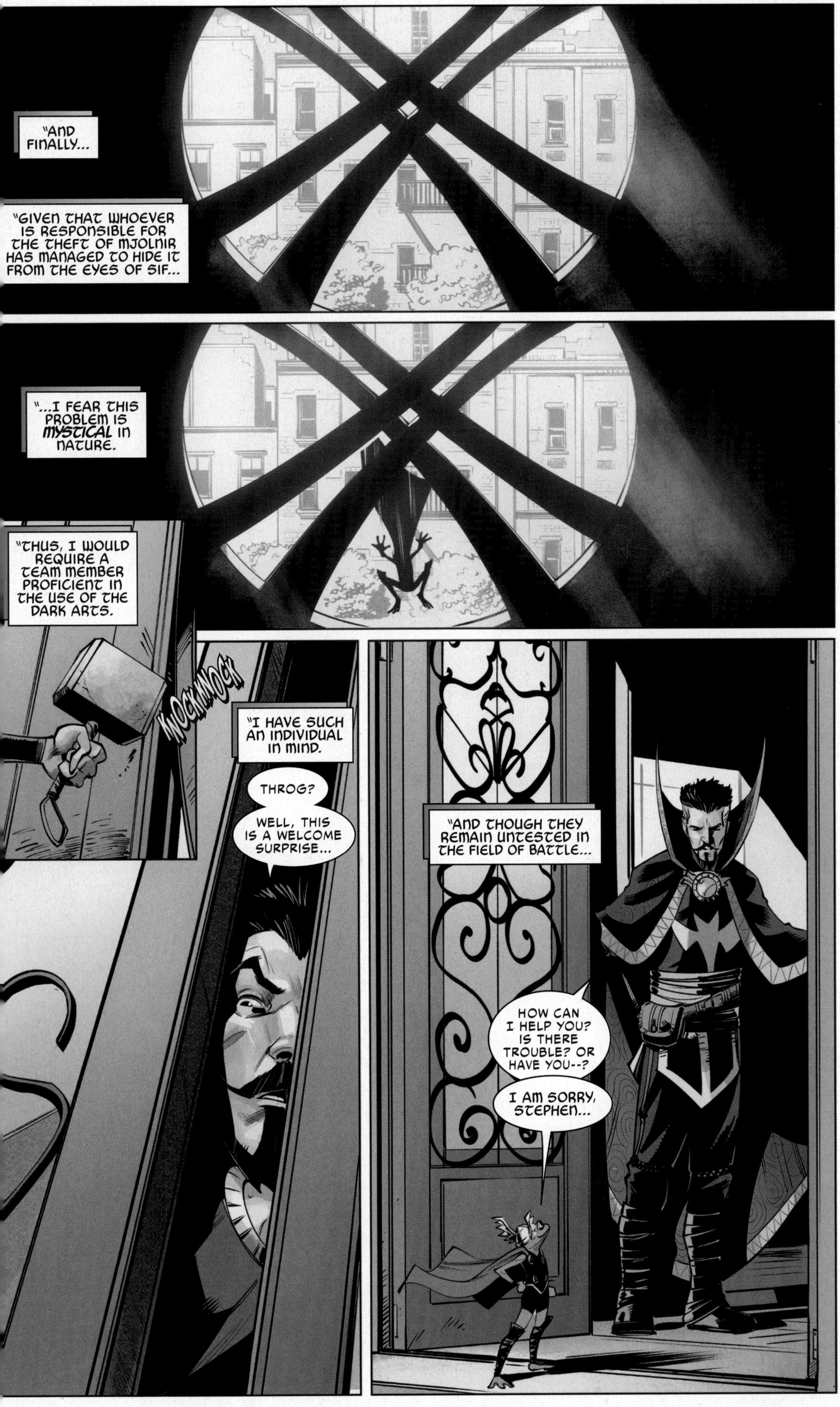
"AND FINALLY...
"GIVEN THAT WHOEVER IS RESPONSIBLE FOR THE THEFT OF MJOLNIR HAS MANAGED TO HIDE IT FROM THE EYES OF SIF...
"...I FEAR THIS PROBLEM IS *MYSTICAL* IN NATURE.
"THUS, I WOULD REQUIRE A TEAM MEMBER PROFICIENT IN THE USE OF THE DARK ARTS.
KNOCK KNOCK
"I HAVE SUCH AN INDIVIDUAL IN MIND.
THROG?
WELL, THIS IS A WELCOME SURPRISE...
"AND THOUGH THEY REMAIN UNTESTED IN THE FIELD OF BATTLE...
HOW CAN I HELP YOU? IS THERE TROUBLE? OR HAVE YOU--?
I AM SORRY, STEPHEN...

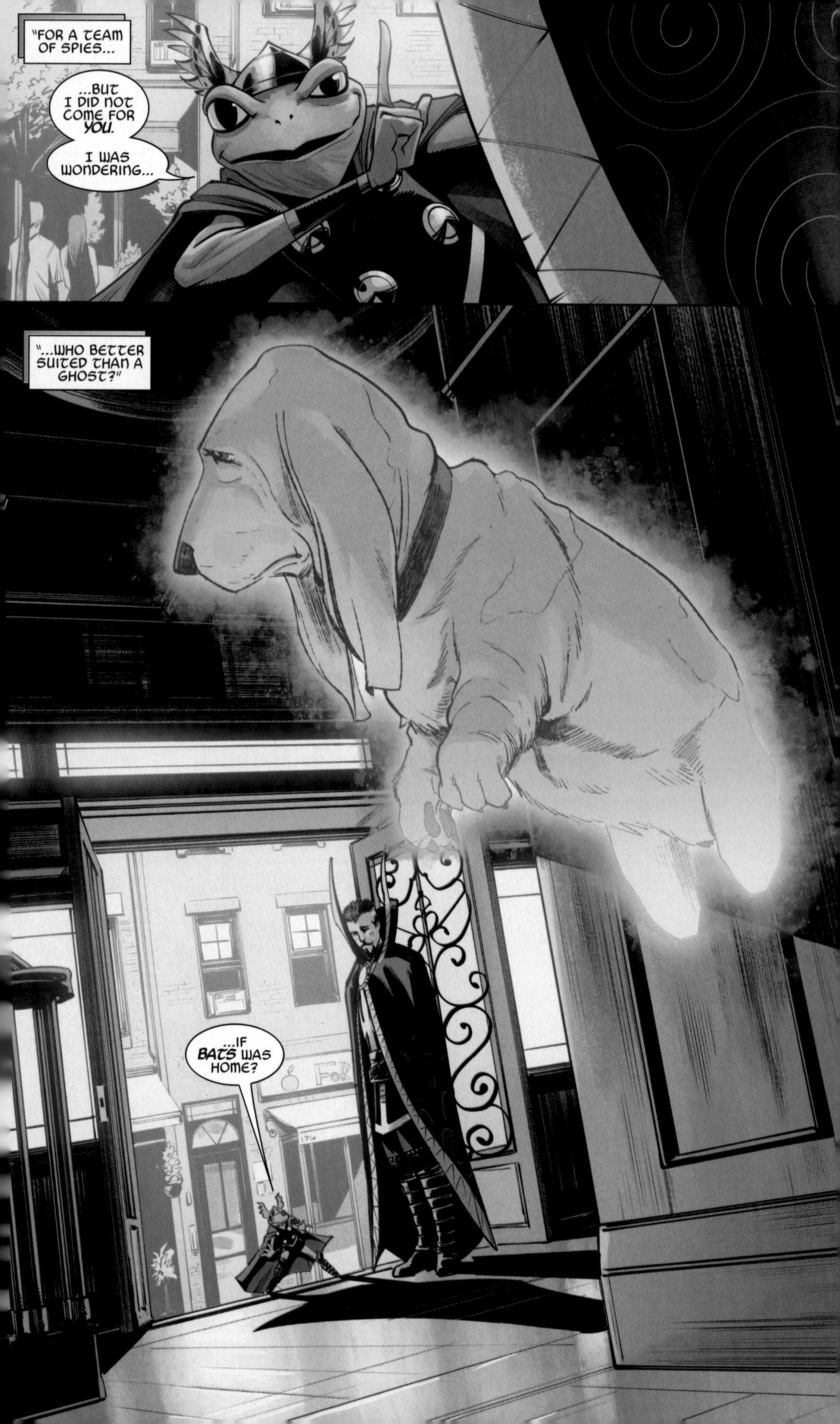
"FOR A TEAM OF SPIES...
...BUT I DID NOT COME FOR YOU.
I WAS WONDERING...
"...WHO BETTER SUITED THAN A GHOST?"
...IF BATS WAS HOME?

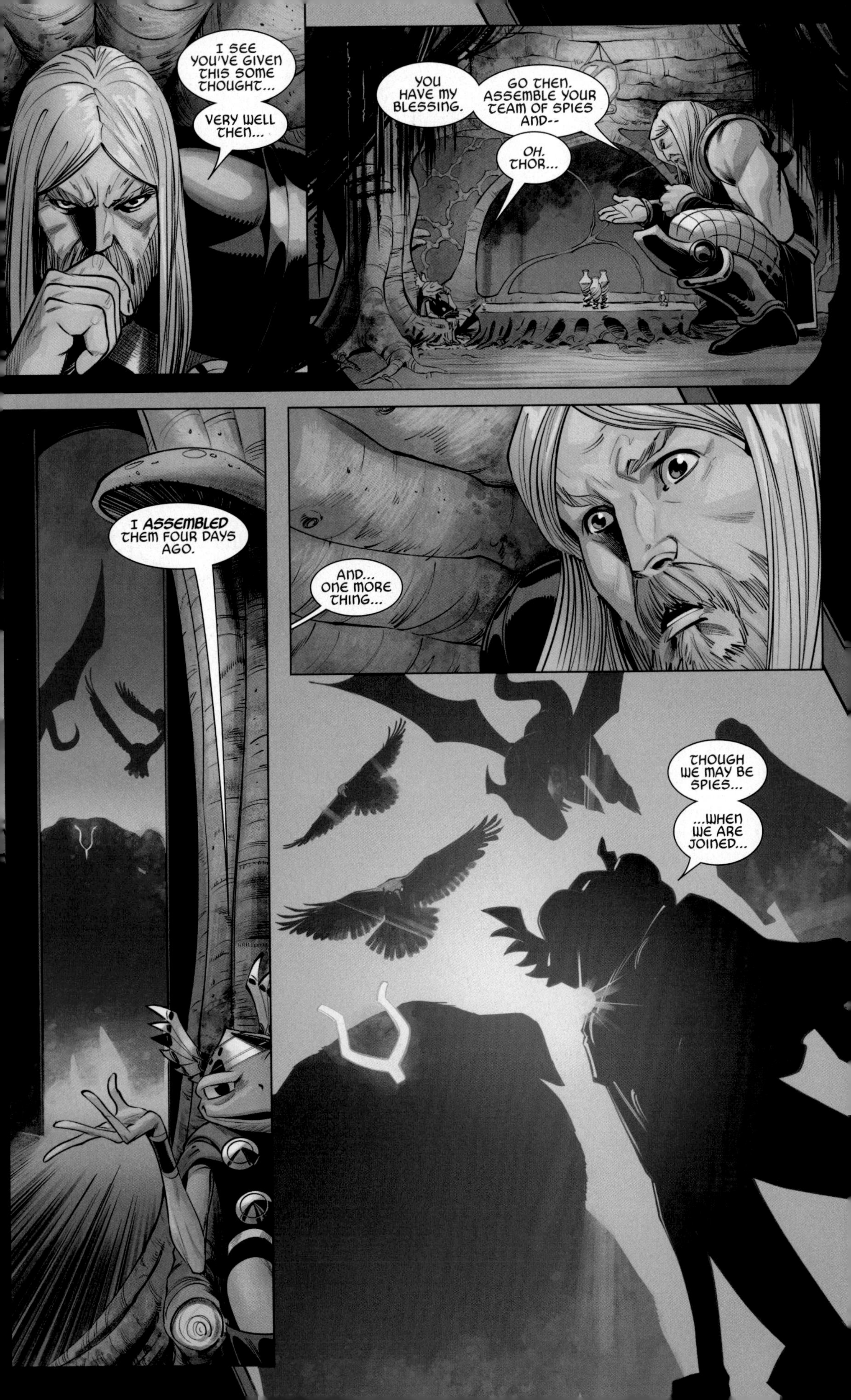
I SEE YOU'VE GIVEN THIS SOME THOUGHT...
VERY WELL THEN...
YOU HAVE MY BLESSING.
GO THEN. ASSEMBLE YOUR TEAM OF SPIES AND--
OH. THOR...
I ASSEMBLED THEM FOUR DAYS AGO.
AND... ONE MORE THING...
THOUGH WE MAY BE SPIES...
...WHEN WE ARE JOINED...

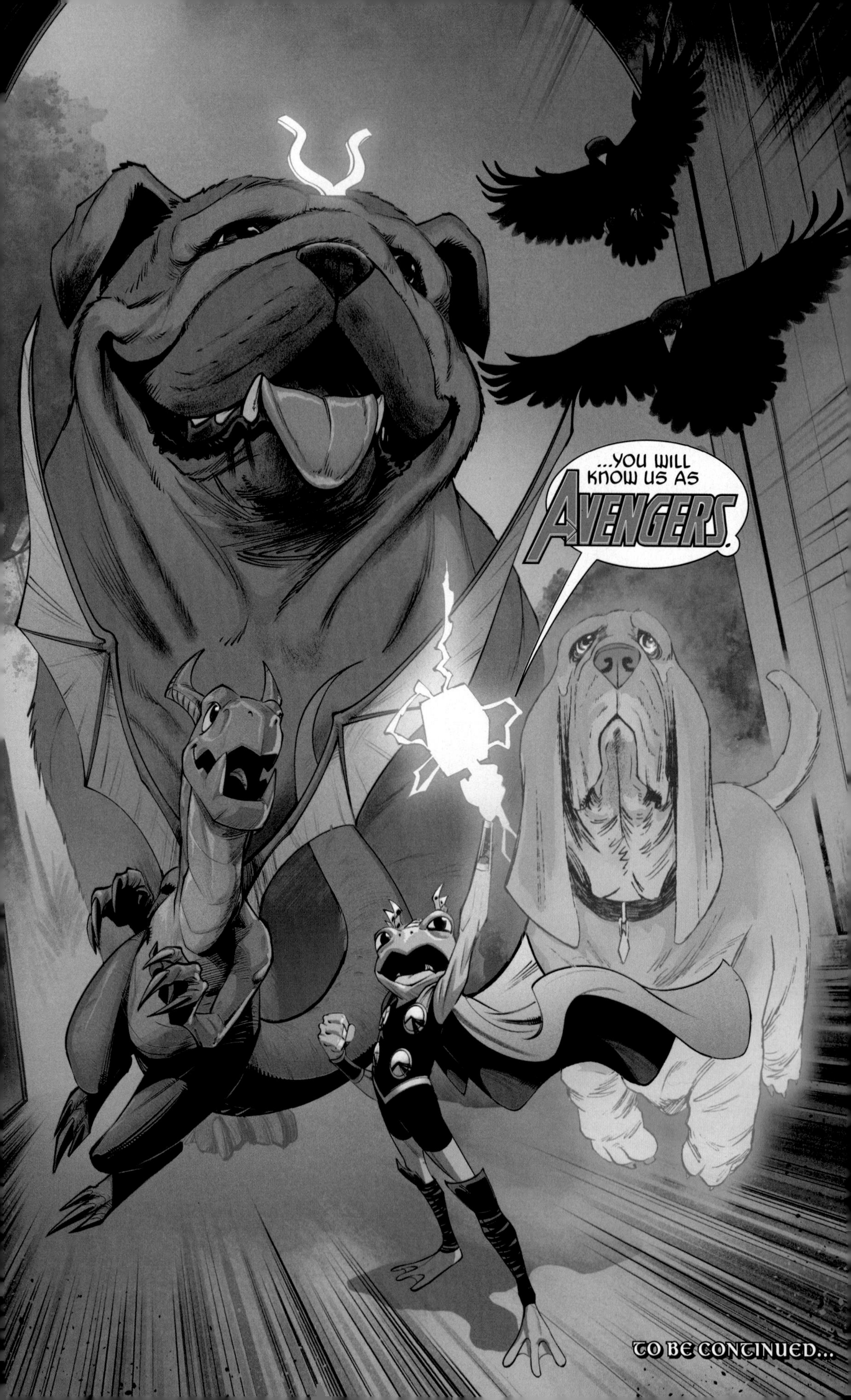
...YOU WILL KNOW US AS AVENGERS.
TO BE CONTINUED...

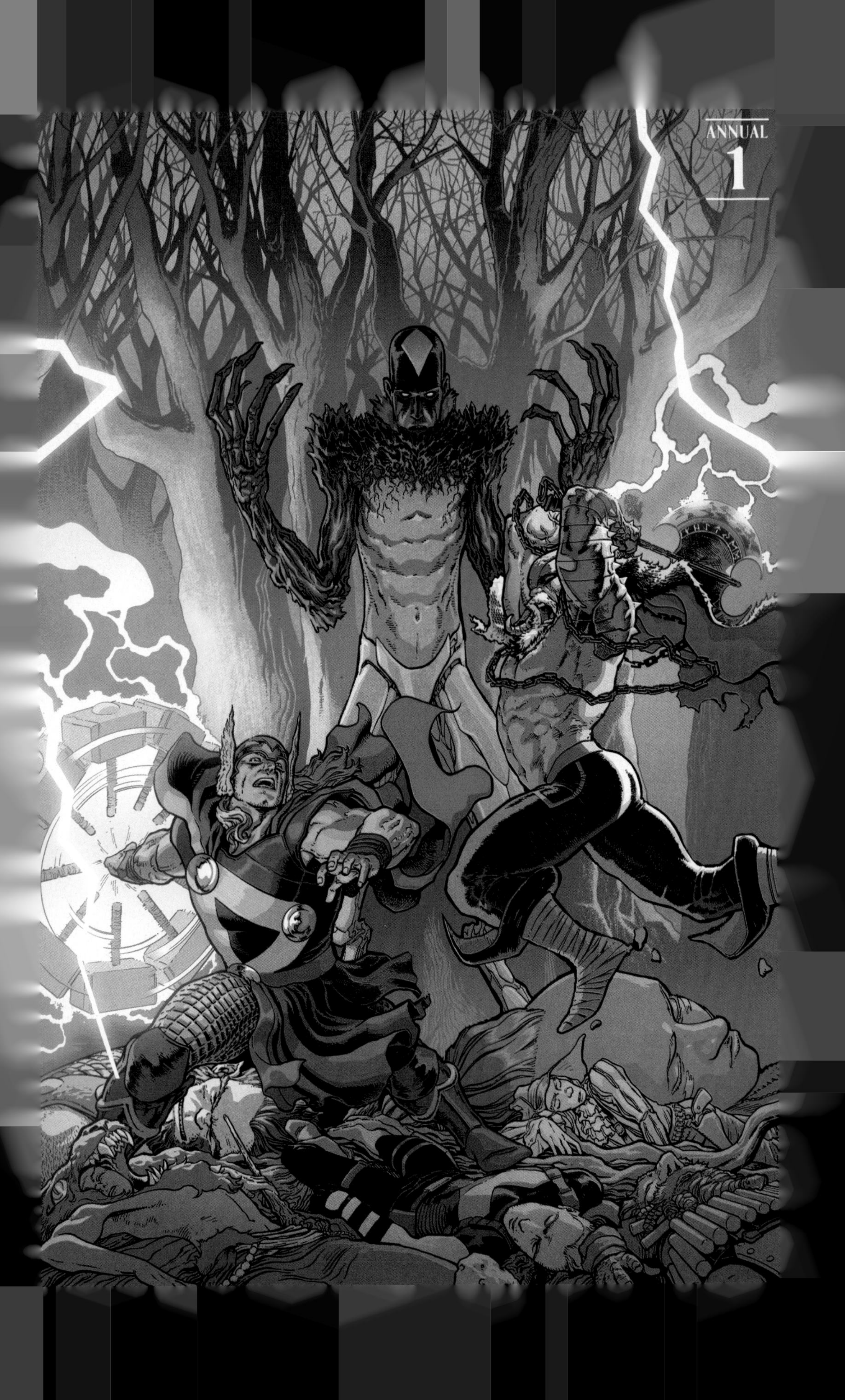
ANNUAL
1

The War of the Realms finally came to an end when the God of Thunder defeated Malekith the Accursed, bringing peace to all the realms. And in the end, that god, a prince, became a king. All hail the new All-Father of Asgard, the Protector of the Realms...

THOR
INFINITE
DESTINIES

Born from the remains of an omnipotent being, the six Infinity Stones, when gathered, grant untold power. They have wiped out half the life in the universe and resurrected it, they have threatened and saved the Multiverse...and now they have been sent out to bond with individuals...No one knows why the Stones bond with each bearer...nor what will happen if they are gathered. Will the story you are about to read reveal another Stone-Bearer or give a clue to the cosmically mysterious intentions of the most powerful artifacts in the universe? Read on, True Believer!

PROLOGUE.

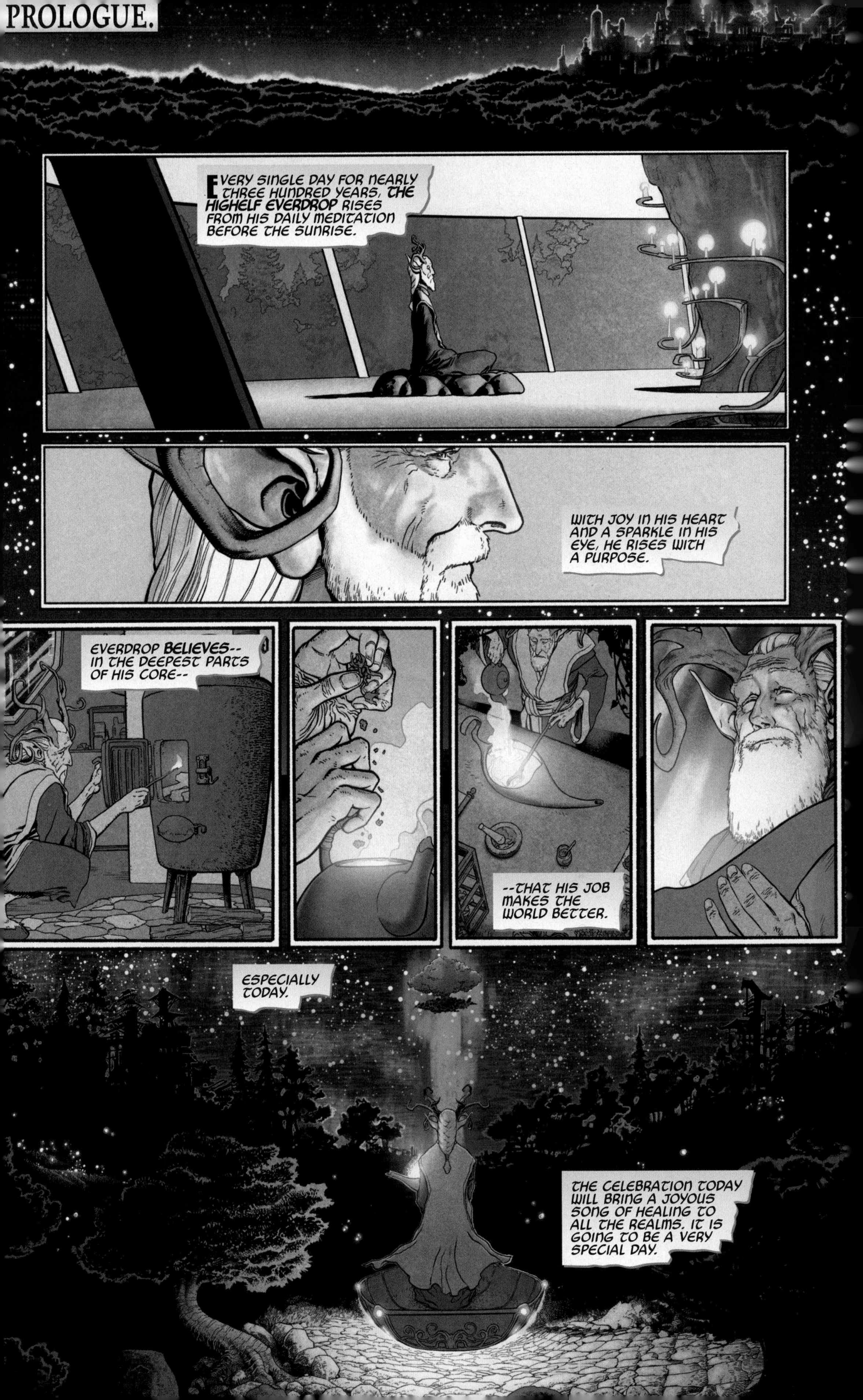
EVERY SINGLE DAY FOR NEARLY THREE HUNDRED YEARS, THE HIGHELF EVERDROP RISES FROM HIS DAILY MEDITATION BEFORE THE SUNRISE.
WITH JOY IN HIS HEART AND A SPARKLE IN HIS EYE, HE RISES WITH A PURPOSE.
EVERDROP BELIEVES-- IN THE DEEPEST PARTS OF HIS CORE--
--THAT HIS JOB MAKES THE WORLD BETTER.
ESPECIALLY TODAY.
THE CELEBRATION TODAY WILL BRING A JOYOUS SONG OF HEALING TO ALL THE REALMS. IT IS GOING TO BE A VERY SPECIAL DAY.

EVERDROP IS THE CARETAKER OF THE QAOYAK TREE. THE QAOYAK TREE WAS ORIGINALLY A SEEDLING FROM YGGDRASIL...*THE TREE OF LIFE* THAT BINDS TOGETHER THE REALMS OF REALITY.

WHEN PROPERLY CARED FOR, QAOYAK RADIATES LIFE, GROWTH, AND JOY FOR ALL WHO ARE NEAR IT.

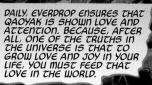

DAILY, EVERDROP ENSURES THAT QAOYAK IS SHOWN LOVE AND ATTENTION. BECAUSE, AFTER ALL, ONE OF THE TRUTHS IN THE UNIVERSE IS THAT TO GROW LOVE AND JOY IN YOUR LIFE, YOU MUST FEED THAT LOVE IN THE WORLD.

EVERDROP CAN FEEL QAOYAK SING.

UNFORTUNATELY...

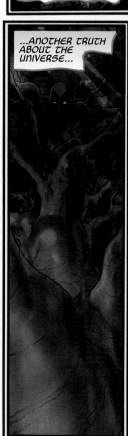

...ANOTHER TRUTH ABOUT THE UNIVERSE...

...IS THAT LIFE...

...JUST ISN'T FAIR.

AAHHHH

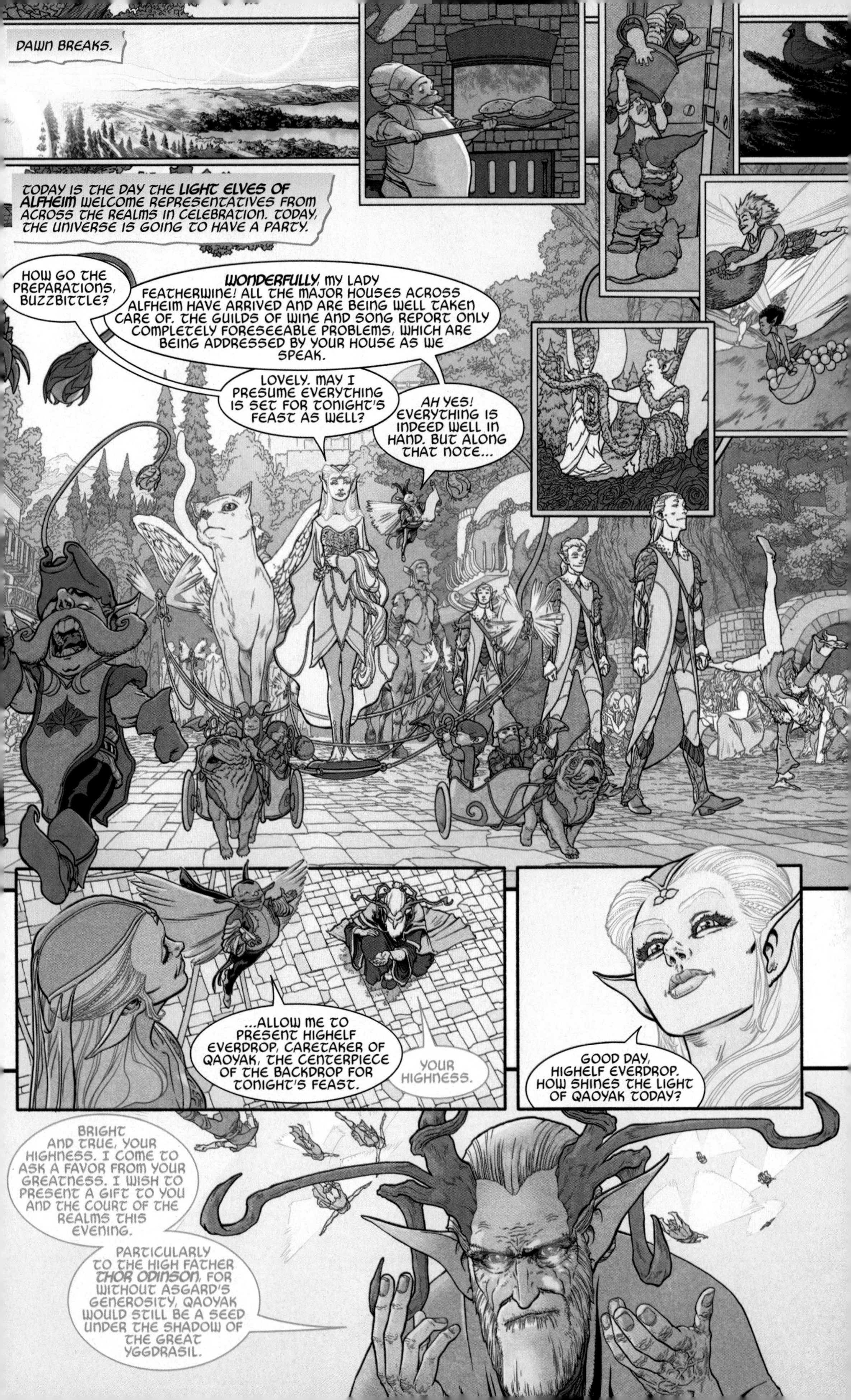
DAWN BREAKS.
TODAY IS THE DAY THE LIGHT ELVES OF ALFHEIM WELCOME REPRESENTATIVES FROM ACROSS THE REALMS IN CELEBRATION. TODAY, THE UNIVERSE IS GOING TO HAVE A PARTY.
HOW GO THE PREPARATIONS, BUZZBITTLE?
WONDERFULLY, MY LADY FEATHERWINE! ALL THE MAJOR HOUSES ACROSS ALFHEIM HAVE ARRIVED AND ARE BEING WELL TAKEN CARE OF. THE GUILDS OF WINE AND SONG REPORT ONLY COMPLETELY FORESEEABLE PROBLEMS, WHICH ARE BEING ADDRESSED BY YOUR HOUSE AS WE SPEAK.
LOVELY. MAY I PRESUME EVERYTHING IS SET FOR TONIGHT'S FEAST AS WELL?
AH YES! EVERYTHING IS INDEED WELL IN HAND. BUT ALONG THAT NOTE...
...ALLOW ME TO PRESENT HIGHELF EVERDROP, CARETAKER OF QAOYAK, THE CENTERPIECE OF THE BACKDROP FOR TONIGHT'S FEAST.
YOUR HIGHNESS.
GOOD DAY, HIGHELF EVERDROP. HOW SHINES THE LIGHT OF QAOYAK TODAY?
BRIGHT AND TRUE, YOUR HIGHNESS. I COME TO ASK A FAVOR FROM YOUR GREATNESS. I WISH TO PRESENT A GIFT TO YOU AND THE COURT OF THE REALMS THIS EVENING.
PARTICULARLY TO THE HIGH FATHER THOR ODINSON, FOR WITHOUT ASGARD'S GENEROSITY, QAOYAK WOULD STILL BE A SEED UNDER THE SHADOW OF THE GREAT YGGDRASIL.

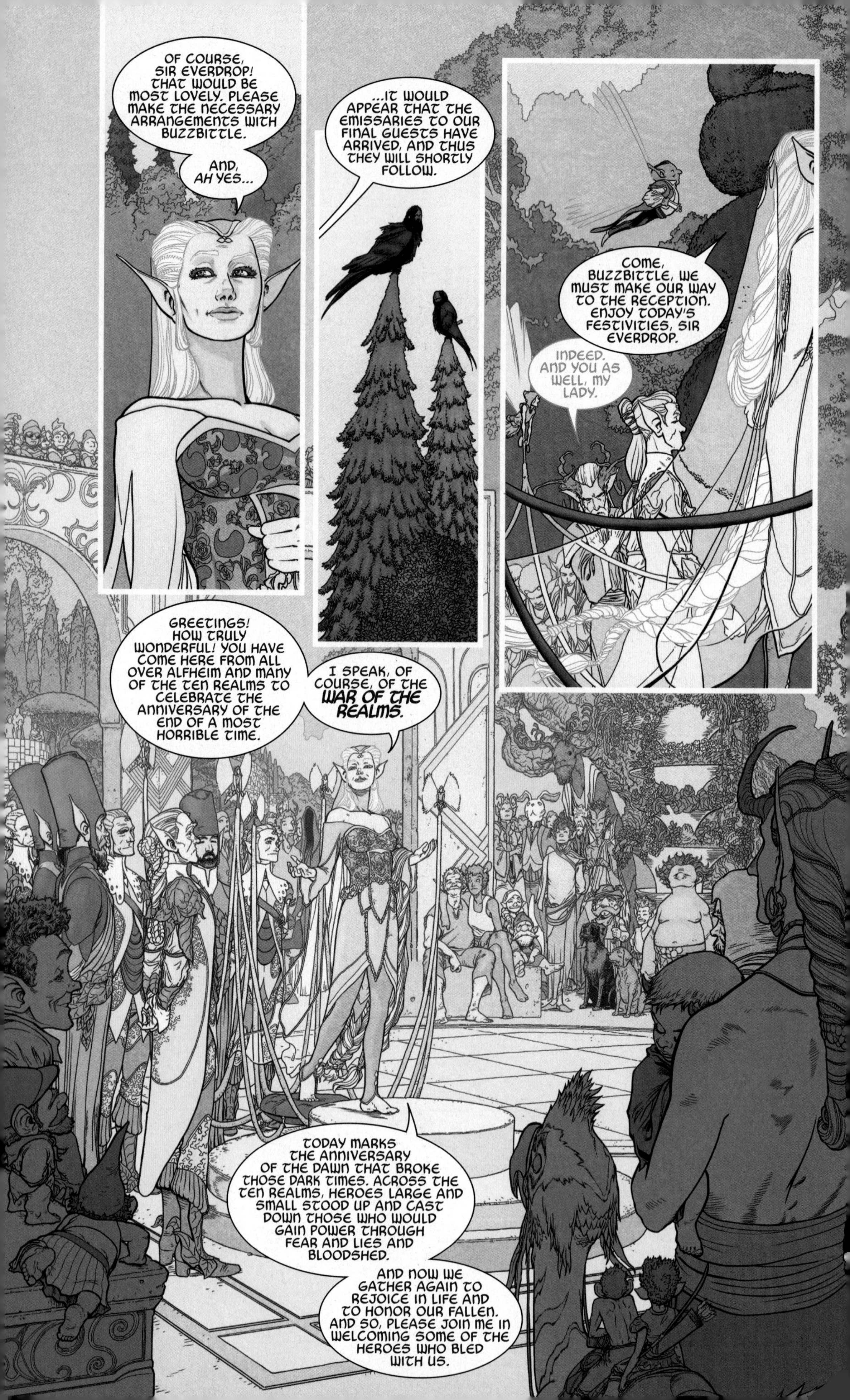

OF COURSE, SIR EVERDROP! THAT WOULD BE MOST LOVELY. PLEASE MAKE THE NECESSARY ARRANGEMENTS WITH BUZZBITTLE.
AND, AH YES...
...IT WOULD APPEAR THAT THE EMISSARIES TO OUR FINAL GUESTS HAVE ARRIVED, AND THUS THEY WILL SHORTLY FOLLOW.
COME, BUZZBITTLE, WE MUST MAKE OUR WAY TO THE RECEPTION. ENJOY TODAY'S FESTIVITIES, SIR EVERDROP.
INDEED. AND YOU AS WELL, MY LADY.
GREETINGS! HOW TRULY WONDERFUL! YOU HAVE COME HERE FROM ALL OVER ALFHEIM AND MANY OF THE TEN REALMS TO CELEBRATE THE ANNIVERSARY OF THE END OF A MOST HORRIBLE TIME.
I SPEAK, OF COURSE, OF THE WAR OF THE REALMS.
TODAY MARKS THE ANNIVERSARY OF THE DAWN THAT BROKE THOSE DARK TIMES. ACROSS THE TEN REALMS, HEROES LARGE AND SMALL STOOD UP AND CAST DOWN THOSE WHO WOULD GAIN POWER THROUGH FEAR AND LIES AND BLOODSHED.
AND NOW WE GATHER AGAIN TO REJOICE IN LIFE AND TO HONOR OUR FALLEN. AND SO, PLEASE JOIN ME IN WELCOMING SOME OF THE HEROES WHO BLED WITH US.

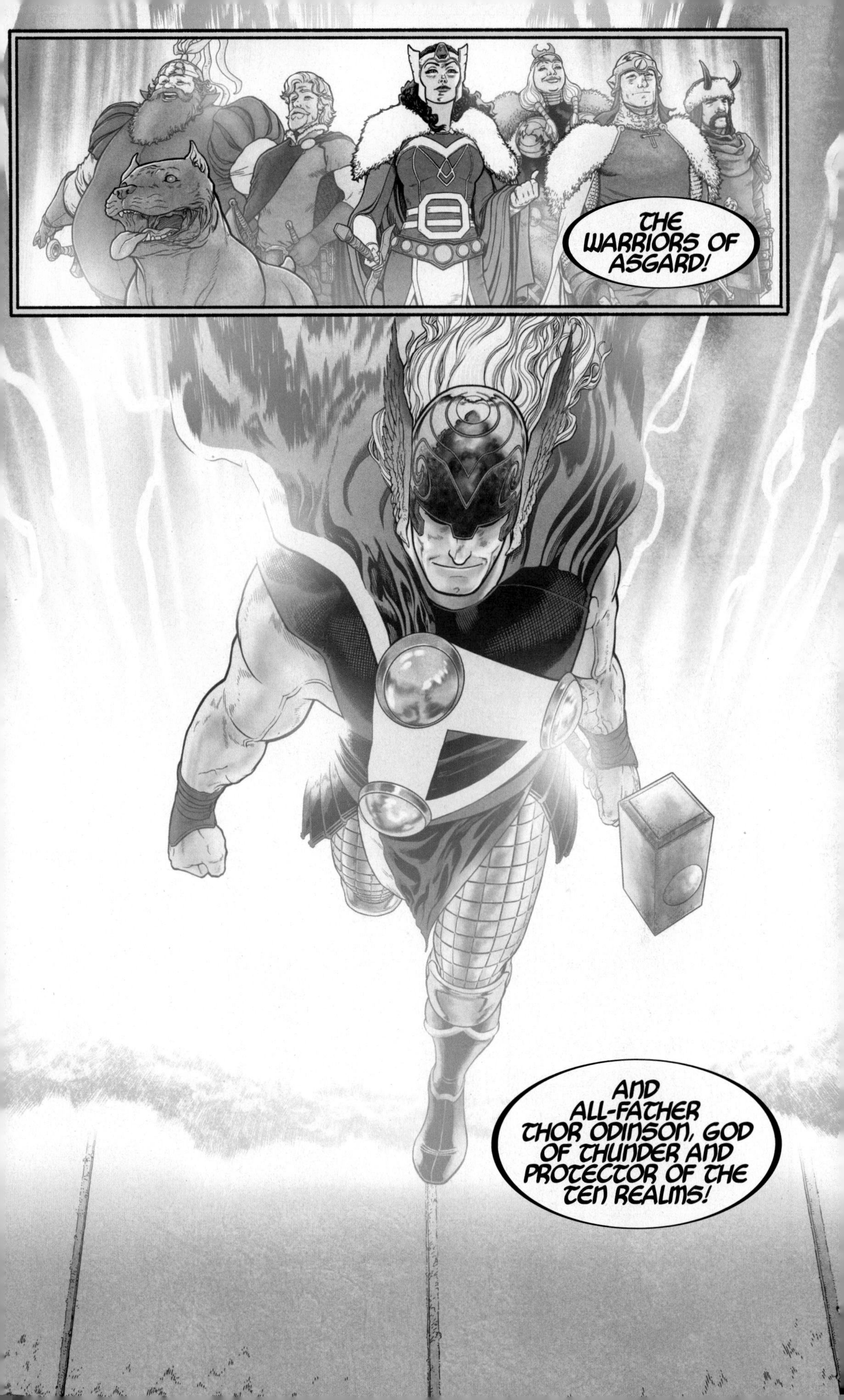
THE WARRIORS OF ASGARD!
AND ALL-FATHER THOR ODINSON, GOD OF THUNDER AND PROTECTOR OF THE TEN REALMS!

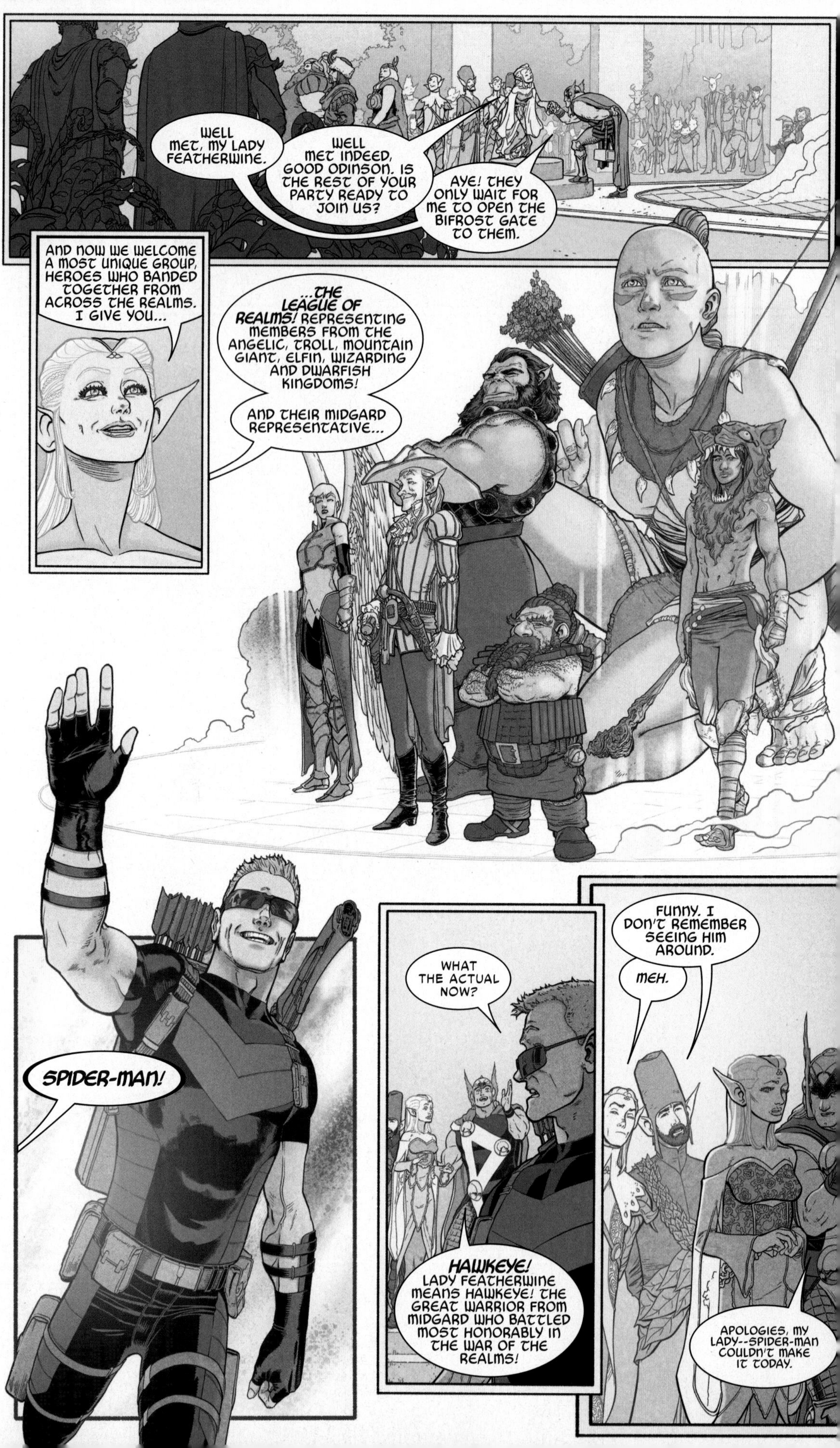
WELL MET, MY LADY FEATHERWINE.
WELL MET INDEED, GOOD ODINSON. IS THE REST OF YOUR PARTY READY TO JOIN US?
AYE! THEY ONLY WAIT FOR ME TO OPEN THE BIFROST GATE TO THEM.
AND NOW WE WELCOME A MOST UNIQUE GROUP, HEROES WHO BANDED TOGETHER FROM ACROSS THE REALMS. I GIVE YOU...
...THE LEAGUE OF REALMS! REPRESENTING MEMBERS FROM THE ANGELIC, TROLL, MOUNTAIN GIANT, ELFIN, WIZARDING AND DWARFISH KINGDOMS!
AND THEIR MIDGARD REPRESENTATIVE...
SPIDER-MAN!
WHAT THE ACTUAL NOW?
HAWKEYE! LADY FEATHERWINE MEANS HAWKEYE! THE GREAT WARRIOR FROM MIDGARD WHO BATTLED MOST HONORABLY IN THE WAR OF THE REALMS!
FUNNY. I DON'T REMEMBER SEEING HIM AROUND.
MEH.
APOLOGIES, MY LADY--SPIDER-MAN COULDN'T MAKE IT TODAY.

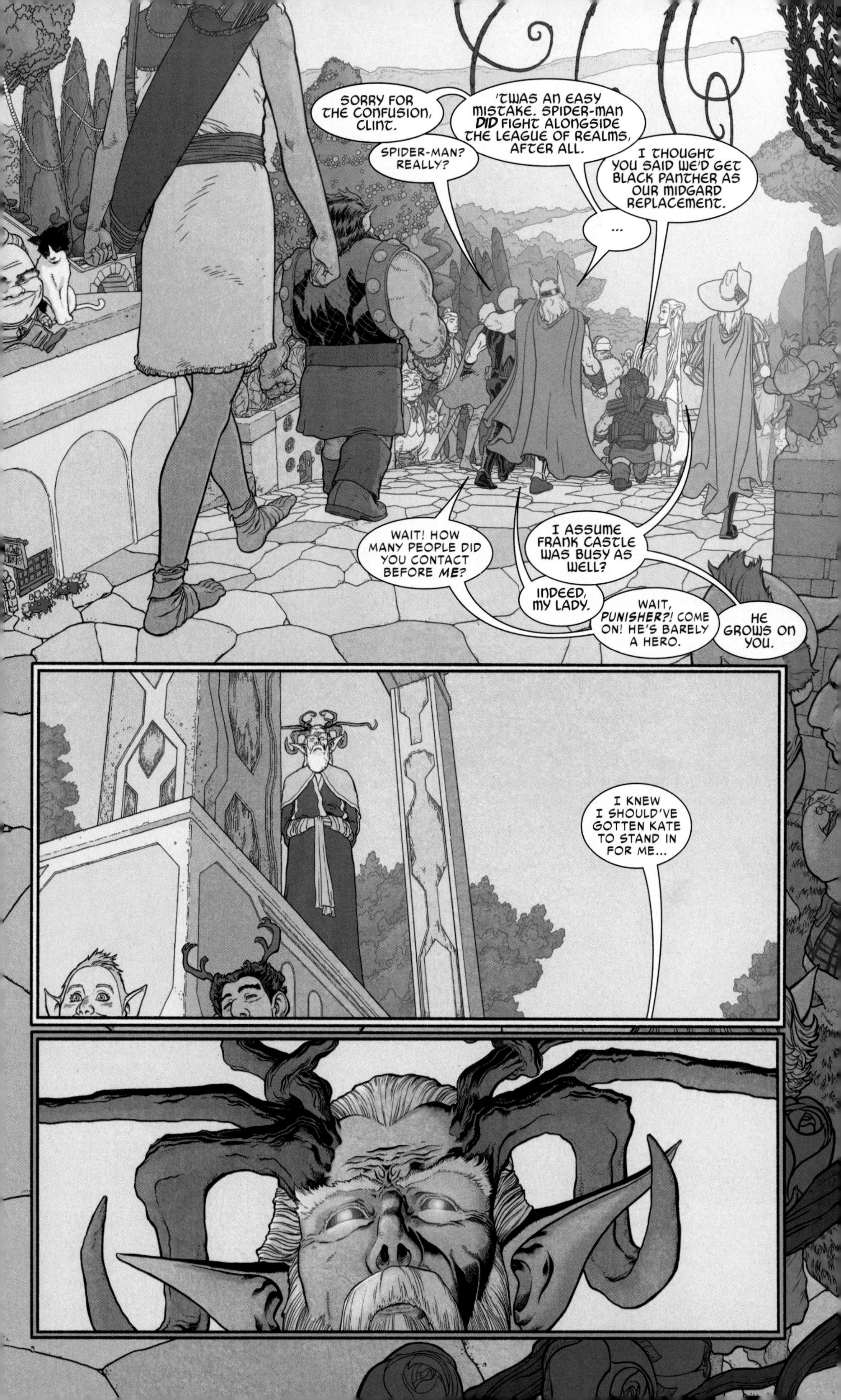
SORRY FOR THE CONFUSION, CLINT.
'TWAS AN EASY MISTAKE. SPIDER-MAN DID FIGHT ALONGSIDE THE LEAGUE OF REALMS, AFTER ALL.
SPIDER-MAN? REALLY?
I THOUGHT YOU SAID WE'D GET BLACK PANTHER AS OUR MIDGARD REPLACEMENT.
...
WAIT! HOW MANY PEOPLE DID YOU CONTACT BEFORE ME?
I ASSUME FRANK CASTLE WAS BUSY AS WELL?
INDEED, MY LADY.
WAIT, PUNISHER?! COME ON! HE'S BARELY A HERO.
HE GROWS ON YOU.
I KNEW I SHOULD'VE GOTTEN KATE TO STAND IN FOR ME...

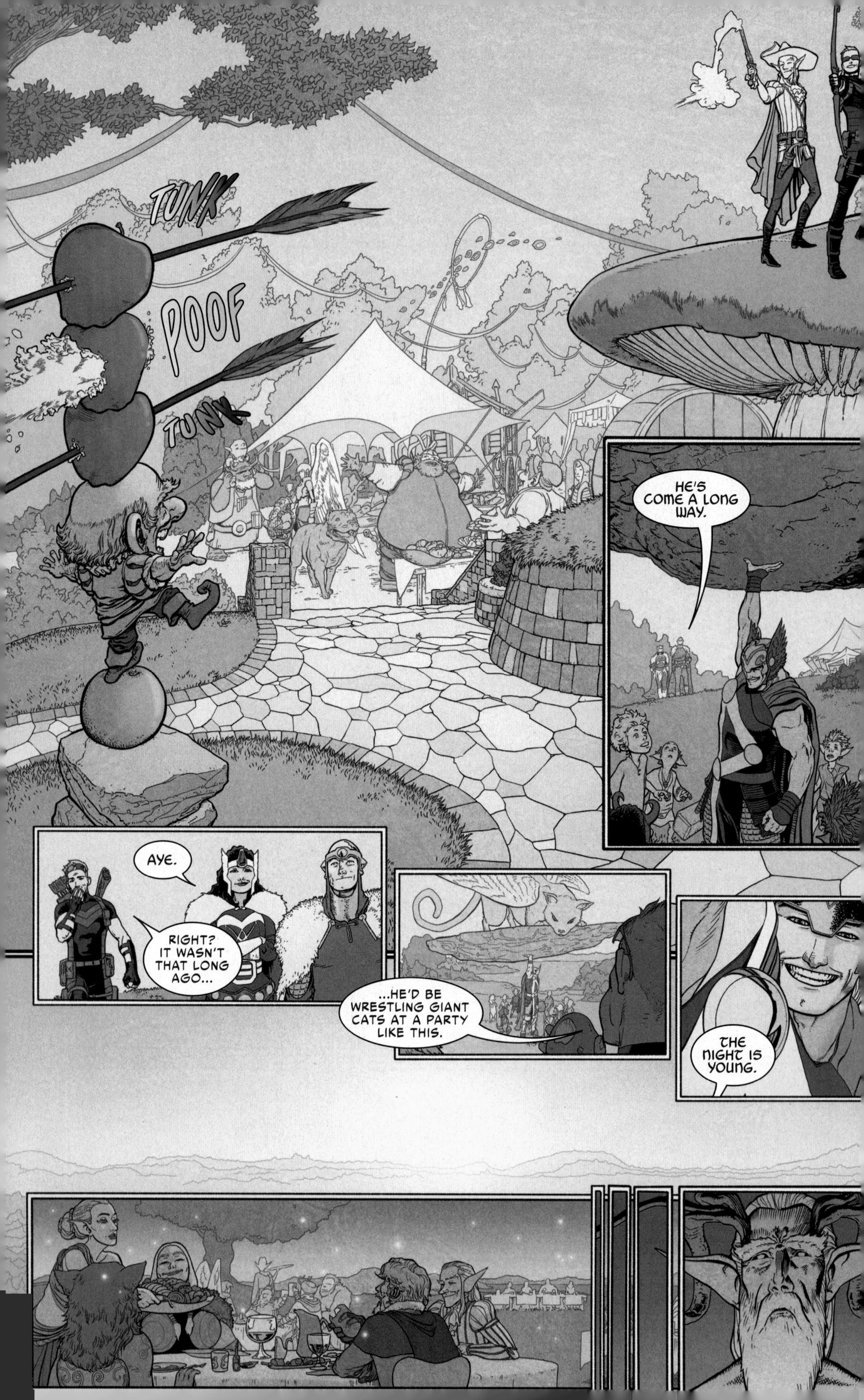

TUNK
POOF
TUNK
HE'S COME A LONG WAY.
AYE.
RIGHT? IT WASN'T THAT LONG AGO...
...HE'D BE WRESTLING GIANT CATS AT A PARTY LIKE THIS.
THE NIGHT IS YOUNG.

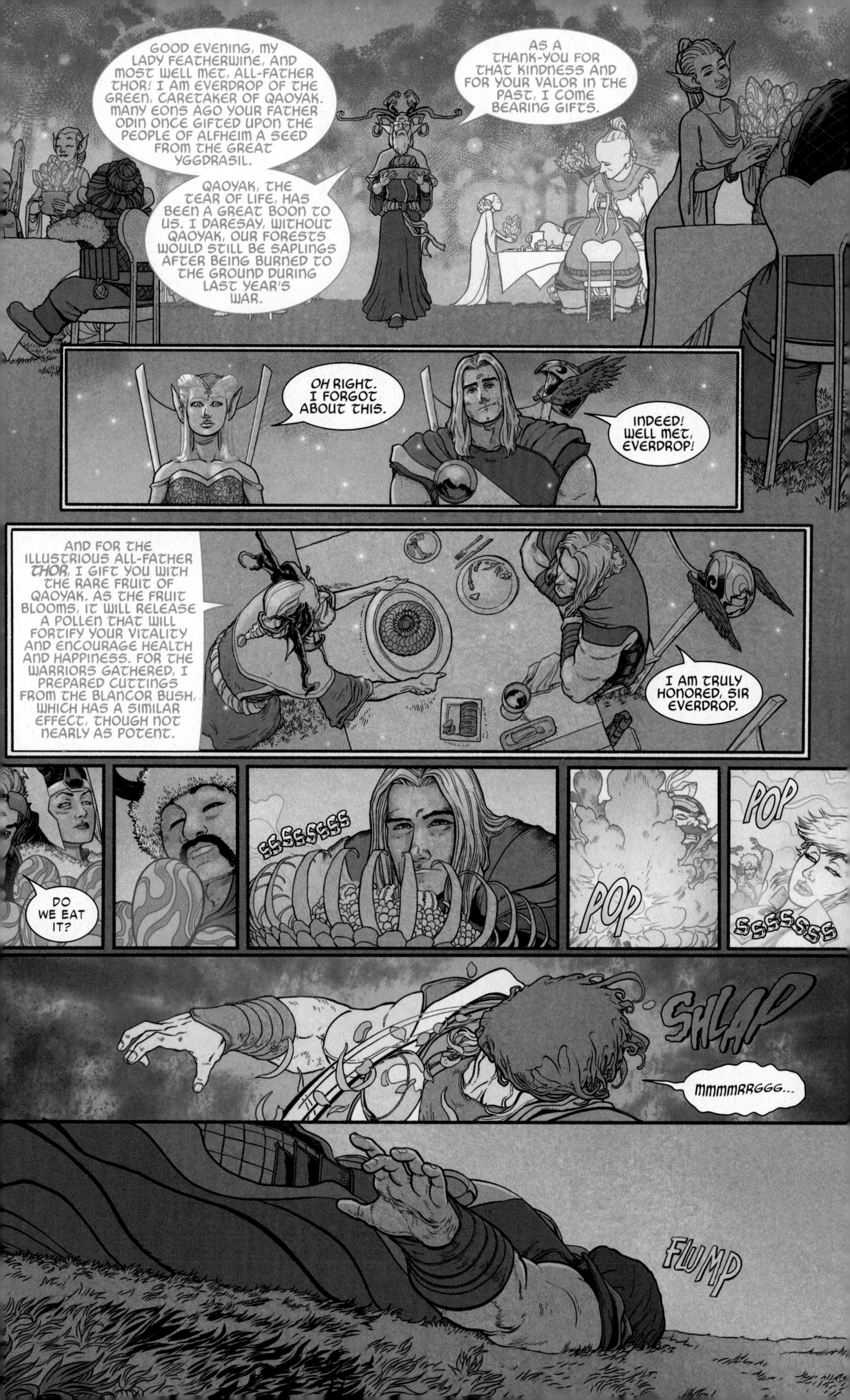
GOOD EVENING, MY LADY FEATHERWINE, AND MOST WELL MET, ALL-FATHER THOR! I AM EVERDROP OF THE GREEN, CARETAKER OF QAOYAK. MANY EONS AGO YOUR FATHER ODIN ONCE GIFTED UPON THE PEOPLE OF ALFHEIM A SEED FROM THE GREAT YGGDRASIL.
QAOYAK, THE TEAR OF LIFE, HAS BEEN A GREAT BOON TO US. I DARESAY, WITHOUT QAOYAK, OUR FORESTS WOULD STILL BE SAPLINGS AFTER BEING BURNED TO THE GROUND DURING LAST YEAR'S WAR.
AS A THANK-YOU FOR THAT KINDNESS AND FOR YOUR VALOR IN THE PAST, I COME BEARING GIFTS.
OH RIGHT. I FORGOT ABOUT THIS.
INDEED! WELL MET, EVERDROP!
AND FOR THE ILLUSTRIOUS ALL-FATHER THOR, I GIFT YOU WITH THE RARE FRUIT OF QAOYAK. AS THE FRUIT BLOOMS, IT WILL RELEASE A POLLEN THAT WILL FORTIFY YOUR VITALITY AND ENCOURAGE HEALTH AND HAPPINESS. FOR THE WARRIORS GATHERED, I PREPARED CUTTINGS FROM THE BLANCOR BUSH, WHICH HAS A SIMILAR EFFECT, THOUGH NOT NEARLY AS POTENT.
I AM TRULY HONORED, SIR EVERDROP.
DO WE EAT IT?
SSSSSSSS
POP
POP
SSSSSSSS
SHLAP
MMMMRRGGG...
FLUMP

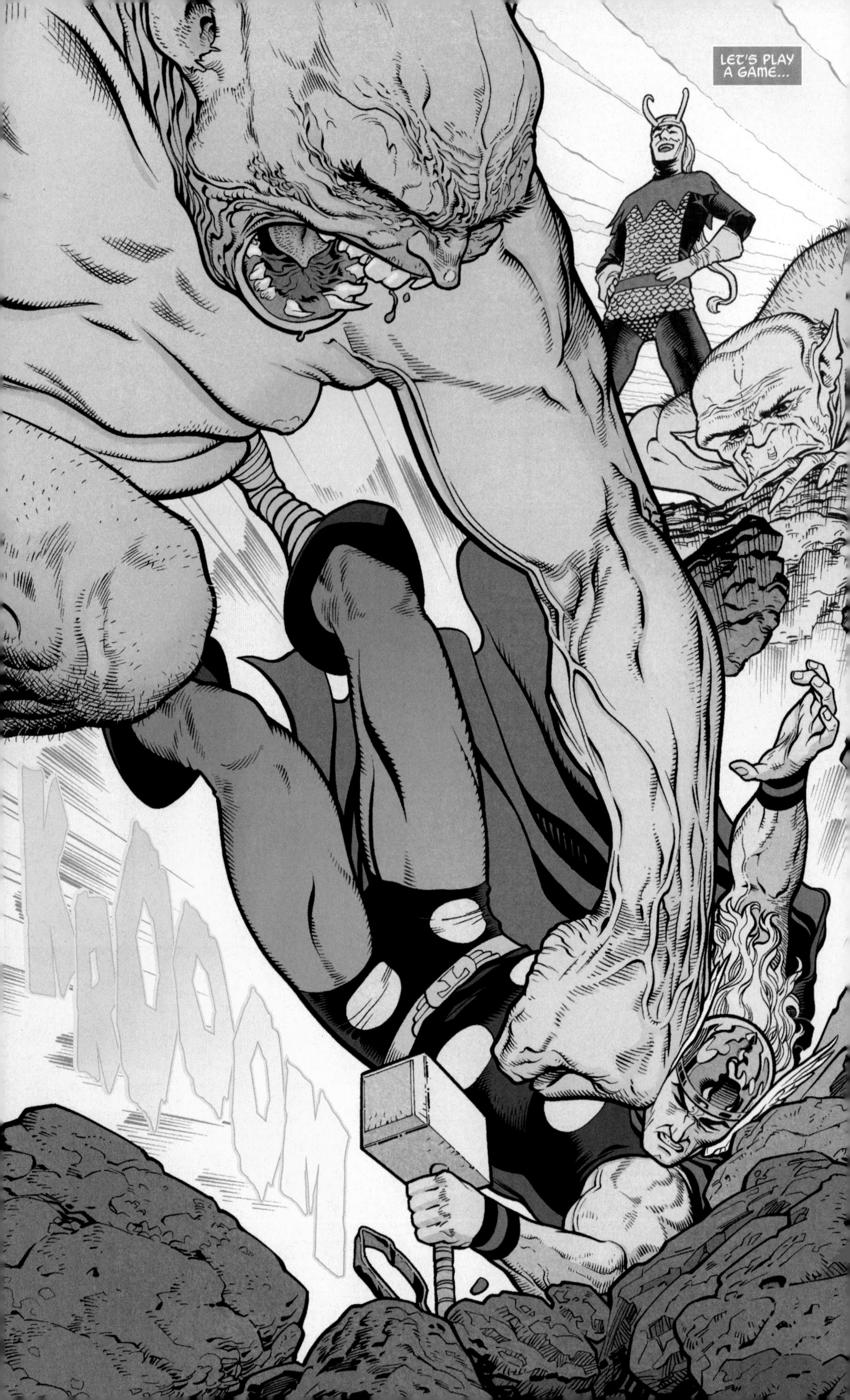
LET'S PLAY A GAME...
KRROOOM

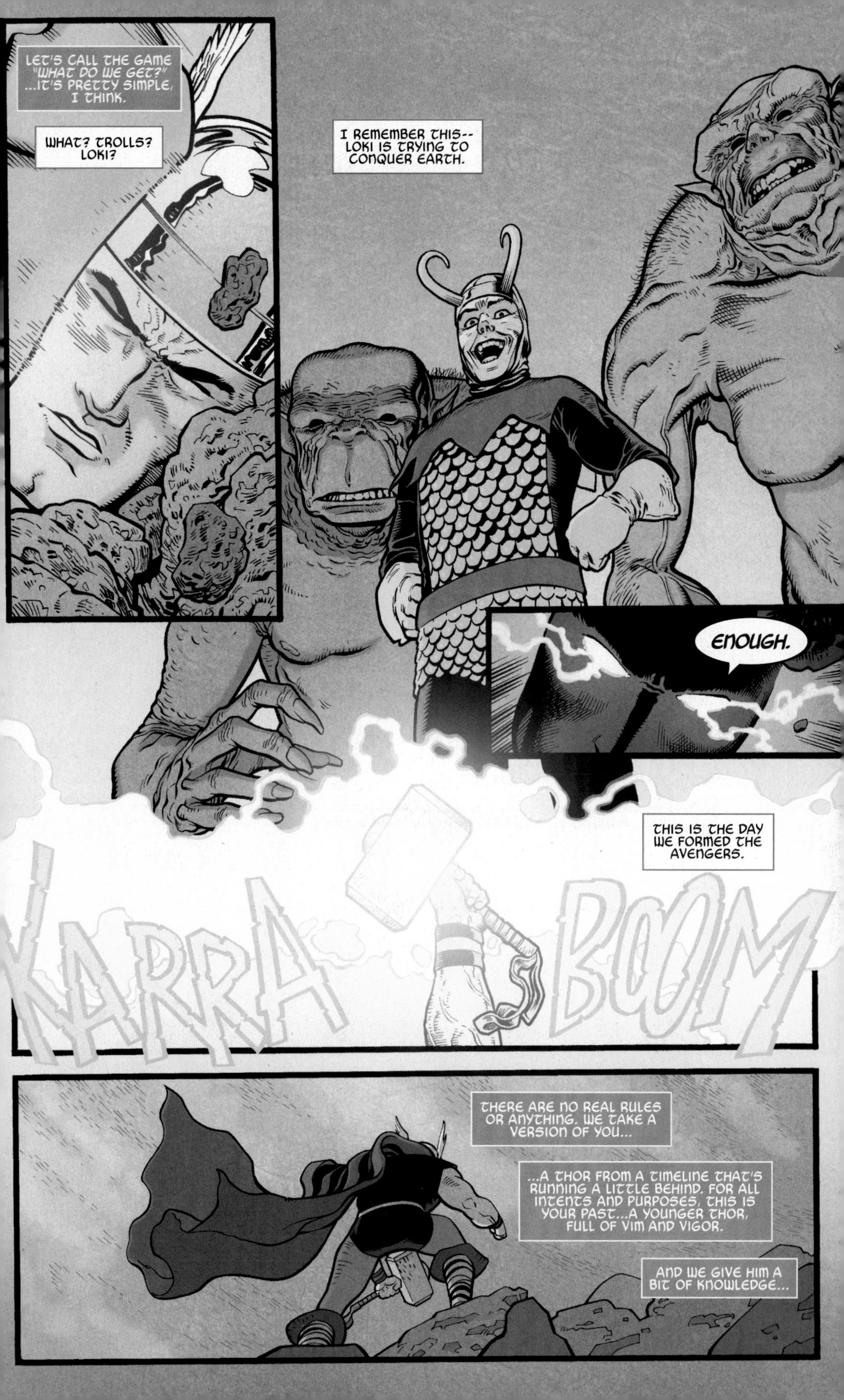
LET'S CALL THE GAME "WHAT DO WE GET?" ...IT'S PRETTY SIMPLE, I THINK.
WHAT? TROLLS? LOKI?
I REMEMBER THIS-- LOKI IS TRYING TO CONQUER EARTH.
ENOUGH.
THIS IS THE DAY WE FORMED THE AVENGERS.
KARRA BOOM
THERE ARE NO REAL RULES OR ANYTHING. WE TAKE A VERSION OF YOU...
...A THOR FROM A TIMELINE THAT'S RUNNING A LITTLE BEHIND. FOR ALL INTENTS AND PURPOSES, THIS IS YOUR PAST...A YOUNGER THOR, FULL OF VIM AND VIGOR.
AND WE GIVE HIM A BIT OF KNOWLEDGE...

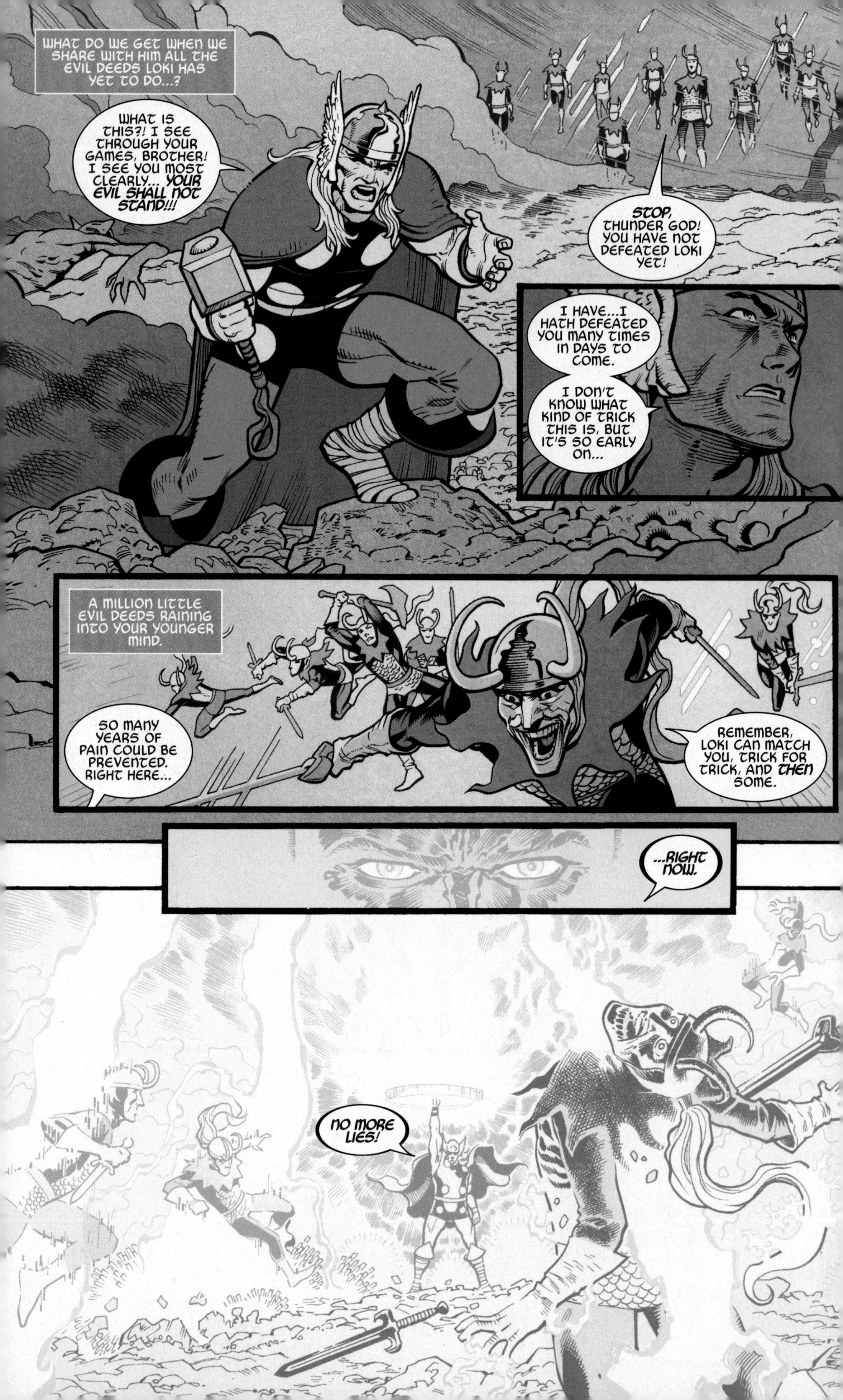
WHAT DO WE GET WHEN WE SHARE WITH HIM ALL THE EVIL DEEDS LOKI HAS YET TO DO...?
WHAT IS THIS?! I SEE THROUGH YOUR GAMES, BROTHER! I SEE YOU MOST CLEARLY... YOUR EVIL SHALL NOT STAND!!!
STOP, THUNDER GOD! YOU HAVE NOT DEFEATED LOKI YET!
I HAVE...I HATH DEFEATED YOU MANY TIMES IN DAYS TO COME.
I DON'T KNOW WHAT KIND OF TRICK THIS IS, BUT IT'S SO EARLY ON...
A MILLION LITTLE EVIL DEEDS RAINING INTO YOUR YOUNGER MIND.
SO MANY YEARS OF PAIN COULD BE PREVENTED. RIGHT HERE...
REMEMBER, LOKI CAN MATCH YOU, TRICK FOR TRICK, AND THEN SOME.
...RIGHT NOW.
NO MORE LIES!

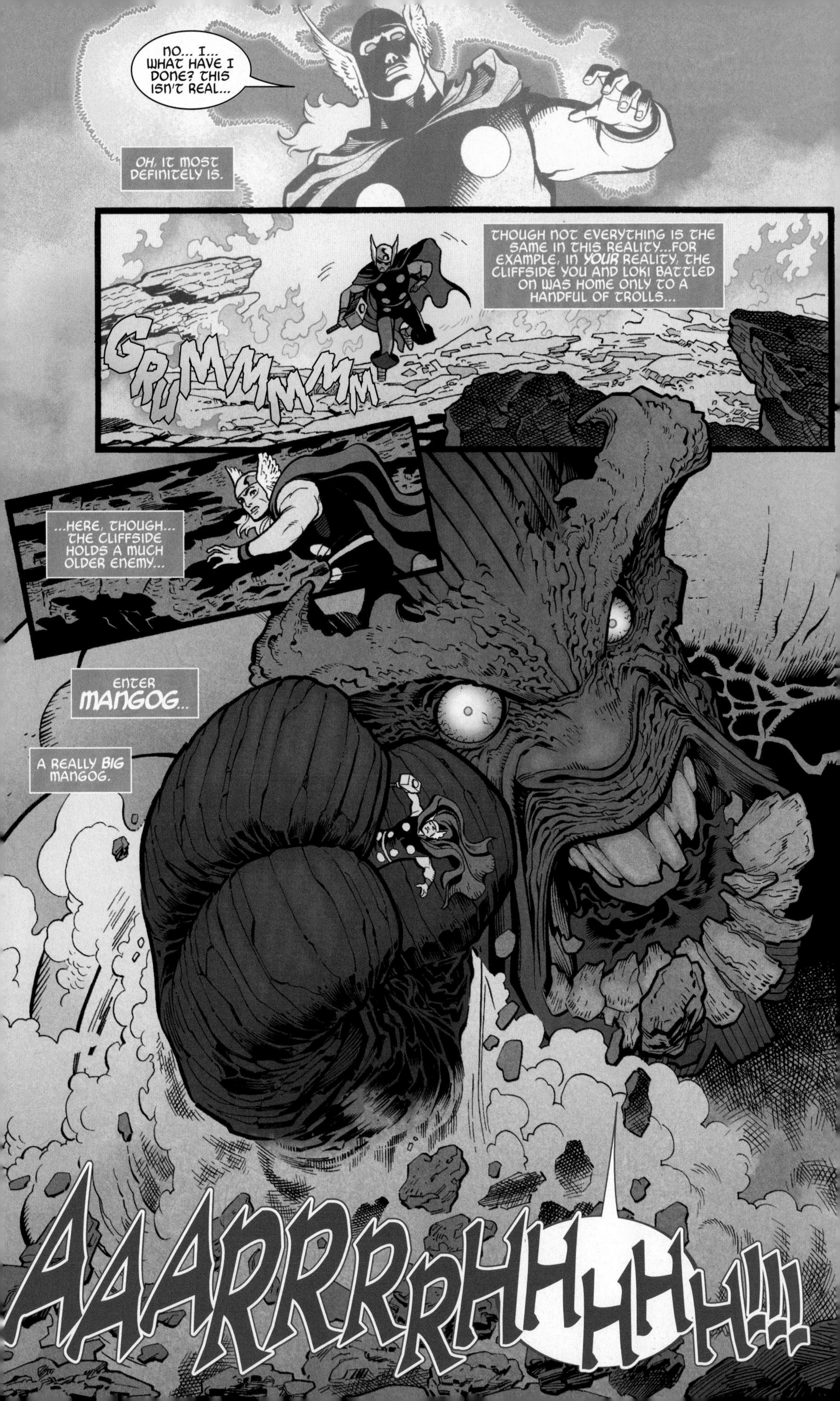

NO... I... WHAT HAVE I DONE? THIS ISN'T REAL...
OH, IT MOST DEFINITELY IS.
THOUGH NOT EVERYTHING IS THE SAME IN THIS REALITY...FOR EXAMPLE, IN YOUR REALITY, THE CLIFFSIDE YOU AND LOKI BATTLED ON WAS HOME ONLY TO A HANDFUL OF TROLLS...
GRUMMMMMM
...HERE, THOUGH... THE CLIFFSIDE HOLDS A MUCH OLDER ENEMY...
ENTER MANGOG...
A REALLY BIG MANGOG.
AAARRRRHHHHH!!!

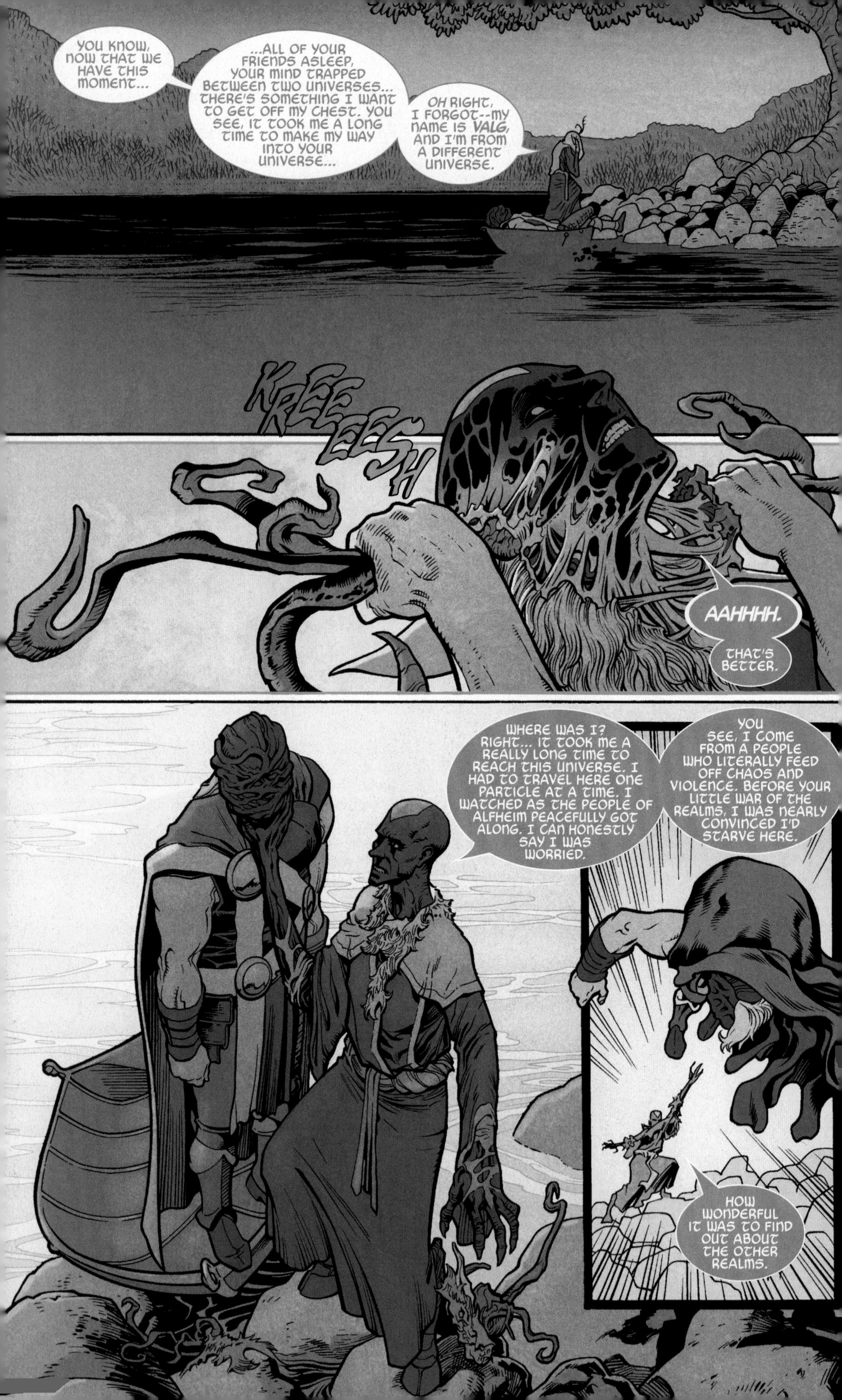

YOU KNOW, NOW THAT WE HAVE THIS MOMENT...
...ALL OF YOUR FRIENDS ASLEEP, YOUR MIND TRAPPED BETWEEN TWO UNIVERSES... THERE'S SOMETHING I WANT TO GET OFF MY CHEST. YOU SEE, IT TOOK ME A LONG TIME TO MAKE MY WAY INTO YOUR UNIVERSE...
OH RIGHT, I FORGOT--MY NAME IS VALG, AND I'M FROM A DIFFERENT UNIVERSE.
KREEEESH
AAHHHH.
THAT'S BETTER.
WHERE WAS I? RIGHT... IT TOOK ME A REALLY LONG TIME TO REACH THIS UNIVERSE. I HAD TO TRAVEL HERE ONE PARTICLE AT A TIME. I WATCHED AS THE PEOPLE OF ALFHEIM PEACEFULLY GOT ALONG. I CAN HONESTLY SAY I WAS WORRIED.
YOU SEE, I COME FROM A PEOPLE WHO LITERALLY FEED OFF CHAOS AND VIOLENCE. BEFORE YOUR LITTLE WAR OF THE REALMS, I WAS NEARLY CONVINCED I'D STARVE HERE.
HOW WONDERFUL IT WAS TO FIND OUT ABOUT THE OTHER REALMS.

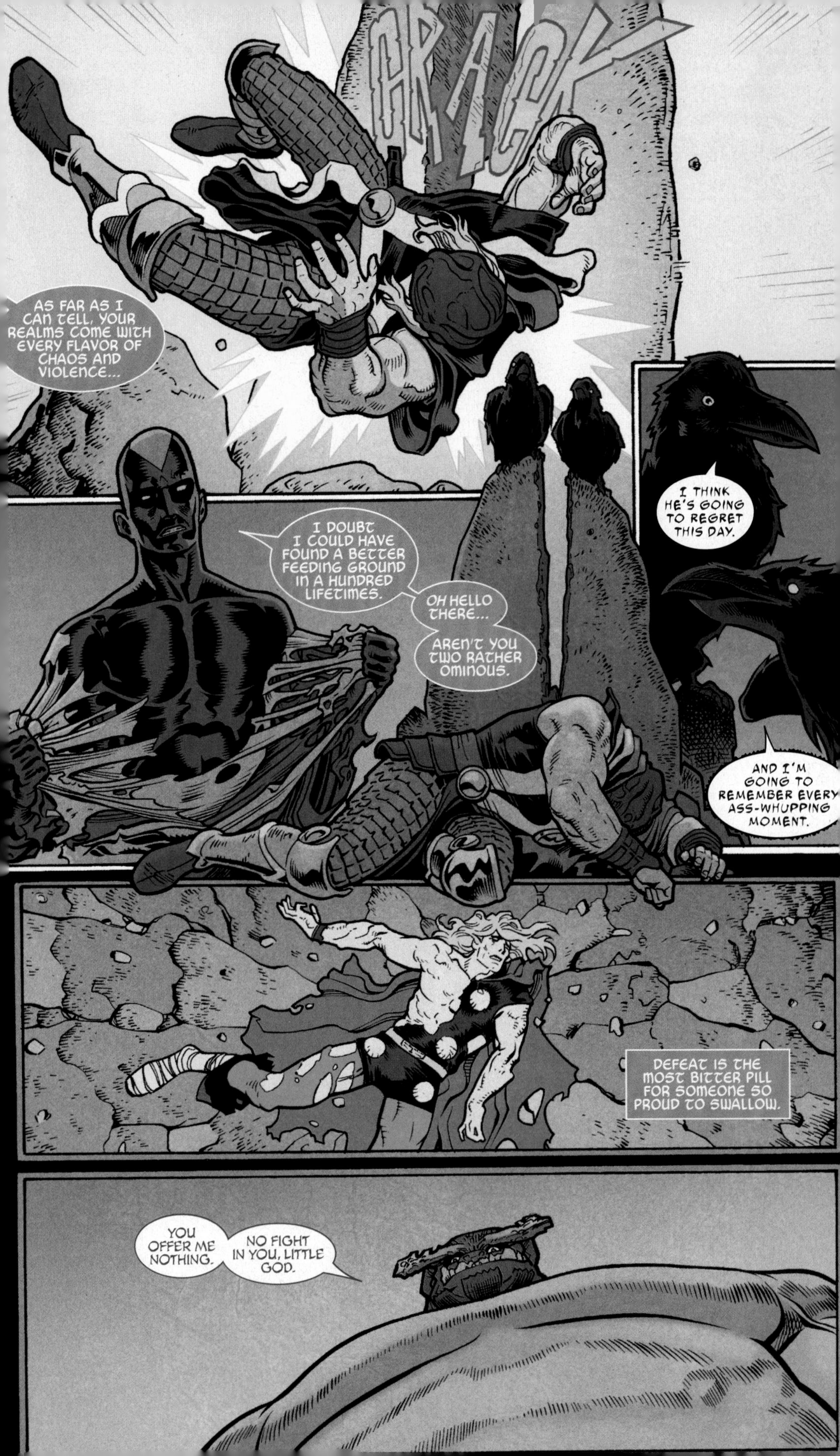
CRACK
AS FAR AS I CAN TELL, YOUR REALMS COME WITH EVERY FLAVOR OF CHAOS AND VIOLENCE...
I DOUBT I COULD HAVE FOUND A BETTER FEEDING GROUND IN A HUNDRED LIFETIMES.
OH HELLO THERE...
AREN'T YOU TWO RATHER OMINOUS.
I THINK HE'S GOING TO REGRET THIS DAY.
AND I'M GOING TO REMEMBER EVERY ASS-WHUPPING MOMENT.
DEFEAT IS THE MOST BITTER PILL FOR SOMEONE SO PROUD TO SWALLOW.
YOU OFFER ME NOTHING.
NO FIGHT IN YOU, LITTLE GOD.

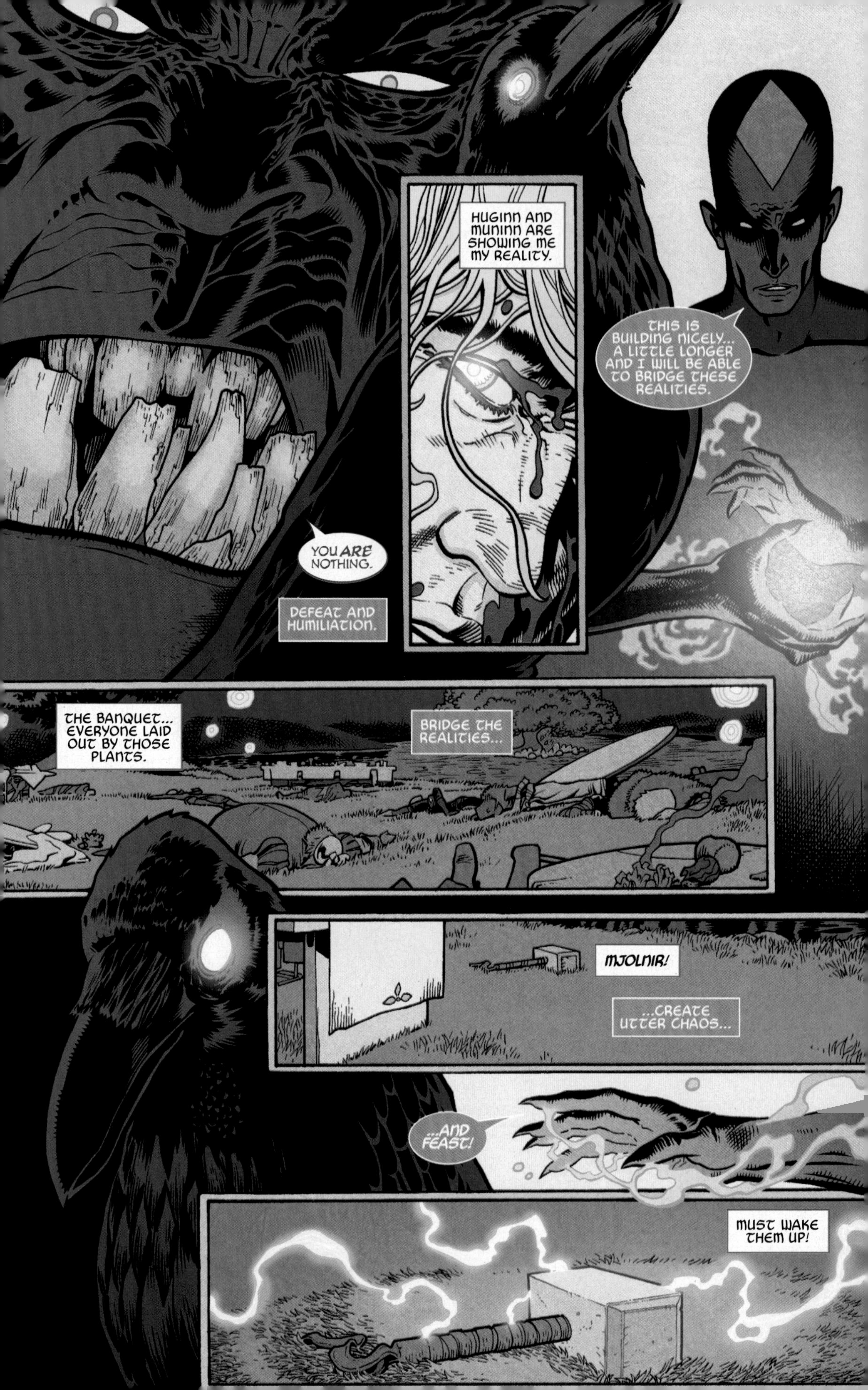
HUGINN AND MUNINN ARE SHOWING ME MY REALITY.
THIS IS BUILDING NICELY... A LITTLE LONGER AND I WILL BE ABLE TO BRIDGE THESE REALITIES.
YOU ARE NOTHING.
DEFEAT AND HUMILIATION.
THE BANQUET... EVERYONE LAID OUT BY THOSE PLANTS.
BRIDGE THE REALITIES...
MJOLNIR!
...CREATE UTTER CHAOS...
...AND FEAST!
MUST WAKE THEM UP!

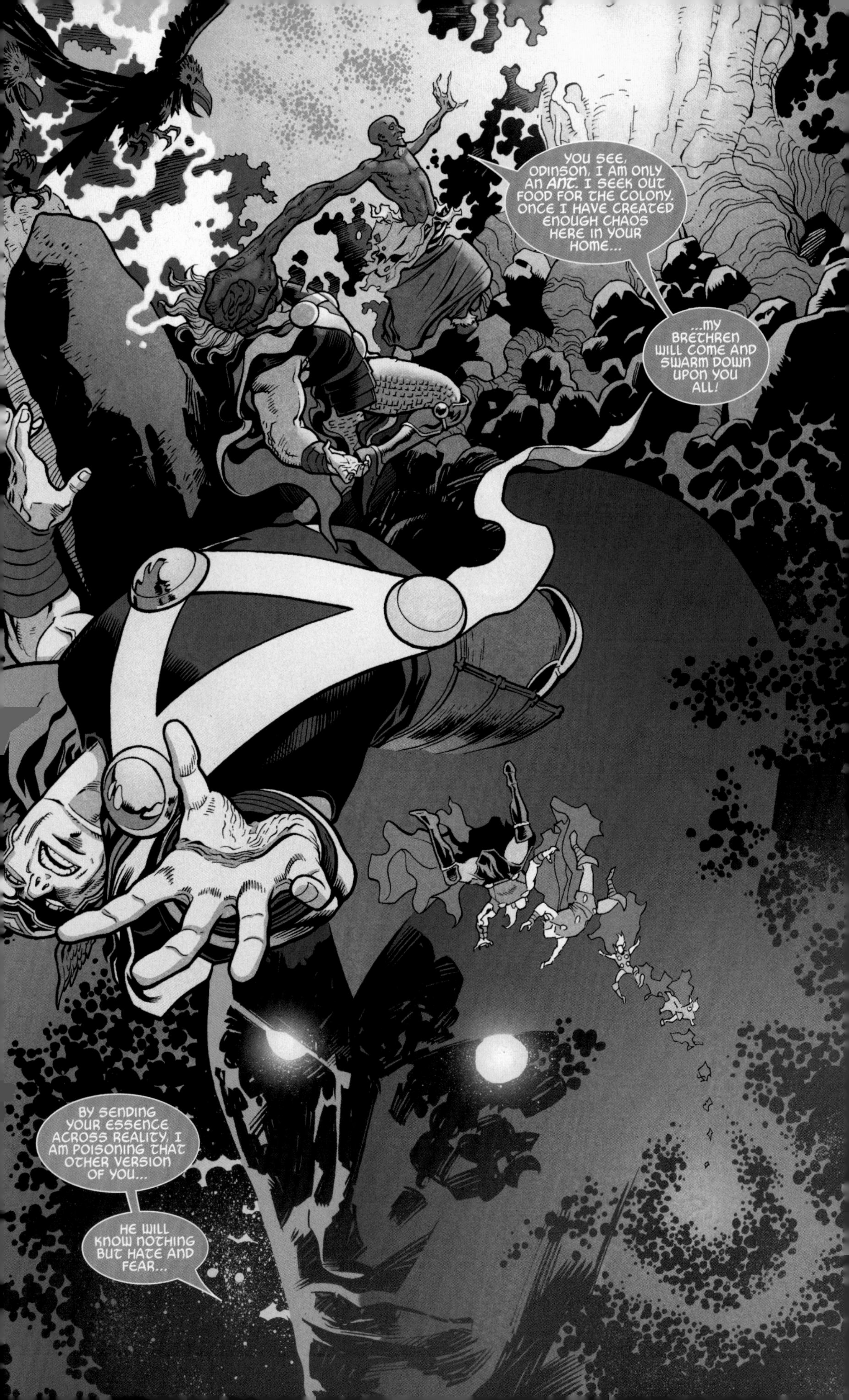
YOU SEE, ODINSON, I AM ONLY AN ANT. I SEEK OUT FOOD FOR THE COLONY. ONCE I HAVE CREATED ENOUGH CHAOS HERE IN YOUR HOME...
...MY BRETHREN WILL COME AND SWARM DOWN UPON YOU ALL!
BY SENDING YOUR ESSENCE ACROSS REALITY, I AM POISONING THAT OTHER VERSION OF YOU...
HE WILL KNOW NOTHING BUT HATE AND FEAR...

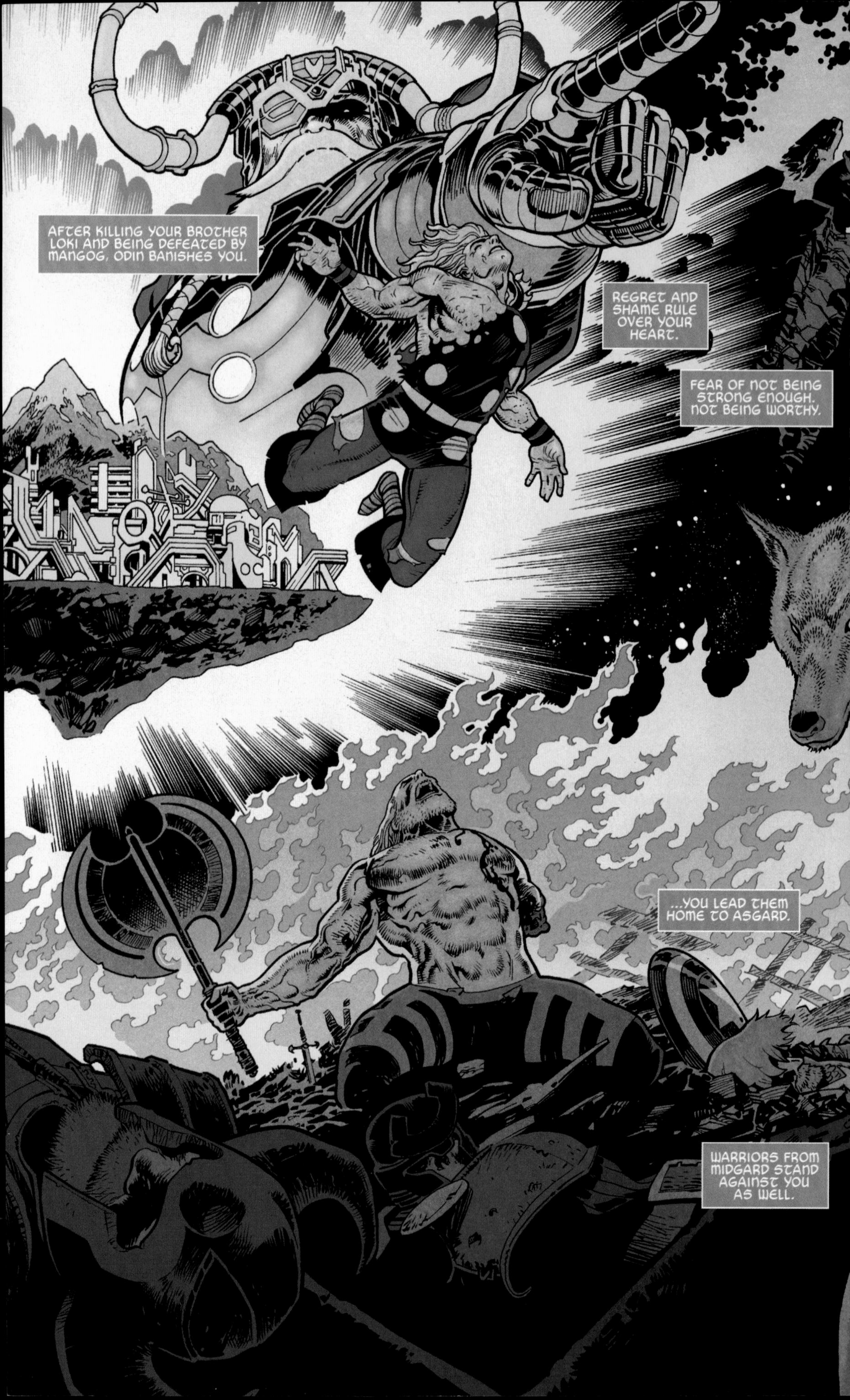
AFTER KILLING YOUR BROTHER LOKI AND BEING DEFEATED BY MANGOG, ODIN BANISHES YOU.
REGRET AND SHAME RULE OVER YOUR HEART.
FEAR OF NOT BEING STRONG ENOUGH. NOT BEING WORTHY.
...YOU LEAD THEM HOME TO ASGARD.
WARRIORS FROM MIDGARD STAND AGAINST YOU AS WELL.

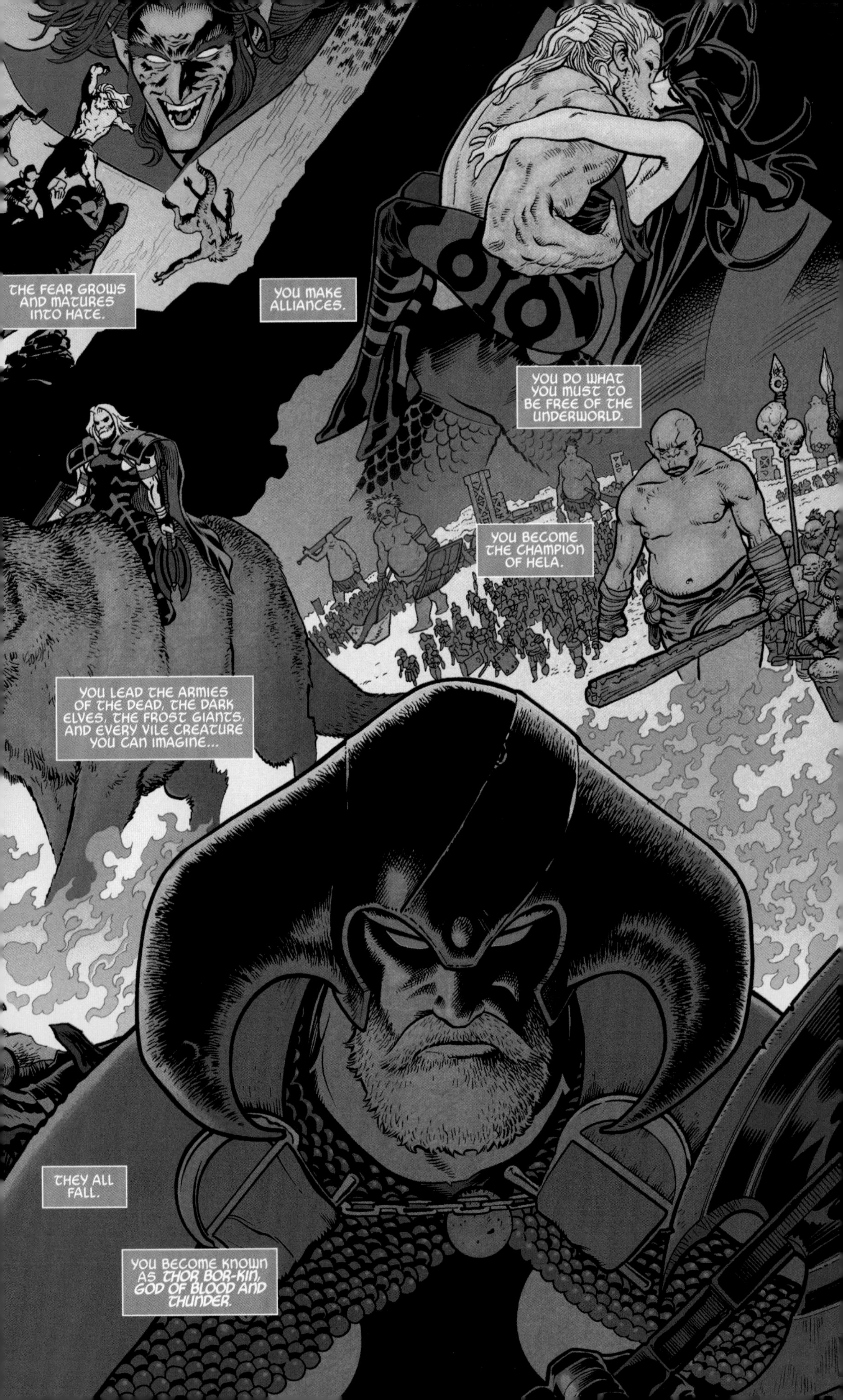

THE FEAR GROWS AND MATURES INTO HATE.
YOU MAKE ALLIANCES.
YOU DO WHAT YOU MUST TO BE FREE OF THE UNDERWORLD.
YOU BECOME THE CHAMPION OF HELA.
YOU LEAD THE ARMIES OF THE DEAD, THE DARK ELVES, THE FROST GIANTS, AND EVERY VILE CREATURE YOU CAN IMAGINE...
THEY ALL FALL.
YOU BECOME KNOWN AS THOR BOR-KIN, GOD OF BLOOD AND THUNDER.

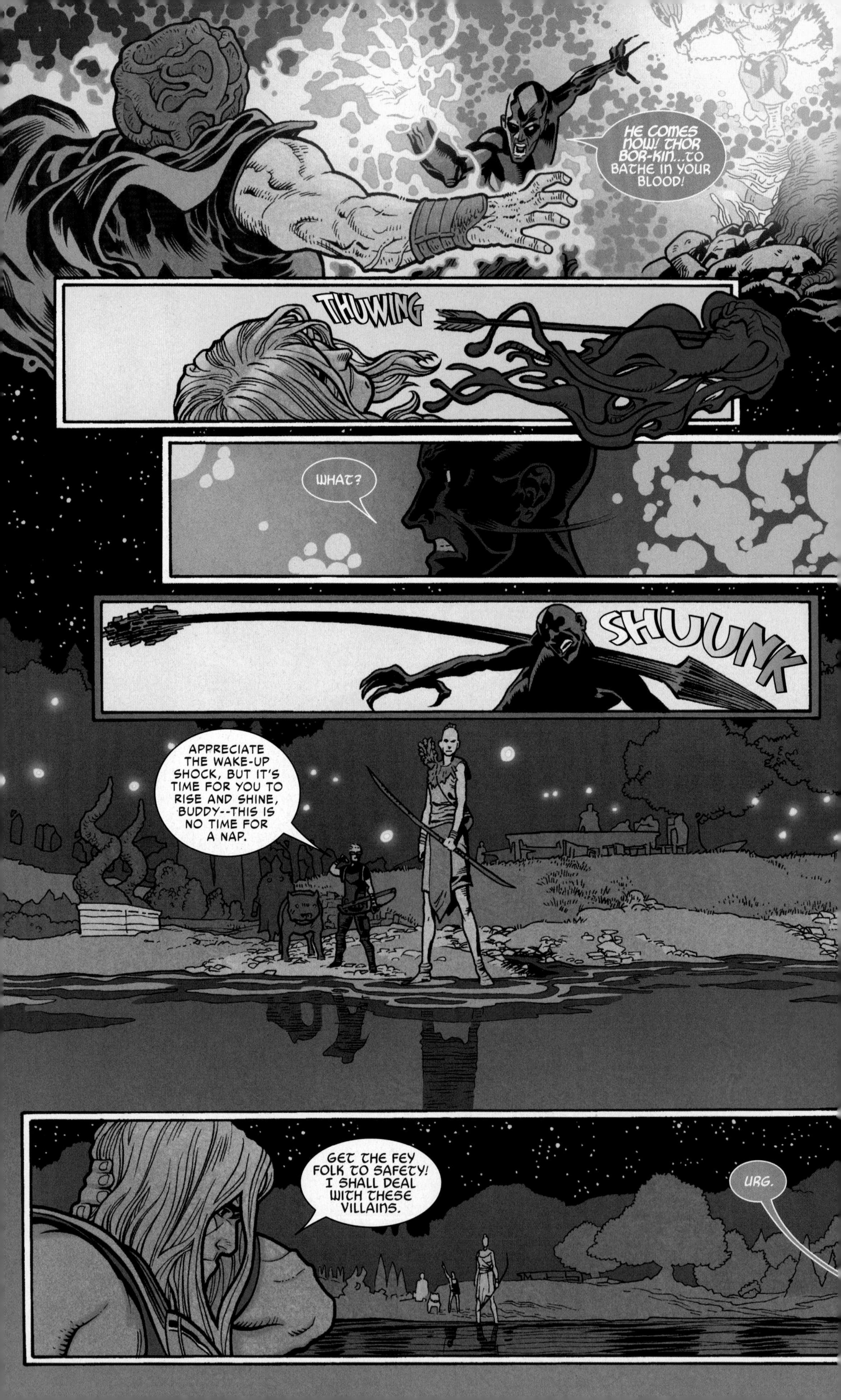
HE COMES NOW! THOR BOR-KIN...TO BATHE IN YOUR BLOOD!
THUWING
WHAT?
SHUUNK
APPRECIATE THE WAKE-UP SHOCK, BUT IT'S TIME FOR YOU TO RISE AND SHINE, BUDDY--THIS IS NO TIME FOR A NAP.
GET THE FEY FOLK TO SAFETY! I SHALL DEAL WITH THESE VILLAINS.
URG.

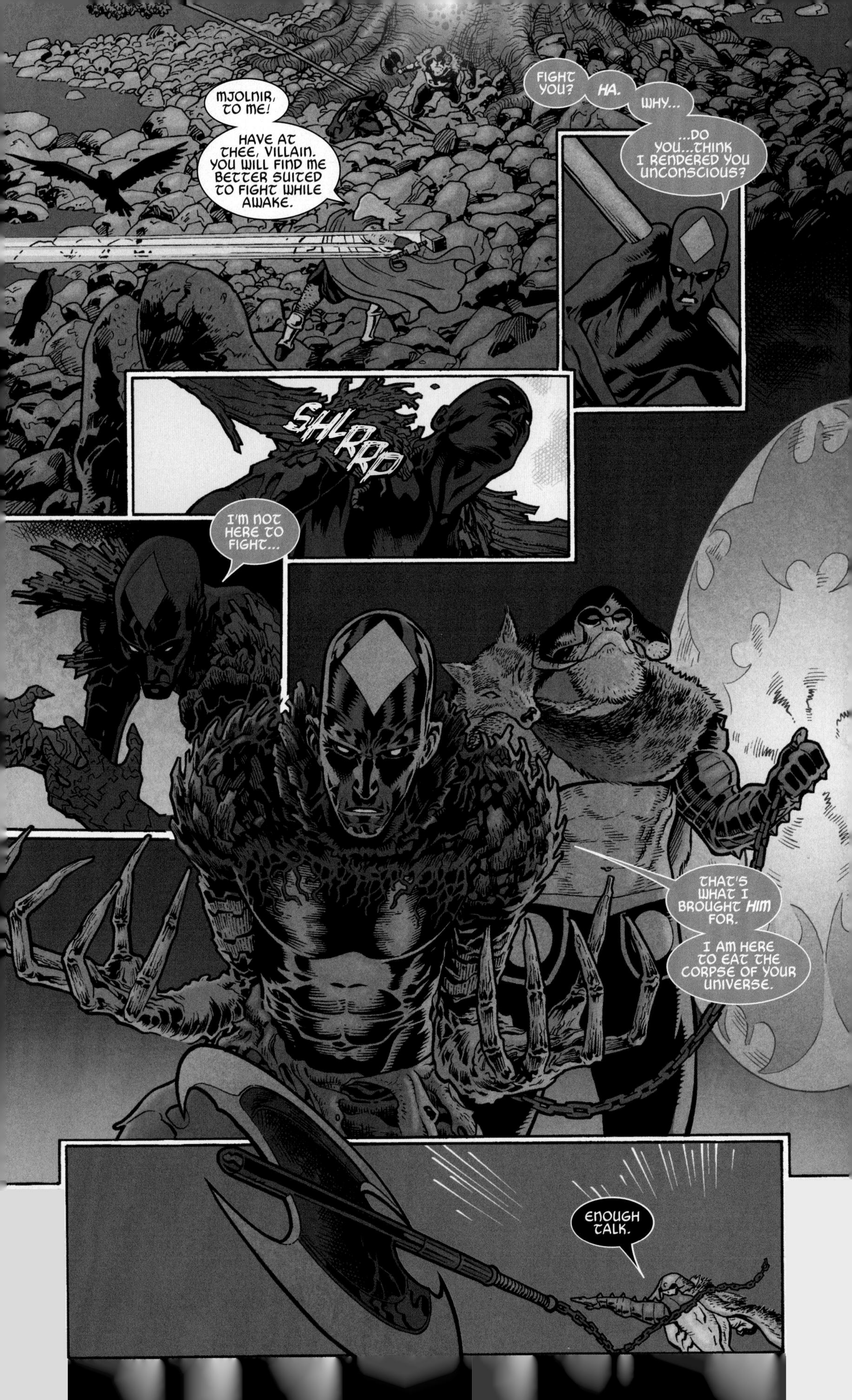
MJOLNIR, TO ME!
HAVE AT THEE, VILLAIN. YOU WILL FIND ME BETTER SUITED TO FIGHT WHILE AWAKE.
FIGHT YOU?
HA.
WHY...
...DO YOU...THINK I RENDERED YOU UNCONSCIOUS?
SHLRRP
I'M NOT HERE TO FIGHT...
THAT'S WHAT I BROUGHT HIM FOR.
I AM HERE TO EAT THE CORPSE OF YOUR UNIVERSE.
ENOUGH TALK.

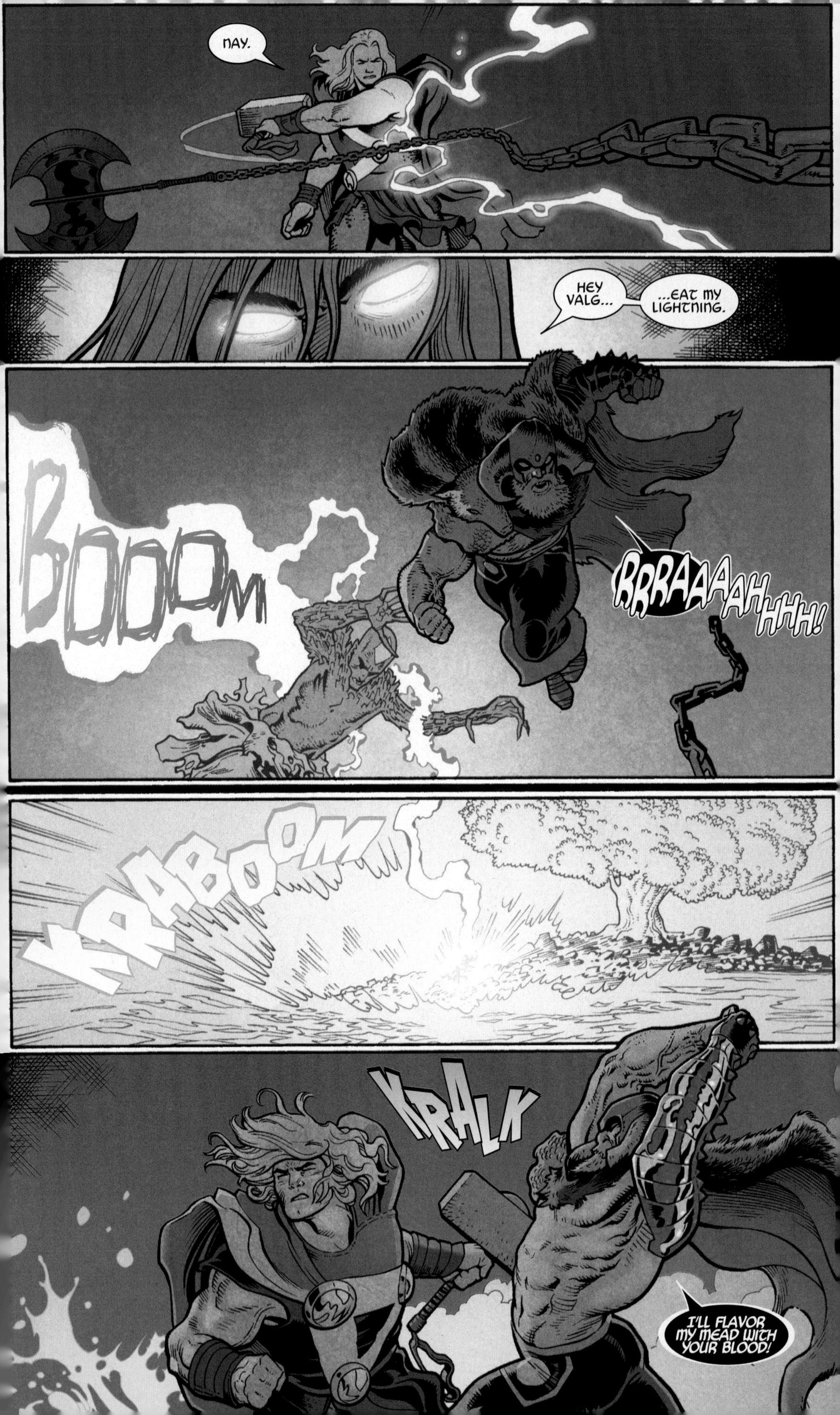
NAY.
HEY VALG...
...EAT MY LIGHTNING.
BOOOOM
BRRRAAAAAHHHH!
KRABOOM
KRALK
I'LL FLAVOR MY MEAD WITH YOUR BLOOD!

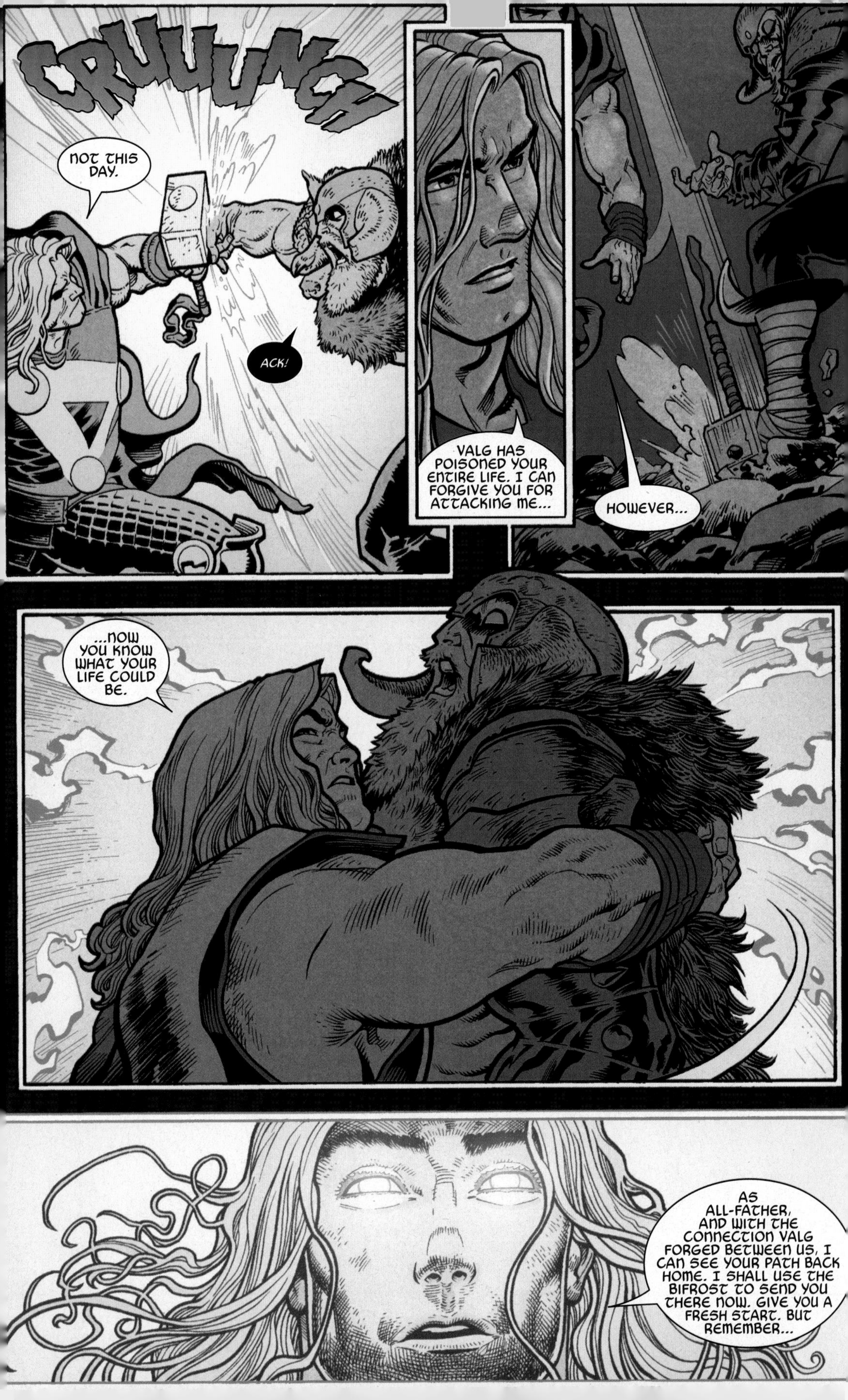
CRUUUNCH
NOT THIS DAY.
ACK!
VALG HAS POISONED YOUR ENTIRE LIFE. I CAN FORGIVE YOU FOR ATTACKING ME...
HOWEVER...
...NOW YOU KNOW WHAT YOUR LIFE COULD BE.
AS ALL-FATHER, AND WITH THE CONNECTION VALG FORGED BETWEEN US, I CAN SEE YOUR PATH BACK HOME. I SHALL USE THE BIFROST TO SEND YOU THERE NOW. GIVE YOU A FRESH START. BUT REMEMBER...

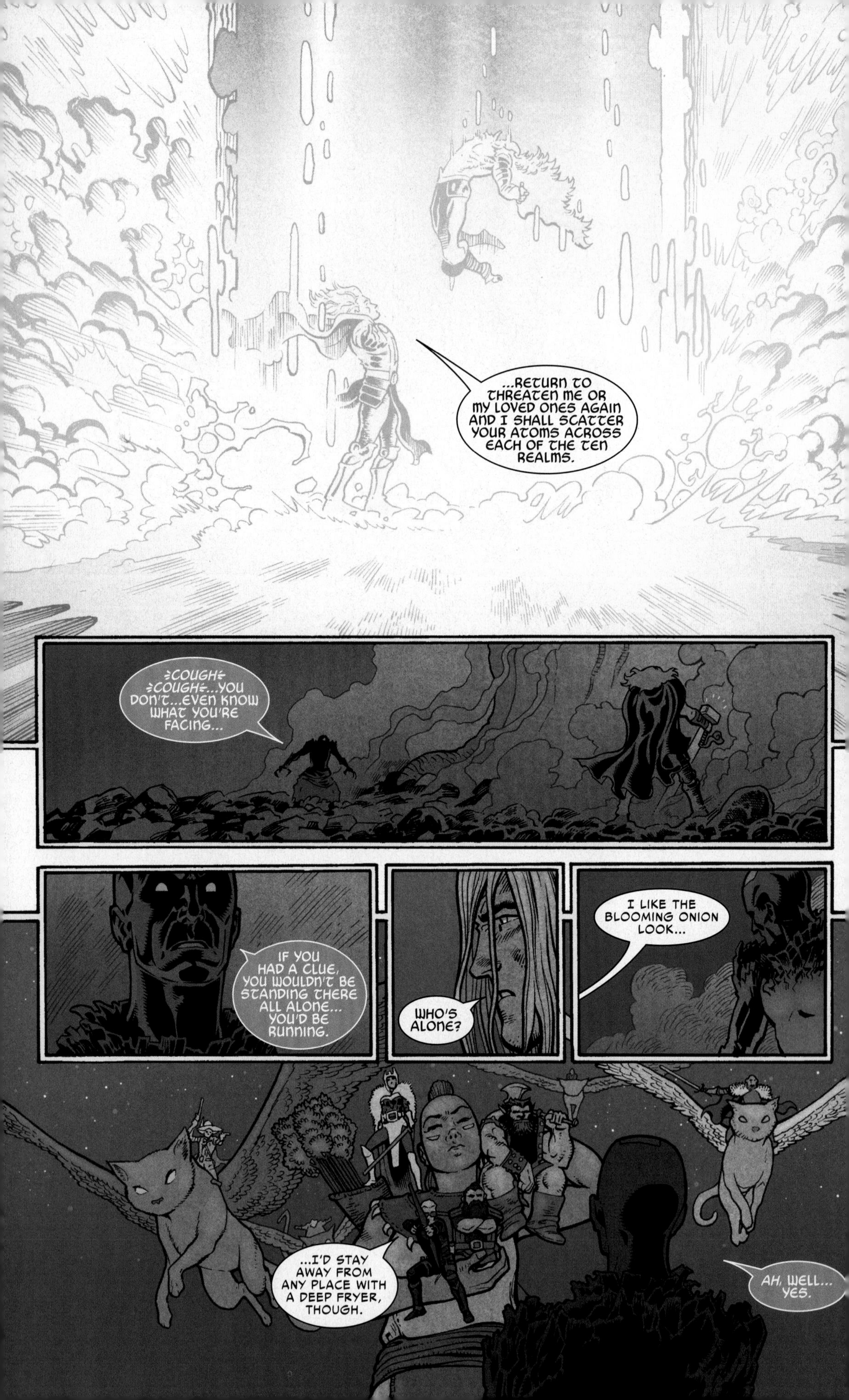
...RETURN TO THREATEN ME OR MY LOVED ONES AGAIN AND I SHALL SCATTER YOUR ATOMS ACROSS EACH OF THE TEN REALMS.
=COUGH= =COUGH= ...YOU DON'T...EVEN KNOW WHAT YOU'RE FACING...
IF YOU HAD A CLUE, YOU WOULDN'T BE STANDING THERE ALL ALONE... YOU'D BE RUNNING.
WHO'S ALONE?
I LIKE THE BLOOMING ONION LOOK...
...I'D STAY AWAY FROM ANY PLACE WITH A DEEP FRYER, THOUGH.
AH, WELL... YES.

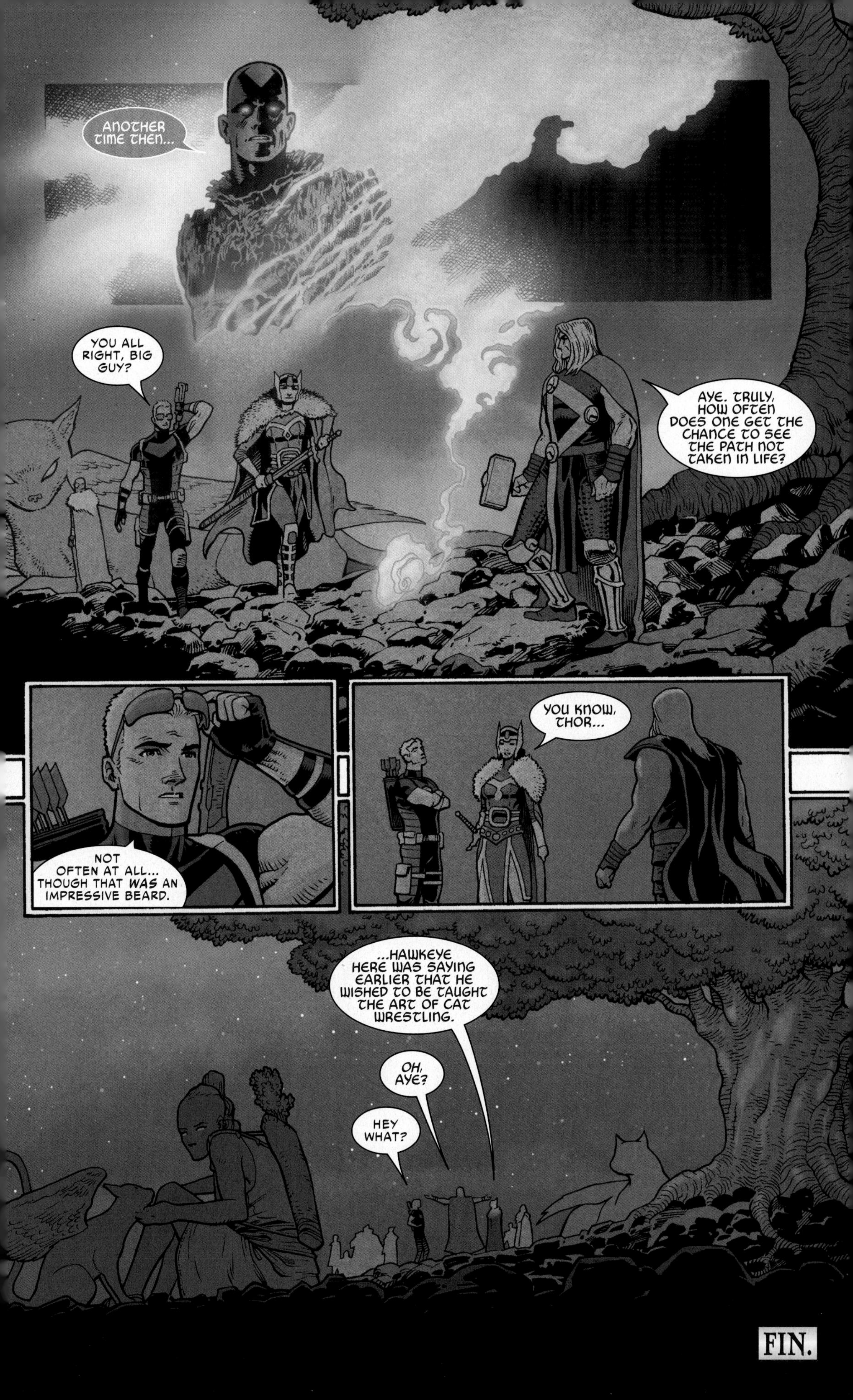
ANOTHER TIME THEN...
YOU ALL RIGHT, BIG GUY?
AYE. TRULY, HOW OFTEN DOES ONE GET THE CHANCE TO SEE THE PATH NOT TAKEN IN LIFE?
NOT OFTEN AT ALL... THOUGH THAT WAS AN IMPRESSIVE BEARD.
YOU KNOW, THOR...
...HAWKEYE HERE WAS SAYING EARLIER THAT HE WISHED TO BE TAUGHT THE ART OF CAT WRESTLING.
OH, AYE?
HEY WHAT?
FIN.

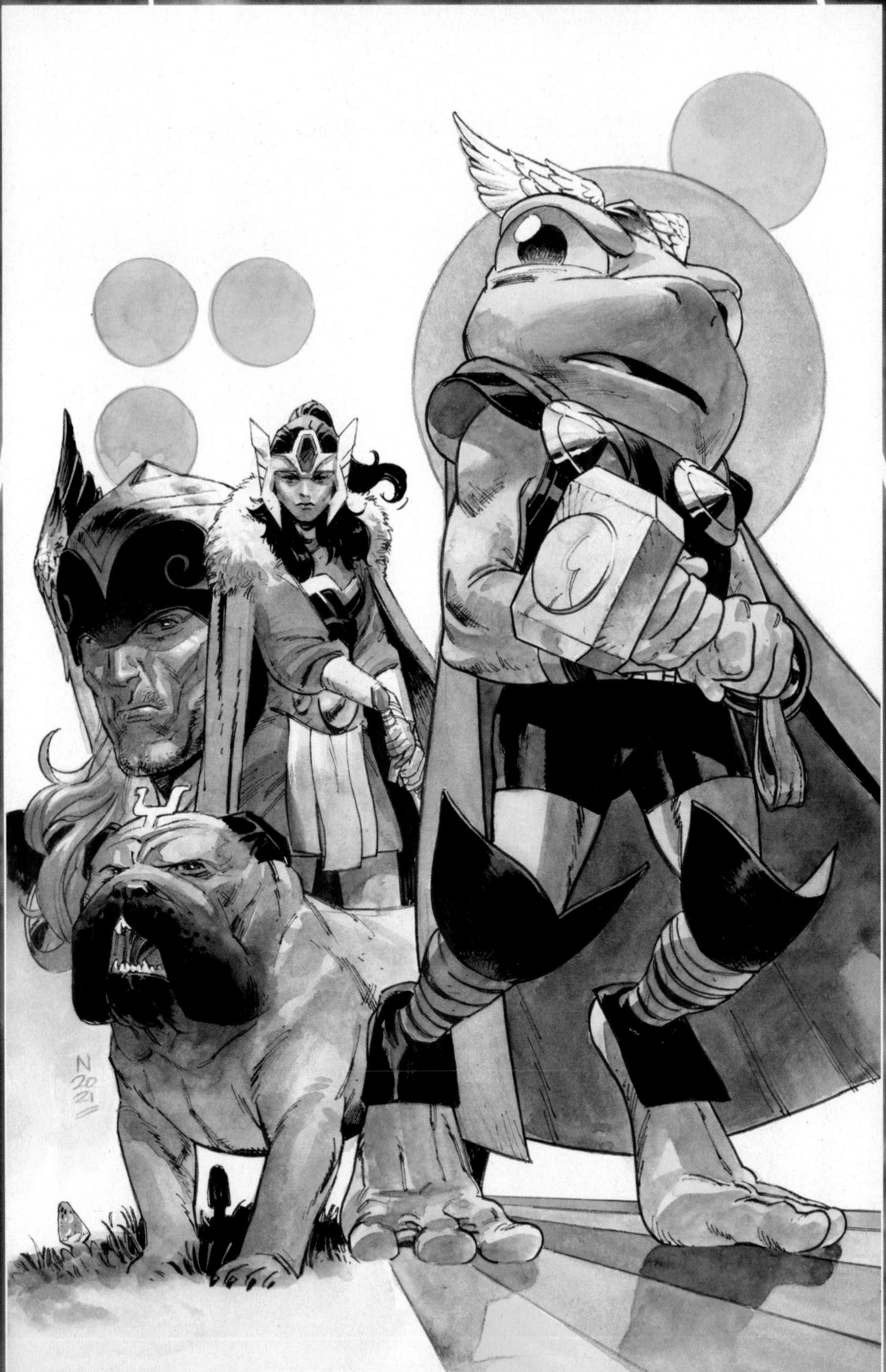
N
20
21

THOR 18 VARIANT BY
Nic Klein

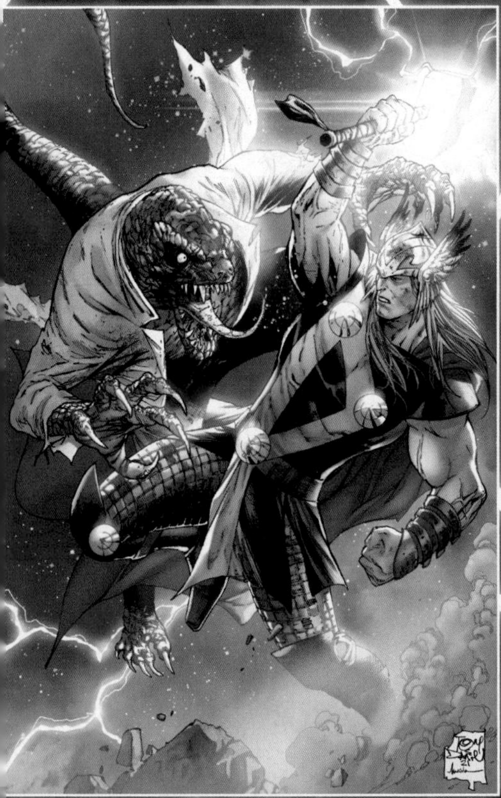

THOR 15 SPIDER-MAN VILLIANS VARIANT BY
Tony Daniel & Marcelo Maiolo

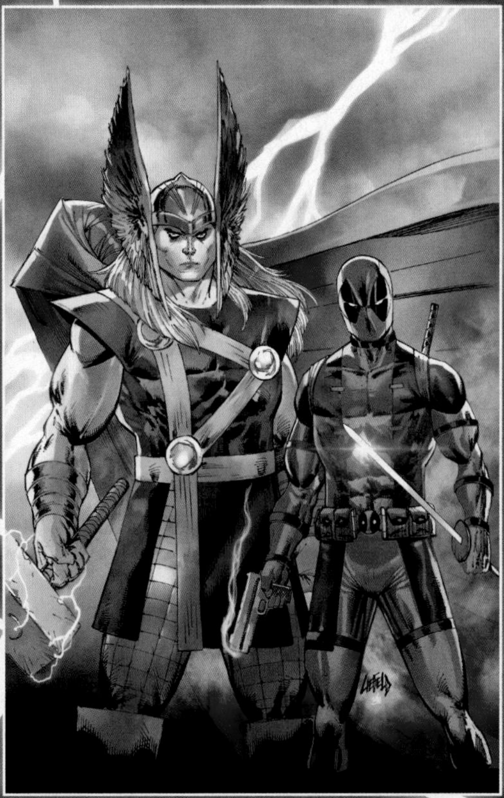

THOR 16 DEADPOOL 30TH ANNIVERSARY VARIANT BY
Rob Liefeld

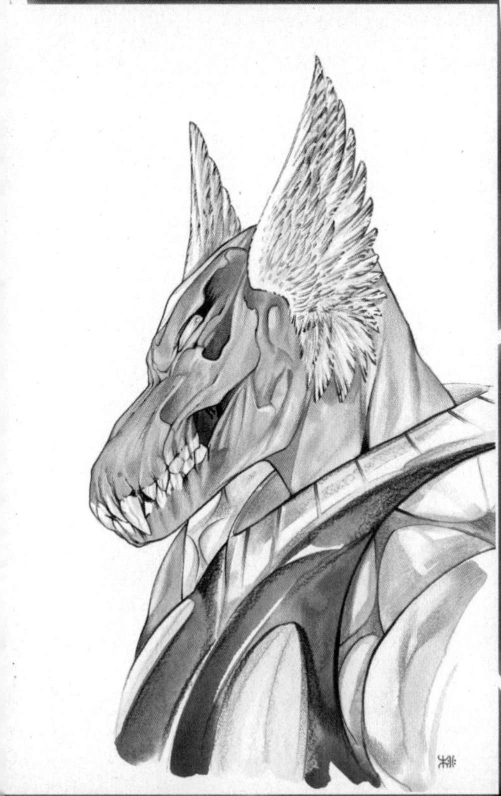

THOR 16 VARIANT BY
Peach Momoko

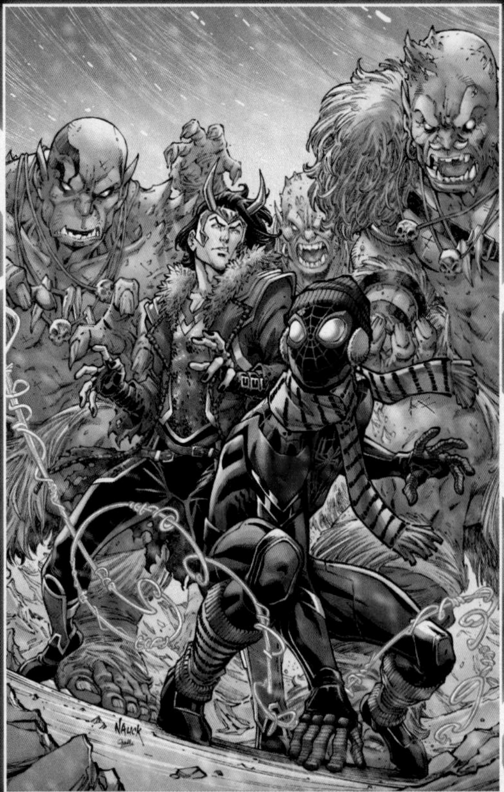

THOR 17 MILES MORALES 10TH ANNIVERSARY VARIANT BY
Todd Nauck & Rachelle Rosenberg

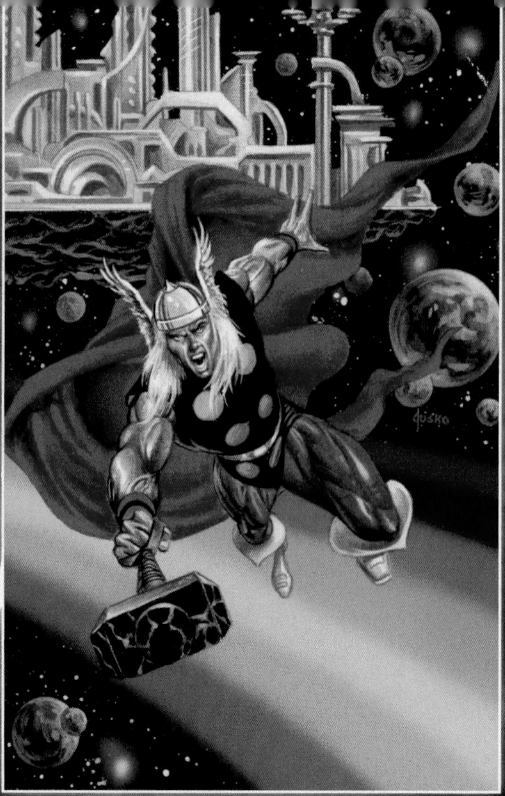

THOR 18 MARVEL MASTERPIECES VARIANT BY

Joe Jusko

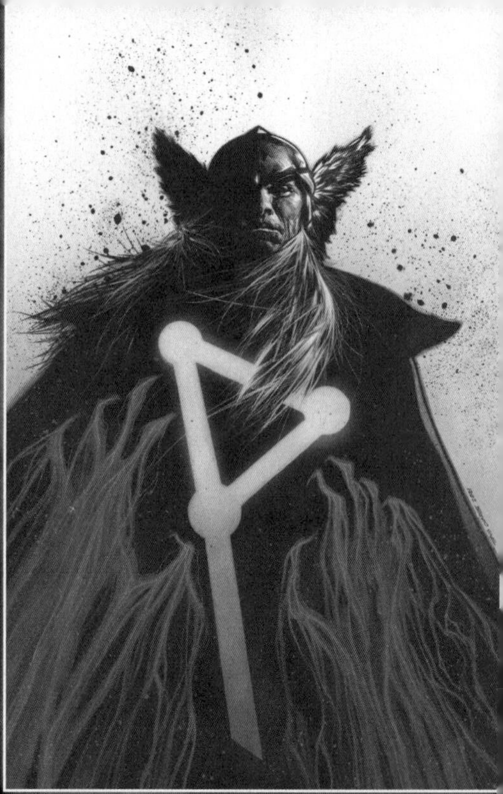

THOR ANNUAL 1 VARIANT BY

Travis Charest

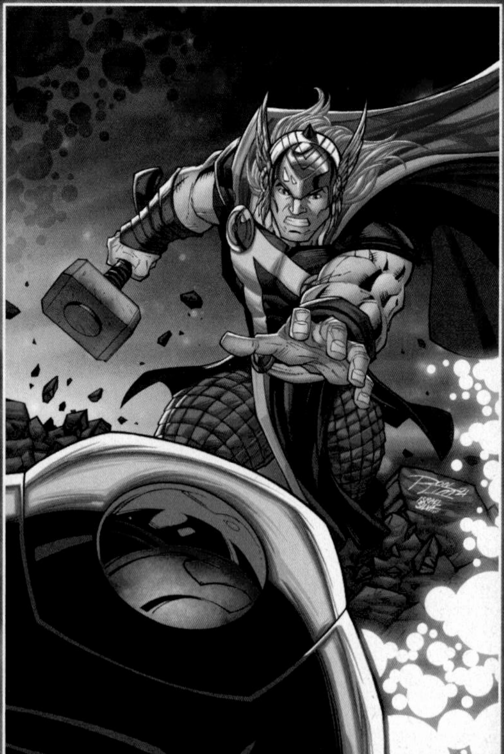

THOR ANNUAL 1 VARIANT BY